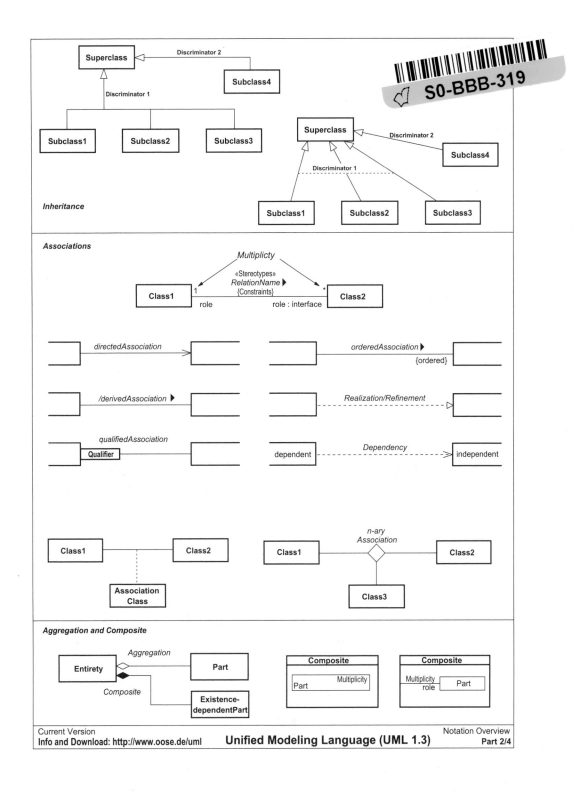

Inheritance

Associations

Aggregation and Composite

Developing Software with UML

Object-oriented analysis and design in practice

Bernd Oestereich

 **Addison-Wesley**

Harlow, England • Reading, Massachusetts • Menlo Park, California
New York • Don Mills, Ontario • Amsterdam • Bonn • Sydney • Singapore
Tokyo • Madrid • San Juan • Milan • Mexico City • Seoul • Taipei

Originally published as *Objekt-orientierte Softwareentwicklung mit der Unified Modeling Language*
© R. Oldenbourg Verlag 1997

English edition © Addison Wesley Longman Ltd 1999
Authorized translation from German language edition published by
R. Oldenbourg Verlag GmbH, Germany

Pearson Education Limited
Edinburgh Gate
Harlow
Essex CM20 2JE
England

and Associated Companies throughout the World.

Cover designed by The Senate, London
Translated and typeset by 46
Printed and bound in the United States of America

First published 1999. Reprinted 1999

ISBN 0–201–36826–5

British Library Cataloguing-in-Publication Data
A catalogue record for this book is available from the British Library

Library of Congress Cataloging-in-Publication Data
Oestereich, Bernd.
    [Objektorientierte Softwareentwicklung mit der UML. English]
    Developing Software with UML: Object-oriented analysis and design in practice / Bernd Oestereich.
       p.   cm. – (Object technology series)
    Includes bibliographical references.
    ISBN 0–201–36826–5
    1. Object-oriented methods (Computer science)   2. UML (Computer science)
    I. Title.   II. Series.
QA76.9.O350713   1999
005.1'17-dc21   98-55553
                    CIP

Contents

Part III
Fundamentals of the Unified Modeling Language   169

Chapter 6
Use Case Diagrams   173

Chapter 7
Class Diagrams (Basic Elements)   185

Preface

To which class of reader do you belong?

You leave unimportant details to others, because you have enough to do. You do not intend to carry out object-oriented analysis or implementation yourself, but you are interested in modern technology and are potentially involved in decision-making on its practical employment.

You know how software is developed because of your many years of practical experience. From your point of view, object-orientation has now reached a degree of maturity, so you feel that you should devote more time to this subject. You would like to have a practice-oriented introduction.

Object-orientation is an established technique in your repertoire. You have been interested in this subject for some time and probably have your own experience with implementation of object-oriented programs. Your interests lean towards analysis and design, and the latest developments in the area of object-oriented methodology and design.

You are interested in software development and have gathered some experience in the field. You have a basic knowledge of the concepts of object-oriented methodology, but feel you need a comprehensive and systematic introduction to the subject.

Dear reader

Starting point

Do you still have time to dedicate yourself to several hundreds pages of technical papers? Do you still read a book from cover to cover? As someone who has suffered enough from the burden of heavy books, I have tried to provide you with a not too bulky, practice-oriented and easily readable book.

Structure

Ways of reading

The book has a modular structure, that is, the individual sections are didactically self-supporting and linked to each other by cross-references (direct page specifications). Thus, you have the option of reading from beginning to end, crosswise or hopping from point to point. A streamlined way of familiarizing yourself with the subject is to read through the chapters *Analysis* and *Design* and to follow the cross-references where needed, to look up and delve deeper into individual subjects in the *Fundamentals* section.

This book provides you with a digest presentation, but with all important information on the Unified Modeling Language (UML 1.3), whose notation and semantics are the current standard in object-oriented modeling. Despite this, the present book is above all an introduction to object-oriented analysis and object-oriented design. Presentation of the UML fundamentals takes place in the context of general problems and discussions about object-oriented software development. To further ease entry into the subject, the UML metamodel is not included in the discussion. Special elements, and elements less relevant in practice, are marked as 'UML advanced' and, where necessary, critically presented.

The use-case driven, architecture-centered, and evolutionary development method underpinning this book is centered on the development of socially embedded corporate information systems, but it is also well suited for technical and other application domains.

About the author

Dipl.-Ing. Bernd Oestereich worked as a consultant and partner with Putz & Partner, Hamburg until 1996, and subsequently as a senior consultant with debis Systemhouse. Since the start of 1998, he has been CEO of oose.de Dienstleistungen für innovative Informatik GmbH.

For over 12 years, the author has been involved with object-oriented software development, in various guises, as a coach, project manager, analyst, designer, developer, trainer and journalist.

Bernd Oestereich is a partner of System Bauhaus (`www.system-bauhaus.com`), a network of internationally renowned, independent specialists for object-oriented software development practicing in the German language area.

Acknowledgments

For their help with this book, I would like to thank all my friends and colleagues, in particular:

Thomas Butschkat, Arne Wallrabe, Christine Sander, Mario Jeckle, Stuart Clayton, Nicolai Josuttis, Peter Hruschka, and Martin Ersche.

Furthermore, I would like to thank Stephan Westphal for his illustrations and the readers of the previous editions and the participants in my seminars for their suggestions and critical remarks.

Bernd Oestereich

Trademark notice

The following are trademarks or registered trademarks of their respective companies.

Windows is a trademark of Microsoft Corporation
Java is a trademark of Sun Microsystems Inc.
Smalltalk is a trademark of Xerox Corporation

Part I

Introduction

To begin with, a little brain teaser.

You are in the cellar of your house. There are three light switches which individually switch on or off three light bulbs in your attic. You may go from your cellar to your attic only once. How can you find out which bulb is connected to which switch?

Initially, all switches are in the 'off' position. Further tools or persons are not available. All bulbs are in perfect working order, you cannot see from the cellar to the attic, metaphysical and esoteric phenomena are not permitted.

If you do not arrive at the solution, take a look at www.oose.de/book. If you think you know the solution, but are interested in the reason behind the puzzle, you will find the answer at the same address.

Chapter 1

Introduction

*Only an idea has the power
to spread this wide.*

Ludwig Mies van der Rohe

This chapter explains the special features of object-oriented software development, its history, and the differences from older methods.

OBJECT-ORIENTED SOFTWARE DEVELOPMENT

Using a bulldozer for potting flowers is as misplaced as using a teaspoon to dig out an excavation for a high-rise building. What matters are the right tools and the right methods.

Demands are rising

Software development is becoming more and more complex – but also more fascinating. Software systems are among the most complex systems created by man – sophisticated software development never gets boring – it requires creativity, precision, the ability to learn and the willingness to analyze and structure new facts intelligently, efficient inbound and outbound communication (within the development team as well as with clients and users), knowledge of and experience with procedures, methods, techniques and tools, clever handling of open questions, ideas which are not fully developed, and so on.

High-quality software development is becoming more and more expensive. The change from alphanumeric interfaces to event-driven graphical user interfaces (GUIs), the introduction of multi-layer client–server architectures, distributed databases, the Internet, and so on, caused a considerable increase in complexity.

Implementation of such software in C++ or similar programming languages is a very labour intensive enterprise. Visual and 4GL development tools, in contrast, bring quick success – but for this very reason lead to skipping the planning and conception stage and use the FBTT (From Brain To Terminal) method instead. Regardless of the way it is realized, each implementation of an application should, however, be preceded by a planning phase – and this is precisely the central point of this book: analysis and design of modern software.

Technical Complexity

Conceptional stability vs. evolution

Software is never completely finished. There is always something to be modified or improved. And even if changes are not mandatorily required, they often remain desirable – until the program is taken off the market. Too many modifications and extensions obviously cause the program to deviate more and more from the original concept. This danger is particularly relevant when the program is successful and is therefore continuously being improved.

For these reasons, it is sensible to look for adequate methods that allow complexity to be mastered, or at least delay the process of decay and help to maintain quality and reliability of the software despite structural disintegration and evolution.

The history of software development is a continuous increase in abstraction – from bit patterns via macro instructions, procedures, and abstract data types to objects, frames, design patterns, and business objects. The significantly stronger abstraction of object-orientation not merely improves and further develops the classical methods, but generates a new way of thinking.

A new way of thinking

Similarities and relationships can always be found, but simplistic statements such as 'messages are only procedure calls' or 'object-orientation – just an old concept with a new label' misunderstand the essence of object-orientation.

Social Complexity

The widespread opinion that software development is mainly a technical task turns out to be only one side of the truth when we take a closer look at the development process. Today, software development is also a complex social process. The decisive reasons for this lie in the fact that software development is very much a person-related process in which psychological and epistemological knowledge together with communication skills play a major role. Many software systems are embedded in a social environment, that is, in an organization involving people – these are the systems (as opposed to technical or other systems) which this book is dedicated to.

Communication is the central point

Experts in the application area and experts in the development team share the same problem: the more specialized you are, the more difficult you are to understand. Correct mutual understanding, however, is the cornerstone of successful cooperation. During the course of a project, models are created of the application world and the software to be developed – most of these to be found in the minds of the people involved. Documentation produced in such a project is at most the tip of an iceberg. Since much more stays in the minds of the developers than will ever appear in the documentation, a consensus about the whole context is indispensable.

Communication, that is, the exchange of the models, the knowledge and the experience present in people's minds is thus a central issue. Since software, more than other technical systems, is intertwined with human abstractions, with all its complexity, its inaccuracies and peculiarities, it resembles human organizational structures far more than typically technical ones.

HISTORY OF OBJECT-ORIENTATION

The object-orientation concept is nearly thirty years old, and the development of object-oriented programming languages is almost as old. There have always been publications on object-oriented programming, but the first books on object-oriented analysis design methods only started to appear at the beginning

At the beginning, there was Smalltalk

of the 1990s. These include publications by Booch, Coad and Yourdon, Rumbaugh *et al.*, Wirfs-Brock and Johnson, Shlaer and Mellor, Martin and Odell, Henderson-Sellers, and Firesmith. An important push was given in particular by Goldberg and Rubin, as well as Jacobson. Many methods are specialized and restricted to specific application areas.

In the early 1990s, the methods of Grady Booch and James Rumbaugh became by far the most popular. The Rumbaugh method was more structure-oriented, while Booch covered the commercial and technical areas, including also time-critical applications, which were reasonably covered. In 1995, Booch and Rumbaugh began to combine their methods, first in the form of a common notation, to create the *Unified Method* (UM). Shortly afterwards, Ivar Jacobson joined in, integrating his so-called *use cases*. Henceforth, the three called themselves 'Amigos'. Since the methods of Booch, Rumbaugh, and Jacobson were already very popular and held a large market share, their combination into the *Unified Modeling Language* (UML) formed a quasi-standard. Finally, in 1997, UML, Version 1.1 was submitted to the Object Management Group (OMG) for standardization, and accepted. Further development of UML is currently being carried out by the OMG.

See UML introduction
⇒ *p. 173*

UML is primarily a description of a unified notation and semantics together with the definition of a metamodel. The description of a development method

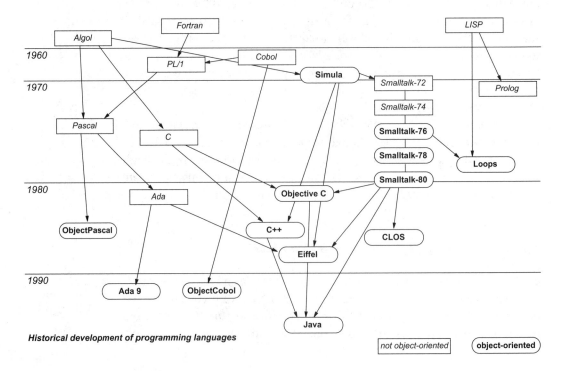

Historical development of programming languages

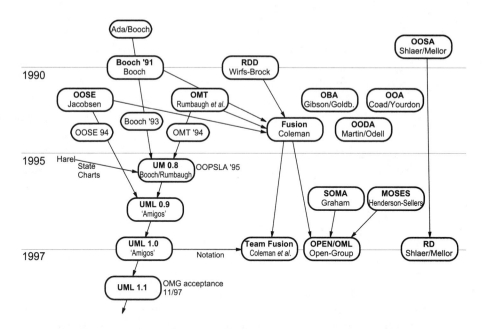

is not part of it. In this book, the analysis and design chapters describe a procedure based on UML which has proved successful when put into practice. This methodology focuses on the development of commercial, socially embedded information systems such as those encountered in service or commercial enterprises. For more technically oriented systems, such as production control, significant adjustments will certainly be needed.

Notation and methodology

UML is multi-facetted and also integrates interesting ideas and concepts from other authors. Thus, besides the ideas of Booch, Rumbaugh, and Jacobson, you will also find those of Harel (state diagrams).

Thanks to the 'Amigos,' different notations have widely converged. On the other hand, independently of the notation, different methodological approaches exist which differ in distinct ways from each other, such as the method of Shlaer and Mellor and the Open Process (with OML – Open Modeling Language as its modeling language). More than 30 active supporters belong to the OPEN consortium, including among others, Brian Henderson-Sellers, Ian Graham, and Donald Firesmith.

The Unified Modeling Language is a modeling language, and as such predestined for translation into programming languages, that is, for code generation. On the one hand, its high expressiveness puts high demands on CASE tools and makes reverse engineering more difficult, on the other hand, it offers extensive modeling capabilities. Currently available tools are far from being able to use UML to its full potential.

Overwhelming Variety of Choices

The fundamental concepts of object-oriented software development methodology are mature and established in practice. On the other hand, UML in particular, offers a notable wealth of detail and is therefore to be used with caution.

The various possibilities of description may be perceived as quite oppressing; a deeper understanding of UML constructs in all their variety requires some effort. As a first approach, one should therefore restrict oneself to the basic elements. Potentially, semantic gaps may remain in the modeling, but in practice, work at this level may be sufficient. Besides, there are lots of places where no systematics at all are applied.

Stereotypes ⇒ p. 221

Moreover, some methodological concepts are only relevant in special or highly detailed circumstances. Here, the choice of elements to be employed is guided by the kind of application (information system, real-time application, and others) and the depth of detail required. Details such as visibility marks, sophisticated stereotypes, and so on, lead not only to better security and higher quality results, but also to higher development efforts and costs. The advantage over other methods is that it takes longer to reach notational or semantic limits, owing to the availability of a wide palette of alternatives of which, however, only the relevant and necessary ones should be applied.

MAKING UP YOUR OWN METHODOLOGY

Introduction of object-orientation

If you wish to establish an object-oriented methodology in your enterprise, it is sensible to analyze what the typical problems and boundary conditions are, and which approaches might be appropriate in dealing with them. It only leads to confusion if your development people are methodologically trained, but are unable to apply their knowledge in practice, because parts of the methodology are not relevant, elementary problems are not sufficiently covered or are not supported by the tools used. Try to work out a simple methodology, omitting all superfluous concepts, and introduce it systematically. An experienced object-orientation analyst can knit the elements together.

The individual concepts and related procedures may be considered proven and reliable. However, their application is certainly not easier than that of the old methods.

Dependencies and relationships between class, activity, collaboration, sequence, and state diagrams can become totally confusing to the eye. Therefore, completeness and consistency of model can be reasonably guaranteed only by appropriate software. Manual modeling is out of the question.

Nevertheless, tools will never be able to make up for the technical and methodological errors of their users – one more reason not to employ all the available possibilities of the method and the tools blindly, but to make an educated selection of those which appear sensible and are necessary for the task.

Do not apply a method blindly

Experience vs Method Observance

You may use a newspaper not only for reading, but also for swatting annoying insects. In a similar way, software development methods and tools may be employed for various purposes.

Many people still consider the software business to be the incarnation of progress itself, but for experienced users, it does not really have a serious reputation. There are still too many annoying problems, and users are becoming more and more demanding. You will probably find no other branch of engineering involving a higher proportion of amateurishness than software development. Another cause may be that too many people who have never been trained in computer science are entrusted with software development.

For the purpose of achieving good programs, it is also sensible to consider the opposite when presenting a method: errors and flaws that may derive from unsystematic development.

If you have ever brought forward (or at least had a chance to observe) the development of a major software project mainly by intuition, that is, without conscious application of a development strategy, you will have noticed how problems become increasingly complex during the course of program development and how more and more sub- and side-problems arise, which continue to intertwine with each other. The results bear a certain similarity to the construction of ambitious Gothic cathedrals which from time to time collapsed before they were finished. The exception being that in those days, the decisive mechanical and physical laws were not yet known. Some typical problems and errors in software development are:

Collapsing constructions

- ◆ Coding is started far too early.
- ◆ Coding is started too late.
- ◆ The procedure is ill-planned and lacking a model of how to proceed.
- ◆ Intermediate and final results are not (or only insufficiently) verified and validated.
- ◆ The application architecture was not planned clearly enough or its development got out of hand.
- ◆ The development is driven by a naïve understanding of object-orientation.

Do-it-yourself approach

- The development is driven by an understanding of object-orientation which is too academic to be used in practice.
- Behind an 'object-oriented' disguise, the spirit of procedural software development is still lurking (particularly when hybrid languages such as C++ are employed).
- Guidelines for analysis, design, and implementation are lacking, are not employed, or are too far removed from reality.
- The documentation of results and design decisions leads a marginal existence in suspended animation.

Complexity of software is often denied, but sometimes trifling errors or lapses in precision, which in isolation are relatively insignificant, accumulated are sufficient to cause unnecessary and tiresome problems.

Basically, the full extent of requirements is underestimated. Delivery dates cannot be kept, the implementation (even without considering the test phase which is practically eliminated) gives in to the pressures of time, and important activities and results are neglected or get lost. If, on top of all this, some elementary system parts are not properly designed or not well thought out, growing complexity leads to persistent or even irreparable problems.

Application of a well-proven procedure helps to avoid such problems.

When applying a method, it is important not to forget the wealth of experience of the developers involved, which allows these people to produce good programs even without the explicit application of a method. Employing methods is not the point of the exercise; the overall purpose is always to be successful. In principle, practical experience is simply the unconscious application of well-proven techniques. The decisive factor is that the quality of the outcome does not happen at random, but systematically.

Methods are not ends in themselves

The important issue is the realization of the ideas that underlie the methods. Rules are 'nothing but generalized prescriptions of behavior that tell us what we should do in order to be able to do what we want to do' (Lübber, 1987, p. 118). Adherence to specific conventions that guide us toward more successful actions, however, also opens up new freedoms and mastery (due to the self-assurance gained).

Good people achieve good results even with poor tools and under difficult conditions. On the other hand, strict adherence to a method alone does not lead to success either. Despite new and advanced methods for better mastering of complexity and problems innate to the development process, demands on the qualifications of developers do not diminish but continue to increase. This applies in particular to object-oriented methodology, since it was designed to be used in complex projects.

HOLISTIC APPROACH

Humans have difficulties in thinking in systems and networks; thinking in terms of individual causal chains seems to come more naturally (*see* Dörner, 1989).

The old structured software development methods help us get to grips with complexity, but reach their limits too quickly: with the traditional separation between data view and functional view, description and implementation of complex software can be no longer mastered or only at a high cost.

Factual descriptions by means of *Structured Analysis* (SA) and *Entity-Relationship Modeling* (ERM) represent different views which, however, complement each other only when applied to areas with little overlap. The incommensurability and difficulty in integrating the approaches at a higher level is even more pronounced between Structured Analysis and *Structured Design* (SD). Through various methodological improvements and integration efforts, the structured methods have achieved a notable degree of performance. Nevertheless, the structural deficits remain obvious. Object-oriented software engineering reflects the existing and proven concepts, but is much more powerful.

SA
SD
ERM

In system theory, reality is perceived as a network: the individual facts and phenomena are no longer reduced to their elements, but are seen as an integrated whole, where the links and interdependencies between the components are an essential part of the entirety (holistic thinking).

Object-oriented software development not only describes data and functions; their interconnection and their relationship with the surrounding world, that is, with other data and functional units, can be defined in a differentiated way. These definitions of mutual relationships and dependencies are always present in the object-oriented model wherever they are needed (from analysis to coding) and are assigned the corresponding responsibilities. This facilitates work and allows programmers to cope with a higher degree of complexity.

Differences from older procedures

The essential differences between structured and object-oriented methods are:

♦ *Holistic objects to work on.* The class concept is used to work with units of data and operations, instead of a separation between data and operations.
♦ *Better possibilities of abstraction.* More than their structured counterparts, object-oriented methods shift the focus of modeling from the solution area towards the problem area.
♦ *Methodological uniformity.* The results of an activity i in the object-oriented development process can easily be taken over into activity $i+1$ and vice versa: all phases of software development operate with the same concepts (classes, objects, relationships, and so on). There is no rupture between different model representations.
♦ *Evolutionary development.* A complex system is not built in one go. All complex systems in nature have developed step by step, each intermediate step had to stabilize first and prove its functional and survival capabilities. In the course of time, this has led to the development of the complicated system called a 'human being'. With object-oriented software development methods, the evolutionary principle can be transferred to software development.

Evolution

The last point about evolutionary development seems to be fairly uncommon in the application development of many enterprises. On the contrary, the argument that everything will have to be redone from scratch is used to create barriers for switching to object-oriented techniques.

In other areas – think of cars, airplanes, and so on – mixed procedures are traditionally practiced: after a given phase of further development and improvement of existing models, entirely new models are developed periodically. The

◆ Human-oriented

In a certain sense, object-orientation is also a *Weltanschauung* (view of the world, in the literal sense of the word). In contrast to conventional software development methods, object-oriented methods are based on a paradigm that places the human being more at the center. This means that the current technocentric view is replaced with an anthropocentric one (*see* Quibeldey-Cirkel, 1994). Traditional software development methods have copied their deductive procedure from empirical sciences, which makes their action oriented towards goals separated from the objective world (see Habermas (1987), 'cognitive-instrumental rationality'). Objectivity, however, only comes into being because 'a community of subjects capable of language and action considers it as one and the same world. A necessary condition for this is that communicatively acting subjects agree with each other on what occurs in the world or what is to be done in it.' (Valk, 1987.)

Deductive separation is replaced with consensual communication. Traditional development methods fail when faced with more demanding tasks because in their deductivism they have not considered the limitations of human communication possibilities – which does not necessarily mean that OO methodology cannot fail as well. Object-oriented procedures, however, are open for the consciousness of a communicative rationality and thus leads to a different view of the world.

The transition from older, more technocentric methods to more holistic, object-oriented procedures can be viewed as a change of paradigm, meaning that one model replaces another one in the same context, and that they mutually exclude each other. Transitions of this kind take place (according to Molzberger, 1984) through three reaction patterns:

◆ *Emotional refusal.* Despite their contradictions, old convictions continue to be adhered to.
◆ *Unreflected euphoria.* Deficits in the old approach have been recognized, but the new ideas have not yet been questioned.
◆ *Déjà-vu experience.* The new paradigm looks so self-evident that one wonders why it has appeared only now, or one even doubts that it is new.

VW Beetle was given up in spite of its success, because the cost of producing the body was no longer competitive. It needed twice the number of welding points than the bodies of big American cars, namely about 6,000 (*see* Railton). Moreover, because of the position of the engine, no trunk could be integrated into the design.

VW Beetle with trunk

The analysis of Bittner *et al.* (1995) shows that, as actually practiced, software development is far more 'evolutionary' than envisaged officially or in procedural models.

In software development, many people share the opinion that permanent further development and enhancement of existing programs is economical and thus is the only practicable road. 'This is, however, a false conclusion if the whole life cycle of the product is taken into account. A small change can affect the entire system. Thus, if stability is crucial, caution requires an analysis of the entire system before the change can be made.' (*see* Valk, 1987). What we need is a middle course.

Permeable Model Representation

One way of clarifying methodological uniformity is to compare the beginning and end of the development process. At the beginning, we may find, for example, the following developer–user dialog:

Developer:	*What is important for you?*
User:	*The customer.*
Developer:	*What is a customer, which features are relevant for you?*
User:	*A customer has a name, an address, and a solvency which we check.*

Customer
name
address
solvency
checkSolvency()

At the end of the process we find a class which, coded in (simplified) Java, looks as follows:

```java
class Customer
{
    String      name;
    Address     address;
    Solvency    solvency;

    public int checkSolvency()
    {
        . . .
    }
}
```

The holistic and human-oriented approach, pursued from the very beginning by the leading pioneers of object-orientation (in the Xerox PARC), becomes clearly visible at many points:

- The class concept facilitates development of software units that do not serve a specific application, but a specific concept or a specific idea of reality and as such can operate in different contexts and therefore in different applications.
- The world of object-oriented software development is a world full of images: terms such as inheritance, message exchange, the tool-material image, and so on are part of the metaphorics and indicate the basic ontological principles.

◆ **Means of abstraction** *Nicolai Josuttis*

Programming is the process of representing facts in a computer. Describing these facts requires abstraction. Items which are irrelevant for the problem are omitted. Otherwise, you would always arrive at bits and quarks.

The faculty of describing things in a sensible way by means of abstraction is also used in everyday life. We normally use two kinds of abstraction:

Part/whole relationship (*has-a* relationship)
The part/whole relationship combines several parts into one object. An object consists of parts. Example: a car consists of engine, body, seats, steering wheel, tires, and so on.
You say 'Look at that car down there' instead of 'Look at that engine with a body, a steering wheel, and four tires down there.' For this purpose, programming languages have structures (records).

Generic relationship (*is-a* relationship)
The generic relationship combines several kinds or variations of objects under one term. An object is a particular variation. Example: a convertible is a car; a car is a vehicle. You say 'There are three cars down there' instead of 'There are a convertible, a sedan, and a station wagon down there.' This means of abstraction is not supported in non-object-oriented programming languages.

- The symbols of the graphical user interface, such as trash can, printer, magnifying glass, folder, brush, scissors, and so forth allow users visual and intuitive action.
- Object-oriented graphical user interfaces help achieve uniform screen organization and coherent operating standards; they induce application developers to adopt these standards and imitate their look and feel.

The structured methods (SA, SD, ERM, and so on) build on similar principles for coping with complexity as the object-oriented ones, but they are methodologically not as uniformly applicable and capable of integration; and in systemic, networked thinking, object-oriented methods go a step further. Object-orientation is the current answer to the increased complexity of software development.

The following points summarize the most important advantages of the object-oriented approach:

Advantages of object-orientation

- Owing to the evolutionary process, new requirements can also be added at later stages of the development process and integrated relatively easily.
- It is possible to deal with more demanding and more complex areas of application.
- Communication between software developers and experts in the application area is improved through the anthropomorphic metaphors.
- Coherent modeling favors the quality of results. The individual development steps remain fairly consistent with each other.

- Concepts uniformly applicable in all development steps facilitate development and improve documentation.
- The holistic view in modeling does better justice to structures, relationships, and dependences in the real world.
- Seen over the whole of their lifetime, object-oriented models are more stable and thus easier to modify. Even essential global system changes are mostly obtained by limited local changes.
- Object-oriented abstractions allow increased reusability of work outcomes.
- Object-oriented software development is more fun.

Nevertheless, object-orientation is not a panacea, and we do not want to be too euphoric: even this approach will not necessarily prevent you from getting lousy results.

SUGGESTED READING

1. Booch, G. (1994) *Object-oriented analysis and design with applications*, 2nd edn., Benjamin/Cummings.
2. Rumbaugh, J., Blaha, M., Premerlani, W., Eddy, F., Lorenson, W. (1991) *Object-Oriented Modelling and Design*. Prentice Hall.
3. Jacobson, I., Christerson, M., Jonsson, P., Övergaard, G. (1992) *Object-Oriented Software Engineering, A Use Case Driver Approach*. Addison-Wesley.
4. Wirfs-Brock, R., Wilkerson, B., Wiener, L. (1990) *Designing Object-Oriented Software*. Prentice Hall.
5. Graham, I., Henderson-Sellers, B., Younessi, H. (1997) *The OPEN Process Specification*. Addison-Wesley (ACM Press), Harlow.
6. Martin, J., Odell, J. (1992) *Object-Oriented Analysis & Design*. Prentice-Hall.
7. Meyer, B. (1988) *Object-Oriented Software Construction*. Prentice Hall.
8. Coleman, D., Arnold, P., Bodorff, S., Dollin, C., Gilchrist, H. (1993) *Object-Oriented Development: The Fusion Method*. Prentice Hall.
9. McMenamin, S. M., Palmer, J. F. (1984) *Essential Systems Analysis*. Yourdon Inc., New York.
10. Yourdon, E. (1989) *Modern Structured Analysis*. Prentice Hall.
11. Booch, G. (1986) *Software Engineering with Ada*. Benjamin/Cummings.
12. Harel, D. (1987) Statecharts: A Visual Formalism for Complex Systems. *In: Science of Computer Programming*, Vol. 8/1987, pp. 231–274.

Chapter 2

Object-Orientation for Beginners

*The only constant in this world
is change.*

Harry Palmer

This chapter provides an easy introduction to the concepts of object-orientation.

Object [lat. *objectum*, 'thing thrown before (the mind)']
Something regarded as external to the mind, separated from the self; the non-ego.

Class [lat. *classis*]
A number of individuals (persons or things) possessing common attributes, and grouped together under a general or 'class' name; a kind, sort, division.

Operation [lat. *operatio*, from *opus, oper*, 'work']
The performance of something of practical or mechanical nature; *Mat.*: The action of subjecting a number or quantity to any process whereby its value or form is affected.

Attribute [lat. *attributum*, subst. use of past participle of *attribuere*]
A quality ascribed to any person or thing, one which is in common usage assigned to him; in *Logic*, that which may be predicated of anything; strictly an essential and permanent quality.

(*From the Oxford Dictionary*)

OBJECT-ORIENTATION FOR BEGINNERS

Novice programmers have fewer problems

Explaining the basics of object-orientation needs only a few examples. Even complete newcomers get rapidly acquainted with the subject, probably even more easily than experienced computer buffs. While professionals are reluctant to abandon their beloved data, function, and process models and always try to fit the new ideas somewhere into their set thinking patterns, computer rookies can light-heartedly get acquainted with object-orientation as an easily accessible approach.

Object-orientation is so called because this method sees things that are part of the real world as objects. A phone is an object in the same way as a bicycle, a human being, or an insurance policy are objects. And these objects are in turn composed of other objects, such as screws, wheels, nose and ears, annual tariffs, and so on. Real-world objects can obviously have a fairly complex structure and cause us some cognitive problems. A complex object, such as a human being, can only be perceived in a simplified way. Obvious external features such as

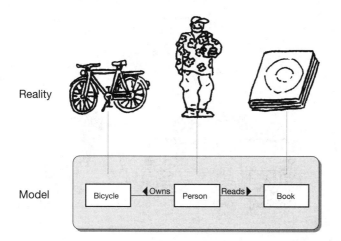

arms, nose and ears can be recognized straightaway, if we neglect detailed components such as blood corpuscles or nerve synapses.

In everyday life, we simplify objects in our thinking – we work with models, as children do. As a boy, I used to play railroad with my father. Not with a real railroad; engine, wagons and crossings were scaled-down representations of reality: we had a model railroad. Software development does essentially the same: objects occurring in reality are reduced to a few features that are relevant in the current situation. Instead of real objects, we work with symbols. Properties and composition of objects only roughly correspond to reality; the model only selects aspects that are useful for carrying out a specific task.

Playing model railroad

Thus, besides their names, in a staff accounting system, employees are reduced to social security numbers, together with allowances and so on, while the internal phone book will show their position, department, and extension.

CLASSES, OBJECTS, INSTANCES

One cow makes moo – many cows make moolah. This phrase, based on an old German farmer's saying has been taken into account in object-orientation. Objects occurring in the real world are thus not only restricted to their most important, mode-relevant properties, but similar objects are also grouped together.

Class = Building plan of similar objects

The objects to be considered in the model are not conceived merely as individual entities. For similar objects, an assembly plan is created, which in object-orientation is called a class. This class is then used to create the concrete objects.

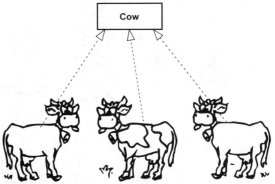

Objects (from left): Uma Udder, Molly Milk, and Patty Pasture

The three cows Uma, Molly, and Patty originate from the prototype class cow. The class cow itself does not exist as an object.

In this book, classes and objects are represented following the notation of the Unified Modeling Language (UML), that is, as rectangles. To differentiate between classes and objects, the names of objects are underlined.

Classes ⇒ p. 186
Objects ⇒ p. 193

Instance
Object

If we want to represent the object–class relationship (instance relationship), we draw a dashed arrow between an object and its class in the direction of the class.

In the case of Uma Udder, this would be read as 'Uma Udder is an instance of the class cow.'

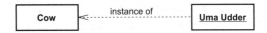

Class A class describes structure and behavior of a set of similar objects ⇒ p. 186.

Object An object is an instance which is present at execution time and allocates memory for its instance variables, and which behaves according to the protocol of its class ⇒ p. 193.

ATTRIBUTES, OPERATIONS, CONSTRAINTS

In the context of classes and objects, we have also talked about their properties. What exactly do we mean by this? What are the significant properties of a
class? The following aspects must be considered:

*Properties of classes
and objects*

- ◆ *Attributes.*   The structure of the objects: their components and the information or data contained therein.
- ◆ *Operations.*   The behavior of the objects. Commonly, the term operations
  is used. However, sometimes the words 'services' or 'methods' or, errone-
  ously, 'procedure' or 'function' are used.
- ◆ *Constraints.*   Conditions, requirements and rules that objects must satisfy
  are called constraints.

⇒ *p. 195*

⇒ *p. 198*
see Glossary
⇒ *p 297*

⇒ *p. 206*

A circle which we want to represent on a screen, for example, has the following properties, amongst others:

Example

- ◆ Attributes: its radius and its position on the screen (x, y).
- ◆ Operations: the possibility of displaying, removing, repositioning, and
  resizing it.
- ◆ Constraints: the radius must not be negative and not equal to zero
  (*radius* > 0).

Operations may or may not have *parameters*. For example, when a new
radius is set, the parameter *newRadius* is passed. Parameters are attached to
the name of the operation enclosed in parentheses. Also, operations without
parameters are followed by a pair of parentheses. This serves to differentiate
them from attributes. Constraints are enclosed in braces.

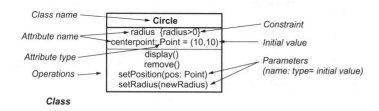

Class

Constraints can be defined not only within classes; they can also apply to
relationships, for example, to define a sorting order. More about this later.

{ordered} ⇒ *p. 239*

On the one hand, during analysis and design, classes are modeled, that is,
their properties and relationships are considered; on the other hand, use case

and sequence diagrams and others are used to represent the interaction between the classes and simulate selected processes. Instead of classes, these diagrams use objects. These are represented in a similar way to classes (in contrast to the class name, the object name is underlined), with the possibility of introducing sample values for the attributes.

Objects: sample attribute values

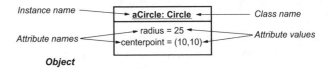

Object

Thus, classes and objects are units composed of attributes, operations, and constraints. The corresponding code in (simplified) Java, for example, looks like this:

```
class Circle
{
  int    radius;
  Point  centerpoint;

  public void setRadius(int newRadius)
  {
    if (newRadius > 0)    // constraint
    {
      radius = newRadius;
      ...
    }
  }
  public void setPosition(Point pos)
  { ... }
  public void display();
  { ... }
  public void remove();
  { ... }
}
```

This example shows only the principle; the actual implementation of the individual operations has been omitted for simplicity's sake.

TAXONOMY AND INHERITANCE

Entomology, the science that deals with insects, has a much longer tradition than computer science. It has been practicing for many decades a method

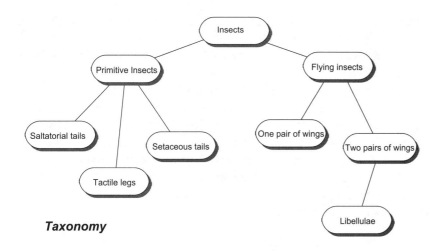

Taxonomy

which in information science is considered as new. Entomologists classify insects present in the whole world using a system called *taxonomy*. Insects are ordered by families and classes. Below the superior group of insects, we find subgroups such as flying insects and primitive insects (without wings). These groups are further subdivided into insects with one pair of wings, two pairs of wings, and so on.

The important factor of this hierarchy (see diagram) is that all insects of a class have identical properties, and that derived subclasses represent a specialization. Subclasses derived from a class automatically have all properties of the superior class. Thus, properties are inherited. This principle is the corner stone of reusability in object-orientation.

Inheritance = Reusing properties

In this way, we can not only classify insects – we can also hierarchically structure objects and concepts used in the area of software development.

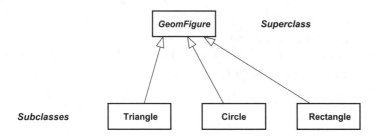

Since this representation reminds us of a family tree and properties are indeed passed from one class down to the next, we also talk about *inheritance* and *hierarchy* of inheritance. The class that bestows its properties is called the *superclass* or *base class*, while the class that inherits something is called the *subclass*. The inheritance relation is represented by an arrow, with the subclass always pointing to the superclass. Arrows can also be bundled, as shown in the illustration on this page.

Generalization
Specialization
Inheritance ⇒ p. 222

This principle is usually called generalization or specialization. The class *GeomFigure* is a generalization of *Circle*, and *Circle* is a specialization of *GeomFigure* – depending on the point of view. This is a case of *is-a* semantics: a circle is a geometric figure. Objects of derived classes can always be

Substitution principle

employed instead of objects of their base class(es) (substitution principle).

Discriminator

Superclasses and subclasses are frequently differentiated by means of a distinctive feature, the so-called *discriminator*. In the following example, we differentiate by figure shape.

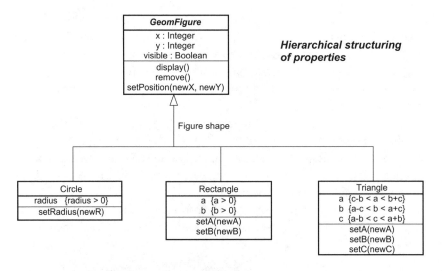

Hierarchical structuring of properties

The above illustration showing the hierarchy of geometric objects is an example of so-called simple inheritance. Besides this form of inheritance, we

Multiple inheritance
⇒ p. 226

also experience multiple inheritance, in which a class can have more than one superclass.

There are various alternatives to inheritance, for example delegation, aggregation, generic programming (such as parameterized classes and C++ templates), and generic design (such as CASE tool macros and scripts), which can sometimes be more advantageous or even unavoidable, so that you should not employ inheritance naively. Inheritance does not have unlimited uses, and it is sometimes not even reasonable to use it.

Structuring of Properties

Differential programming is a politically correct name for object-oriented legacy-hunting. In the generalization or specialization process of classes, a subclass inherits the properties of its superclass, but it must also assume its responsibilities and tasks, at least in principle. Particular features may be specialized, that is, further developed, and new features may be added. Existing properties, however, should neither be suppressed nor restricted.

Differential programming

But how are properties arranged inside an inheritance hierarchy? Fundamentally, properties are situated precisely in those classes where, according to their semantics, they are effectively a property of the class.

Structuring by semantic aspects

This means that properties are not distributed simply according to optimization and non-redundancy criteria, and that they are not placed in a superclass for the sole purpose that subclasses can make practical use of them. Class hierarchies are not designed with such goals in mind, but follow the individual view of the world to be modeled (which must probably be agreed upon and which, moreover, will be potentially different from the real world itself).

The class diagram shown on the previous page shows an example of generalization and specialization of geometric figures. It is assumed that all figures can be displayed on a screen, and that they can be removed and repositioned.

Since these properties are to apply to all figures, the corresponding properties should already be situated in the *GeomFigure* class, together with the attributes for screen position and visibility status. The *visible* attribute indicates whether the figure is currently being displayed. The x and y coordinates specify the center point of the figure.

Further properties cannot be generalized; thus the model looks as shown. The *GeomFigure* class includes the attributes x, y, and *visible*, together with the operations *display()*, *remove()*, and *setPosition()*.

In the derived classes *Circle*, *Rectangle*, and *Triangle*, the sides (a, b, c) or the *radius* are defined, together with constraints on these attributes and operations for modifying the attributes.

The corresponding Java program code for the class model looks as follows (simplified and only for the classes *GeomFigure* and *Rectangle*):

```java
class GeomFigure
{
  int x, y;
  boolean visible;

  public abstract void display();
  public abstract void remove();
  public void setPosition(int newX, newY)
  {
    if (visible) {
      remove();
      x = newX;
      y = newY;
      display();
    } else {
      x = newX;
      y = newY;
    };
  }
}
...
class Rectangle extends GeomFigure
{
  int a, b;  // sides
  public void setA(int newA)
  {
    if (newA > 0) { a = newA; };
  }
  public void setB(int newB)
  {
    if (newB > 0) { b = newB; };
  }
}
```

All geometric figures have one thing in common: they have a position (*x, y* of the figure's center point), they can be displayed, removed, and repositioned. Displaying and removing are common properties of all geometric figures, but they must be implemented individually. A circle is drawn in a different way from a triangle. In the superclass *GeomFigure*, the operations *display()* and *remove()* must therefore be abstract operations. Only inside the classes *Circle*, *Triangle* and so on do they become concrete operations (see the following sample code).

Abstract operations ⇒ *p. 198*

The *setPosition()* operation too is a common property and therefore situated in the *GeomFigure* class. However, it need not be an abstract operation, because it can be concretely implemented by means of the properties *x, y, display()*, and *remove()* already present in the *GeomFigure* class, as shown in the next piece of sample code.

Individual properties in the example are, amongst others, the *radius* of the circle, the *a* and *b* sides of the rectangle, and the *a, b,* and *c* sides of the triangle. In addition, special constraints can be formulated for the sides and the radius. Thus, for example, the value of the *radius* attribute in the *Circle* class must neither be negative nor zero.

Special properties

Constraints ⇒ *p. 206*

Since they use individual properties of the figures, the operations *setRadius(newR)*, *setA(newA)*, and *setB(newB)* are not general properties of the GeomFigure class, but special properties of the subclasses. Things would have been different if we had defined an operation *resize(byFactor)* – this would have been a common abstract property of all geometric figures.

```
class GeomFigure extends Object
{
  int x, y;
  boolean visible;

  public abstract void display();
  public abstract void remove();
  public void setPosition(int newX, newY)
  {
    if (visible) {
      remove();
      x = newX;
      y = newY;
      display();
    } else {
      x = newX;
      y = newY;
    }
  }
}
```

```
class Rectangle extends GeomFigure
{
   int a, b;

   public void display()
   { ... }
   public void remove()
   { ... }
   public void setA(int newA)
   {
      if (newA > 0) { a = newA; };
   }
   public void setB(int newB)
   {
      if (newB > 0) { b = newB; };
   }
}
```

In the diagram below, the *Square* class is modeled as a subclass of *Rectangle*, because it is a special form of rectangle. The *Square* class is a specialization of the *Rectangle* class; the sides *a* and *b* must be equal, which is formulated as a constraint. Thus, objects of the *Square* class have a redundant attribute (the *b* side), because the specification of one side would be sufficient. However, we usually put up with this redundancy because it corresponds to our normal view of the world that a square is a special form of rectangle.

The redundancy-free alternative would consist of realizing the rectangle as a specialization of the square: first, we would create a class with a side *a*, then derive a subclass with a second side *b*. This would be optimal with regard to memory requirements, but we could no longer specify a reasonable discriminator.

Pathological discriminator

A further argument speaks against the rectangle as a specialization of the square: take two variables *s* and *r*, which are of the types *Square* and *Rectangle*, respectively. Now you could assign the variable *s* a rectangle,

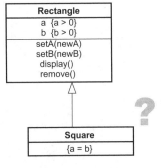

because according to the class hierarchy, a rectangle is compatible with a square – this possibility can, however, hardly be intended.

```
class Rectangle extends Square { ... }
Rectangle r;
Square s;
...
s = r;  // assignment allowed because type
        // compatible, but not sensible
```

A problem of the variation shown in the class diagram (*Square* is a subclass of *Rectangle*) is, however, constituted by the fact that *Square* contains a constraint on attributes of the superclass. In the present example, reduced to the essential as it is, the consequences are clearly visible and not very critical. Generally, however, use of such constraints is strongly discouraged, because subclasses that define constraints on attributes of superclasses cannot enforce that all operations of the superclasses observe them. They have no possibility of knowing the constraint, because inheritance is a one-way process in the direction of the subclasses. Moreover, the properties constrained in one class (*Square*) would be (at least partially) implemented in another class (*Rectangle*).

Substitution principle

After all, objects of the *Rectangle* class can well be squares or become squares, if by chance their sides are equal. This is probably an adequate solution and thus the end of the discussion of this design problem: the *Square* class is not modeled at all; instead, the following operation is envisaged for the *Rectangle* class:

```
public boolean isSquare() {
   return (a == b)
}
```

This discussion shows that generalization and specialization are not solely motivated by optimization and elimination of redundancy, but also by the adopted semantics – and that this too is not always easy.

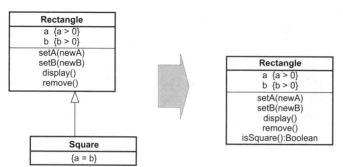

Square rectangles

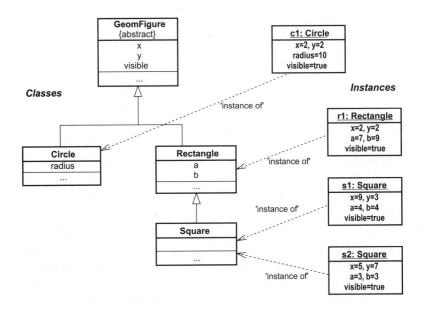

A similar design problem can also be found in the comparison of sides in the *Rectangle* and *Triangle* classes. In both classes, we have the sides *a* and *b* – this redundancy may, however, continue to exist because it has no semantic significance. In the present examples, figures are discriminated by shape, not by number or kind of sides.

ABSTRACT CLASSES

Basics ⇒ p. 190

Classes of which no concrete instances can be created, that is, of which there will never be any objects, are called abstract classes. In our example, there will be objects of the classes *Circle*, *Rectangle*, and *Triangle*, but none of the *GeomFigure* class, because *GeomFigure* is merely an abstraction. It is only included in the model to sensibly abstract the (common) properties of the other classes. Abstract classes are marked by the property value *{abstract}* below the class name or by the class name set in italics.

Tagged values ⇒ p. 211

This does not mean that there can only be objects of the most specialized class in the hierarchy. To illustrate this, the class hierarchy has been extended by a *Square* class (which, as discussed earlier in this chapter, can be problematic). The illustration also shows that an object always includes the attributes of its own class and all its superclasses.

CRC CARDS

CRC cards are filing cards on which the class, its responsibilities and other collaborators are noted. CRC is an abbreviation of Class–Responsibilities–Collaborators. Sometimes, instead of CRC cards, the term class card is used. They are a simple, but practical tool particularly for analysis purposes.

Classes, responsibilities, collaborators ⇒ *p. 124*

What Are Responsibilities?

A class is responsible for the knowledge its objects should have (attributes) and for the operations its objects must carry out to fulfill their tasks and reach their goals.

Attributes
Operations

What Are Collaborators?

These are other classes for which relationships must exist to enable the class to fulfill its tasks. A class may not be able to fulfill all of its responsibilities by its own force; in many cases it must cooperate with other classes. Thus, collaborators are partners in cooperation.

Collaborators are cooperation partners

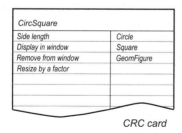

CRC card

CircSquare see ⇒ *p. 35*

CRC cards are suitable for teamwork – as in the Metaplan technique, they can be organized together and stuck to pinboards. The arrangement of the cards usually follows static semantics (that is, generalizations, specializations, associations, and aggregations) or dynamic semantics (that is, the flow of messages).

OBJECTS COMMUNICATE WITH EACH OTHER

As we have seen on the previous pages, classes have attributes, operations, and constraints, and can be ordered hierarchically by means of the generalization principle. However, the objects must also be able to act. They need to call on each other's operations to be able to fulfill their tasks. The classes that another class can communicate with must be explicitly specified. Therefore, CRC cards are used to specify with which classes a class must cooperate for that purpose.

A precondition for cooperation is that the instances of the classes know each other. In the inheritance relationships presented above, this is the case. If no inheritance is involved, cooperation can take place on the basis of association and aggregation, which we are now going to discuss in more detail.

Association

Basics ⇒ p. 228

An association is a relationship between different objects of one or more classes. A simple example is the relationship between a window and a set of geometric figures.

Difference relation/association ⇒ pp. 241 ff.

In the simplest case, an association is represented by a single line between two classes. Usually, however, associations are shown in as much detail as possible. Then, the association receives a name and a numerical specification *Multiplicity, cardinality ⇒ p. 228* (multiplicity indication) of how many objects on one side of the association are connected with how many objects on the other side. Furthermore, the role names are added, which describe the meaning of the classes involved or their objects in more detail (for example, *employee, employer*). Associations are also called *use relationships* – even if this may seem somewhat cheeky in the example below.

Generally, we can differentiate between directed (one-way), bidirectional, and undirected (direction not yet specified) associations. UML (unfortunately) makes no distinction between bidirectional and undirected associations.

Aggregation

Basics ⇒ p. 243

A particular variation of association is aggregation. This is again a relationship between two classes, but with the peculiarity that the classes relate to each other as a whole relates to its parts.

Aggregation is the composition of an object out of a set of parts. A car, for example, is an aggregation of tires, engine, steering wheel, brakes, and so on. These parts may in turn be aggregations: a brake consists of disk, pads, hydraulic cylinder, and so on. Aggregations are *has relationships*: a car *has* an engine. Instead of aggregation, some people talk about *part–whole hierarchy*. Another example of aggregation is shown below.

Has relation
Whole-part hierarchy

A special form of aggregation is one in which the individual parts depend on the aggregate (the whole) for their existence; such a case is called a composition. An example is the relationship between an invoice item and the invoice. An invoice item always belongs to an invoice. If the whole (for example, the invoice) is to be deleted, all existence-dependent parts (for example, the invoice items) are deleted together with it. In a normal aggregation, only the object and its relationship with the other object would be deleted.

Composition ⇒ p. 245 (aggregation with existence-dependent parts)

An example of a normal aggregation is the relationship 'car has wheels': wheels necessarily belong to a car insofar as this is an aggregation, but they can also be regarded as separate entities that can exist without a car – in contrast to some humans who feel incomplete without a car (so-called pathological reverse composition).

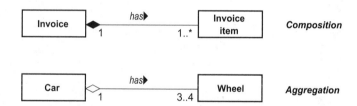

An aggregate may temporarily (mostly at the beginning) also be without parts, that is, a cardinality of 0 is allowed. As a rule, however, the sense of an aggregate is to collect parts.

An essential property of aggregates is that the whole acts as a proxy for its parts, that is, takes on operations which are then propagated to the individual parts. In the aggregation 'invoice has invoice items' for example, these would be operations such as *computeInvoiceTotal()* and *numberInvoiceItems()*.

Propagating operations

In an aggregation, the side of the whole is marked by a lozenge. Compositions are marked by solid lozenges and have always a multiplicity of 1 (or 0..1) on the side of the aggregate. The individual parts of an existence-dependent aggregation can only belong to and depend on one whole. An individual part whose existence depended on different aggregates would be a contradiction. However, besides that one existence-dependent relationship, an individual part may have any number of normal associations and (non-existence-dependent) aggregations with other classes.

Parts of normal aggregations can simultaneously be part of different aggregates which may be instances of different classes or of the same class. The following example shows that one employee can simultaneously work for several departments. Nevertheless, the department is seen as an aggregate because it represents a unit which unites several employees.

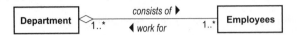

The class diagram shown on the next page contains a further example of a composition, namely a new class *CircSquare* whose objects form an aggregate (here, a graphical overlay) of a square and a circle. As attributes, *CircSquare* therefore only aggregates one circle and one rectangle with equal sides (square). This is a composition because the two partial objects circle and rectangle that make up a CircSquare are existentially related to it. Since a CircSquare must know its partial objects, but the latter need not know who aggregates (uses) them, directed relationships are indicated.

CircSquare,
see Class card ⇒ p. 31
Directed relations
⇒ p. 241

The code for the *CircSquare* class looks as follows in (simplified) Java:

```
class CircSquare extends GeomFigure
{
  Circle    k;
  Rectangle r;

  public void display()
  {
    c.display();
    r.display();
  }

  public void remove()
  {
    c.remove();
    r.remove();
  }

  public void setA(int newA)
  {
    c.setRadius (newA / 2);
    r.setA(neuA);   // this turns the rectangle
    r.setB(neuA);   // into a square (a=b)
  }

  public void resize(float factor)
  {
    setA(r.getA() * factor);
  }
}
```

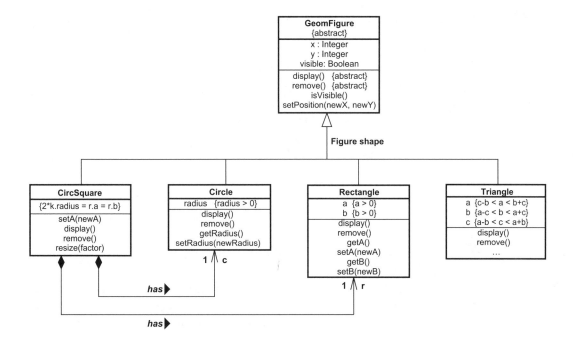

MESSAGE EXCHANGE

Communication between objects is achieved by exchanging messages. The objects send messages to each other. These messages lead to the operations, which means that an object understands precisely those messages for which it has operations.

A message is represented by means of the name of an operation (with arguments enclosed in parentheses, if required) and an arrow. The arrow indicates the direction of the message.

We return to our example of geometric figures and look at the class *CircSquare* and its relationships with *Rectangle* and *Circle*. Let us assume that an object of *CircSquare* is sent a *resize()* message. As the following code fragment shows, inside the *resize()* operation, the object sends a message to itself (*setA()*), which in turn generates messages to *Circle* and *Rectangle*. Thus, *CircSquare* delegates the proper task of resizing to its parts.

```
class CircSquare extends GeomFigure
{
  ...
  public void setA(int newA)
  {
    c setRadius (newA / 2);
    r.setA(newA);
    r.setB(newA);
  }
  public void resize(float factor)
  {
    int a;
    a= r.getA();
    setA(a * factor);
  }
```

(where the local variable *a* has been introduced for a better understanding of the following argumentation).

Difference operation/message

Now, one might think that message exchange between objects is no more than a function or procedure call in traditional procedural programming languages. However, this is not exactly the case. The following three arguments hold against it:

◆ In contrast to conventional programs, operations and data build a unit. An object contains all operations needed for processing its data contents, and all of its further behavior. Facts that are related to each other by their contents, are concentrated inside the object. In traditional programs, they are strewn all over, or stand unconnected one behind the other. In contrast to a procedural solution, in an object-oriented solution operations or messages can only be accessed via the object:

```
Object message: argument.        Smalltalk
Object.message(argument);        // C++, Java
```

for example:

```
aCircle radius: 17.              Smalltalk
aCircle.setRadius(17);           // C++, Java
```

◆ Moreover, object attributes are usually encapsulated and accessible from outside only via appropriate operations (such as the radius which can only be accessed via the *getRadius()* and *setRadius(newRadius)* operations). In procedural languages, these mechanisms can only be realized with a lot of good will and self-discipline (in this case, *aCircle* is, for example, a pointer to a data structure):

```
setRadius(aCircle, 17);
```

◆ The most important issue is, however, that a message can only be interpreted by an object if the object possesses a *matching* operation (in Smalltalk, messages can even be propagated to other objects without any operation at all). However, in the classes that define an object, this operation can have multiple definitions (for example, the operations *display()* and *remove()*). The operation to be used is decided dynamically. Further explanations can be found in the section on polymorphism.

Basics of sequence diagram ⇒ *p. 262*

While the class diagram represents the relationships between the classes in a sort of building plan, collaboration and sequence diagrams are used to show a specific operation or situation. A collaboration or sequence diagram reflects a scenario and shows the individual messages between the objects that are needed to cope with the selected operation. While sequence diagrams emphasize the temporal course of action, collaboration diagrams start from the relational structure of the objects involved. Otherwise, the represented states of affairs are identical.

Collaboration diagrams ⇒ *p. 257*

The following two diagrams show such a scenario. An object of the *CircSquare* class receives a *resize(factor)* message, which means that the two

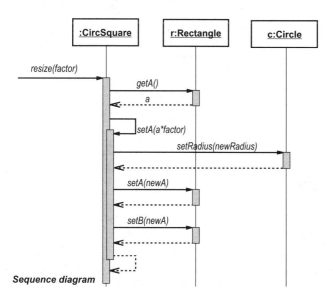

Sequence diagram

Class diagram ⇒ p. 35
Code example
⇒ pp. 36 ff.

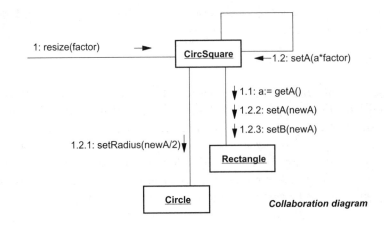

Collaboration diagram

aggregated individual figures are to be resized by the specified factor (for example 1.5).

The *resize(factor)* scenario leads to the following message exchange. It is based on the class diagram and the code samples shown on the two preceding pages.

1.1 The object *CircSquare* sends the rectangle the message *getA()*. The rectangle answers with the value of the current side length, and *CircSquare* stores the answer temporarily in the variable *a*.

1.2 Subsequently, *CircSquare* sends the message *setA(a*factor)* to itself.

1.2.1 Within the *setA(newA)* operation, the *CircSquare* object first sends the message *setRadius(newA/2)* to the circle.

1.2.2 Subsequently, the rectangle is sent the message *setA(newA)*.

1.2.3 Followed by the message *setB(newA)*.

Thus, if the initial side length is 12 and the specified factor 1.5, the new radius is 9 and the new side length is 18.

COLLECTIONS

Container classes

Collections are classes usually defined in the standard class libraries and have in common that they collect and manage sets of objects. Collections are also called container classes. They have all the operations for adding and removing objects, checking whether a given object is contained in the set, and determining how many objects are currently contained in the set.

Ordered collection

A main distinction can be made between sequential collections and associative collections. In sequential collections, objects are collected in a sequential structure; the best known example is the *array*. Associative collections not only store objects, but also an additional key for each object through which it can be identified. An example for this is the *dictionary*.

Sequential and associative collections

The individual collection classes differ with regard to their sorting possibilities and to whether objects may occur more than once, whether objects of different classes may coexist, whether objects may be inserted only at the beginning and the end, whether the number of their elements is variable, whether duplicates may exist, and so on.

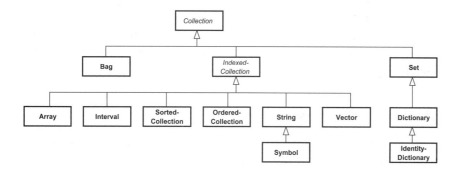

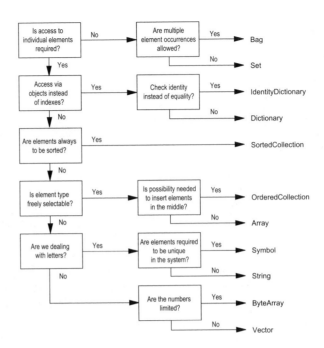

Depending on programming language and class library, the class hierarchy of collection classes may vary. The class hierarchy excerpt shown on the previous page is taken from a Smalltalk library. The overview above (taken from Wallrabe and Oestereich, 1997) shows which of these classes are suitable for which purposes.

POLYMORPHISM

This is in reality one of the cornerstones that makes object-orientation so powerful. The inheritance principle together with dynamic typing of some programming languages or the interface concept of Java form the basis for polymorphism. Polymorphism means that an operation may behave differently (in different classes). There are two kinds of polymorphism: static polymorphism (overloading) and dynamic polymorphism.

Static Polymorphism

Generic operators   Polymorphism is already known from the procedural world, namely in the form of operators such as + or −. These (generic) operators can be applied to both integer and real numbers. Object-oriented programming languages (or hybrid ones such as C++) provide the possibility of using these operators also for user-defined data types or classes. Precisely speaking, operators are nothing more than operations with special names. Therefore, the same effect can also be achieved for normal operations.

A further aspect of polymorphism consists in interface variations of operations of the same name (here in a C++ sample):

```
class TimeOfDay {
  public:
    void setTime(char[8] time);
    void setTime(int h, int m, int s);
};
...
TimeOfDay aClock;

aClock.setTime(17, 1, 0);
aClock.setTime(«11:55:00«);
```

In this example, two operations of the same name exist which differ only by their signature, or which, in other words, only need to be supplied with different parameters. Depending on which parameters are specified (hour, minute, and second as individual values or as a character string), one or the other operation is activated. Users of this class behave in the same way. This should, indeed, always be the case – otherwise, if homonymous operations of a class did not have the same effect, they would sooner or later be used in the wrong way.

Dynamic Polymorphism

A precondition for dynamic polymorphism is the so-called *late binding*. From a physical point of view, binding is the point in the life of a program at which the caller of an operation is given the (memory) address of that operation. Usually, this happens when the program is compiled and linked. Most of the traditional programming languages have this form of binding exclusively, which is called *early binding*. Smalltalk exclusively has late binding.

Late binding

In late binding, the precise memory location of an operation is only determined when the call takes place, that is, when the corresponding message is sent to the object. Thus, the association between message and receiving operation does not occur at compile time, but dynamically at runtime of the program. Why all this fuss?

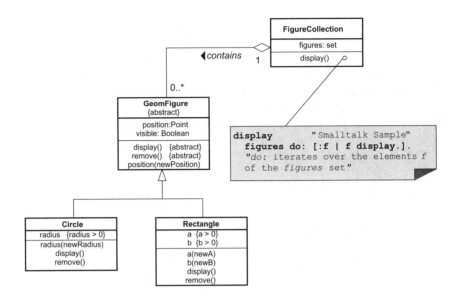

Inheritance ⇒ p. 222

Inheritance means that a class inherits all the properties of its superclass. Thus, without having to define its own attributes and operations, it can have inherited ones. It is, however, free to redefine an inherited operation and to overwrite it with the new definition. Which of these operations is to be used at runtime in response to a corresponding message, that is, which class the called operation comes from, is only decided at runtime.

Example

See the figure above for an example where the classes *Circle* and *Rectangle* are both derived from the superclass *GeomFigure*. A feature shared by all geometric figures is that they can be displayed, removed, and repositioned. Therefore, the superclass already contains these properties – including the *display()* and *remove()* operations, although these are abstract and can only be filled with contents by the derived classes *Circle* and *Rectangle*, because rectangles are displayed (or drawn) differently from circles.

Collections ⇒ p. 38

The figure collection shown in the illustration contains a set of geometric operations, namely circles and rectangles. In a (*do:*) loop, the *display()* operation of the *FigureCollection* class calls the figures one by one and sends them the *display()* message. At this point, it is not known whether the addressed object is a circle or a rectangle.

The object understands the *display()* message in any case, because *display()* is a property of the *GeomFigure* class, from which *Circle* and *Rectangle* are derived. Although the GeomFigure class cannot know how a circle or a rectangle is displayed, it can nevertheless include this function, albeit with no concrete contents.

Circles and rectangles

At the moment in which the *display()* message encounters an object, it is decided which concrete operation will be used: if the object is a rectangle, the *Rectangle.display()* operation is called. Use is always made of the operation of the most specialized class. Thus, although an operation of the *GeomFigure* class calls operations which it also contains itself, the homonymous operation of another class (namely *Rectangle*) is activated. This is polymorphism.

OBJECT IDENTITY

Identity is a property that differentiates an object from all other objects. This term is often confused with addressability, equality of attributes, or a unique name. Particularly in relational databases, names or similar things are used as keys. Usually, these keys are then also employed to create relationships between objects or entities.

Equality vs identity

However, such names are only partly suited to identify an object, because the identity of an object (for example a car) does usually not depend on its attributes (for example the number plate). Names may change; different objects may have the same name. Sometimes, unique names are available (for example social security number), but can or must not be used (for example for reasons of protection of personal data). To avoid these problems from the very start, artificially generated keys are used which have no substantial reference

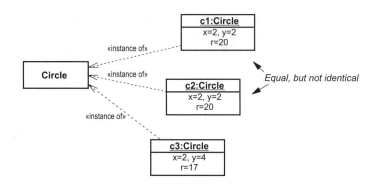

to the properties of the objects and keep their value unchanged forever. Examples of this are unique time stamps or counters (ID numbers).

Object-oriented database systems and CORBA implementations (*Common Object Request Broker Architecture*, an architecture for cross-compatibility in heterogeneous systems, independent from programming languages, operating systems, and computers) include their own mechanisms for this purpose, thus guaranteeing the identity of the objects. Objects that are active in a program are usually uniquely identified by their memory address, that is, by a pointer. Object-oriented databases are often based on system-generated ID numbers and corresponding pointers. The illustration above shows three objects: two of these have identical attribute values; as objects however, they are not identical.

Persistence ⇒ below

Inheritance ⇒ p. 222

PERSISTENCE

Database linkage ⇒ p. 163

Objects are created at runtime of the application program, and if nothing else is done about them, they are deleted at program termination. If objects are to be kept in existence beyond the runtime of the application, they need to be stored in a non-volatile storage medium, that is, a database. Thus, persistent objects are long-term storable objects. All other objects are transient objects. Objects that are stored, but do not exist in the running program, are called *passive objects*, while instances that exist at runtime are called *active objects*.

Persistent objects may contain data exclusively contained in the active object. The data is computed during creation or loading of the object or is added during execution, but is not taken into consideration for later storage. Creation and loading of objects is carried out by special operations.

DESIGN PATTERNS

Design patterns are well tried ideas for the solution of recurring design problems. They are, however, not readily coded solutions, but describe the solution path. Design patterns exist for design problems of all sizes:

Architecture patterns

- ◆ Architectural patterns describe solutions to problems with coarse design, such as the structure of a multi-layer architecture.
- ◆ (Normal) design patterns describe solutions to problems with fine-grained design; examples follow below. They are independent of a specific programming language or environment.

Idioms

- ◆ Idioms are programming language specific solution descriptions.

Many of the design patterns known today were originally implemented in Smalltalk, that is, they were idioms. After undergoing a thorough abstraction process, they have now become language-neutral design patterns.

See framework
⇒ *p. 135*

The following paragraphs briefly list some design patterns. There is no particular, finished theory behind the concept of design pattern; instead, there are various authors who have systematically collected and published such ideas for solutions. For a detailed discussion of design patterns, we recommend the publication by Gamma, Helm, Johnson and Vlissides (1995).

Adapter

Examples

An adapter provides an existing class with a new interface. This can be sensible, for example, if an existing class is to be used, but its interface in the existing form does not fit in with the remaining implementation.

Bridge

A bridge separates the interface of a class from its implementation, thus achieving a higher degree of independence from a concrete (for example platform-specific) implementation.

Composite

The composite pattern is used to create (assemble) tree-like aggregations which can be used equally as individual objects and as a combination of objects. We will explain it in more detail with the aid of a couple of illustrations.

See design pattern notation ⇒ *p. 256*

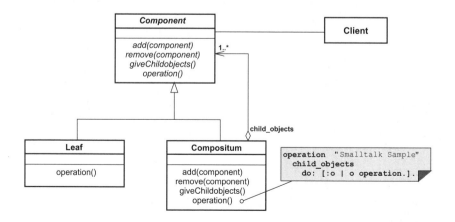

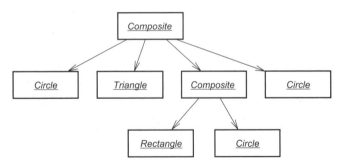

GeomFigure
⇒ *pp. 23 ff.*

Assuming that *Leaf* was the *GeomFigure* class known from the previous examples (with its subclasses *Circle*, *Triangle*, and *Rectangle*), this structural pattern could be used to build groups of geometric figures.

Decorator

The decorator pattern allows the properties of a concrete object to be dynamically changed and extended independently of its class.

Façade

A façade is used to give a set of classes, a subsystem, or a class category a single simple interface that shields it against the complexity of the subsystem classes.

Memento

The memento pattern shows a simple way to restore previous states of objects, for example, for an implementation of undo functions.

Observer

This pattern describes a mechanism that allows all other objects that depend on a given object to be informed about changes in its state (for example, changes of attributes).

Visitor

The visitor pattern shows how an iterative operation can be performed on a set of objects without the involved objects having to know who is iterating over them and how.

SUGGESTED READING

1. Booch, G. (1994) *Object-Oriented Analysis and Design with Applications*, 2nd edn., Benjamin/Cummings.
2. Rumbaugh, J., Blaha, M., Premerlani, W., Eddy, F., Lorenson, W. (1991) *Object-Oriented Modelling and Design*. Prentice Hall.
3. Jacobson, I., Christerson, M., Jonsson, P., Övergaard, G. (1992) *Object-Oriented Software Engineering, A Use Case Driver Approach*. Addison-Wesley.
4. Wirfs-Brock, R., Wilkerson, B., Wiener, L. (1990) *Designing Object-Oriented Software*. Prentice Hall.
5. Martin, J., Odell, J. (1992) *Object-Oriented Analysis & Design*. Prentice Hall.
6. Meyer, B. (1988) *Object-Oriented Software Construction*. Prentice Hall.
7. Gamma, E., Helm, R., Johnson, R., Vlissides, J. (1995) *Design Patterns: Elements of Reusable Object-Oriented Software*. Addison-Wesley.
8. Alexander, C. *et al*. (1977) *A Pattern Language*. Oxford University Press.
9. Alexander, C. *et al*. (1979) *The Timeless Way of Building*. Oxford University Press.
10. Buschmann, F., Meunier, R., Rohnert, H., Sommerlad, P., Stal, M. (1996) *Pattern-Oriented Software Architecture: A System of Patterns*. Wiley.
11. Larman, C. (1998) *Applying UML and Patterns – An Introduction to Object-Oriented Analysis and Design*. Prentice Hall.
12. Schader, M., Korthaus, A. (Eds.) (1998) *The Unified Modeling Language – Technical Aspects and Applications*. Physica, Heidelberg.

Chapter 3

The Development Process

Aye make yourself a plan
They need you at the top!
Then make yourself a second plan
Then let the whole thing drop

Jonathan Jeremias Peachum in 'Song of the insufficiency of human endeavour'
(Bertolt Brecht, The Threepenny Opera)

This chapter describes an application-driven, iterative-incremental, and architecture-oriented life cycle for software development

Business-Oriented Software Engineering Process (BOE Process)

The basis for the process model for object-oriented software development discussed in this chapter is a more comprehensive process model which cannot, however, be systematically described in its entirety in the framework of this book. It would require a whole book to itself.

For this reason, we limit ourselves to an example which describes selected important aspects and alternative techniques and, it is hoped, provides a number of useful suggestions. The discussion in this chapter focuses on medium to large projects with specific boundary conditions, and reflects experiences from several real projects. Thus, the process is practice-oriented and realistic, but has nevertheless an exemplary character.

The BOE process is not a closed, finished process model, but provides a framework which must be adapted to concrete application areas on the basis of process patterns. Depending on application architecture, technical surroundings, and other boundary conditions, specific implementations are required.

AIMS

The object-oriented application development life cycle, as discussed in this book with the use of UML, follows a model for commercial software systems with the following features. It is:

- use case-driven,
- architecture- and component-centered,
- iterative, and
- incremental

Special features of this process model are the subdivision of development activities into small units and the coordinated interlocking of activities with different levels of detail. The development from the rough to the detailed need not be done simultaneously in all areas of the system, but depends on priority and requirements of the problem domain.

Process models that need to consider boundary conditions such as a specific architecture must be adaptable to the customer's enterprise and the specific project. This is not a book on process models and project planning; neither does it describe sophisticated generic process patterns. It is merely intended to present a typical example.

Use Case Driven

At the beginning, use cases are identified systematically. They form the basis for further activities. For example, use cases can be assigned priorities, thus defining which use cases are to be implemented first.

Use case driven means that we intend to employ use cases for determining the requirements. Use cases describe the basic processes in the application area from the users' point of view.

Architecture-Centered

The process of application development must be able to take properties and peculiarities of an existing application domain into account. The application architecture determines which artefacts need to be developed. Frequently, application architectures are layer models and include, for example, the following levels:

- process control,
- dialogs, dialog control,
- business classes,
- persistency.

In addition, systems are often subdivided into components and subsystems.

The architecture describes how the entire system is divided into parts and how these interact. This can be used to decide which parts need to be developed at all. Thus, if the architecture envisages a process level, it is highly probable that process control classes will need to be developed.

Basically, 'architecture-centered' means that the development process supports development of artefacts specified by the architecture in the best possible manner.

Iterative and Incremental

The system is developed in several phases, some of which can be worked on simultaneously. Formerly, application development followed the so-called waterfall model, that is, the complete requirements for the system were defined first, then the design was carried out for the complete system, and finally all parts were implemented.

Waterfall model

The use case-driven approach is more flexible. First, as mentioned above, all use cases should be identified. These form a kind of rough requirement

Example Component creation ⇒ *p. 130*

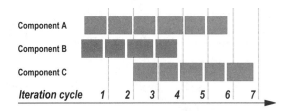

specification. Large systems are then usually structured into subsystems (modularization), which can be done on the basis of the use cases, as we will see later. Subsequently, the subsystems can be developed by separate teams.

Synchronization of partial results

To be able to proceed in an iterative and incremental way, the partial results of the component teams must periodically be synchronized. The components should be developed independently from each other as far as possible, but they need to be coordinated centrally, so that at specific points in time meaningful and, above all, scheduled results are achieved. These intermediate results are then validated in internal and external reviews. This is accomplished inside the project by acceptance test preparation and quality assurance (QA), externally by the customer's business departments, future users, or others.

Component teams

Thus, each team tries to achieve specific expected results by certain times which are planned independently of the completion times of individual components. This requires that the development process of each individual team be divided into iterable steps. Each step consists of fine-grain planning (specification of iteration goals) and an analysis–design– implementation sequence.

Thus, iterative means the decomposition of the development into several similar steps. Each iteration produces a partial result.

Incremental means that the total functionality of the system under development grows with each step.

OVERVIEW OF DEVELOPMENT PHASES

Very roughly, the development process can be divided into the phases of requirement analysis, problem domain analysis, iterative-incremental development and introduction, as illustrated in the following figure.

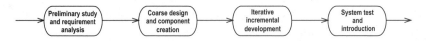

Development phases

Each phase is in turn structured into a number of individual activities. The phases of preliminary study, problem domain analysis and introduction usually proceed consecutively, while the interactive incremental development phase represents the development process proper. The first phases run consecutively to establish a sufficient basis for fundamental project planning, that is, to allow reliable estimation of expenditure, cost, schedules, organization, and staffing.

The following sections describe the individual phases and their development activities in more detail, with the aid of activity diagrams, such as the requirement analysis on page 56. These are slightly extended activity diagrams as briefly explained in the box on page 61.

See requirement analysis diagram ⇒ p. 56

Extended activity diagram ⇒ p. 61

REQUIREMENT ANALYSIS

What is a requirement analysis good for – why don't we model the system straightaway?

Why do we need to analyze requirements at all?

Requirement analysis is justified by the fact that software developers are usually not specialists in the application domain. To develop successful software, information on the underlying problem must be collected. Development planning can be addressed only after the task in hand has been comprehensively described and potential misunderstandings have been eliminated. Requirement analysis is also becoming increasingly important because of the continuously rising demand for quality software.

It is indispensable for analysts to get acquainted with the application domain. This can be done by consulting the professional literature, working guidelines, legal or contractual conditions, and so on.

The most important part of familiarization is to communicate with the (future) users and to get to know the application domain in practice. System analysts must see how future users are currently carrying out their tasks. It may even be helpful to perform the users' tasks or at least get the same basic training as a new customer employee.

Familiarization, getting to know the practice

Developers and users (or other experts) must help the others to achieve a basic understanding of their own field. Thus, the experts on the client's side are, at least marginally, confronted with problems and facts of electronic data processing, and the developers get an idea of the business area for which the software is needed.

The more comprehensive a project is, the more it is important that clients and/or users get a feel for the complexity and susceptibility of software, but also for its flexibility and possibilities. Prototypes can also be used to bring the two perspectives closer to each other. Including future users in the process from the very beginning is important for the success of a project.

Asking questions,
listening, discussing

Analysis consists of putting questions, listening, discussing, getting to grips with the application, and memorizing and documenting the received information in one of the following forms (which will be explained in more detail at a later stage):

- business process models,
- use case models,
- activity models,
- specialized dictionary,
- CRC cards,
- mind maps,
- materials collection,
- dialog blueprints,
- business class models.

Requirements formulated in this way include properties and constraints that the software under development must satisfy. This is, however, not a description of the software system to be developed, but a description of **what** the system is supposed to do (and maybe why), but not of **how** this is to be achieved. The step from *what* to *how* only begins with the dialog design.

What?
Not How?

Besides the features mentioned above, there should also be an introduction to the subject and a general description of the context which have, more or less, the following content:

- Introduction to the subject and the task.
- Fundamentals of the system conception and of the development and future application environments.
- Limits, constraints, priorities, and, if required, step-by-step planning.
- Task, role, and responsibility distribution among all people involved (clients, users, developers, and so on).
- Reliability and quality requirements, that is, description of the effort required for the achievement of specific goals (a flight monitoring system must satisfy higher standards than a flight reservation system).
- Speed requirements, required response time behavior.
- Expected data volume.
- Principal reactions to unwanted results and incorrect handling.

The contents must be coordinated with the client. This requirement description can be used at a later stage to verify if and how the finished product meets the requirements, although only very roughly because detail requirements emerge gradually during the course of the development process. In any case, the requirements should include the criteria for acceptance of the system by the customer.

Cooperation with Domain Experts

Analysis is inconceivable without close cooperation with experts (domain experts) and collaborators for the application area. These are the people to interview, to elicit designs from, and to discuss requirements with.

Domain experts need not necessarily be (part of) the future users – they are just people who know an awful lot about the application domain. Experts may be somewhat peculiar or weird. Often, the more specialized someone is, the more difficult that person is to understand. Analysts are simply exposed to the quality (or expertise) of the experts – how good these are is almost impossible for them to judge, except on the basis of plausibility and absence of contradictions. Experts may have a very peculiar view of the application domain, and different experts may have different views or see only a limited section.

Domain experts

Users and experts involved in the analysis should have a basic knowledge of the following issues:

- How are software projects fundamentally carried out?
- What are 'use cases'? How are they used to determine and define requirements?
- Which possibilities of interaction and presentation are offered by graphical user interfaces? What are buttons, scroll bars, option fields, tool bars, and so on?

Special knowledge of object-orientation as such is neither required from the customer nor from the customer's staff and experts involved.

Activities of Requirement Analysis

The activity diagram on the next page shows the individual activities that typically occur in requirement analysis. Following sections are coded (A1, P1, and so on) to refer to activities on the diagram. The listed activities need not necessarily be carried out in every project, but should be seen as dependent on border conditions and properties of a concrete project commission.

For smaller-scale projects, internal developments, and projects with well-known long-term customers, some of these activities will probably be considered only minimally. Things are different in a large-scale project with a

Each project is different

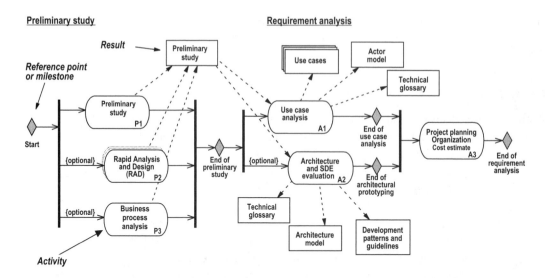

new customer which technologically breaks new ground and might even have to be carried out at a fixed price.

Alternative solutions   **PRELIMINARY STUDY.** Frequently, before a concrete software development project is actually started, a preliminary study is carried out which describes what the nature of the task or the problem as such is, and which principal alternatives are conceivable for its solution.

RAD WORKSHOP. Before the first development cycle, a two to four weeks RAD (Rapid Analysis and Design) workshop might be organized, where the most important business processes, use cases, business objects, and components are contemplated, and first application prototypes or prototypical application fragments are designed and implemented.

BUSINESS PROCESS ANALYSIS. As a rule, the application domain in which the system under development will be employed is integrated into existing business processes or will be in future. To clarify how the system to be developed *Integration* can be optimally integrated, the business processes must be analyzed in the *into the context* context of the new system.

USE CASE ANALYSIS. With the aid of use cases, the requirements to be satisfied by the system under development are defined, that is, *what* it should do, and in which working contexts (but not *how* it should do it).

EVALUATION OF ARCHITECTURE AND SOFTWARE DEVELOPMENT ENVIRONMENT. To reduce technological risks and pave the way for the application development as such (that is, to force a more efficient software development) the corresponding problem zones could, for example, be analyzed as prototypes.

Depending on the peculiarities of a project, other types of preliminary studies might be indicated. Recently, for example, I participated in an analysis of a project which involved the development of a new application (a new, object-oriented client–server technology), but on the basis of a reference application of the supplier (in old procedural technology). At the customer's site, a so-called gap analysis was performed which helped to determine which requirements were already covered by the old existing solution, which requirements were newly formulated for this customer, and at which points the reference system had to be adapted. Thus, the requirements for the new development were the sum of the reference solution and the identified 'gap'.

Gap analysis

Preliminary Study

P1

Before attempting to solve a task, there is much to be said, first of all, for defining what this task or problem effectively consist of; subsequently showing the principal solution variations; and finally deciding for a concrete solution variation. The following procedure has worked well in practice:

- *Specification of general aims*.   Together with the customer, the general aims and the border conditions to be considered are specified. Resulting documents: conference protocols, and the like.
- *Information sources*.   Documents are viewed and existing ideas regarding the problem are collected. How is the problem currently being handled? Resulting documents: list of existing information sources and contact partners.
- *Is-state*.   Questionnaires and interviews are used to obtain a rough outline of the current state.
- *Clarification of requirements*.   Meetings and conversations with the technical departments are used to determine the general functional and non-functional requirements and ideal aims of people affected and involved. Resulting documents: conference protocols.
- *Delimitation of the problem area*.   What does no longer belong to the task? Where do we find interfaces with the outside world? Output: task description, context diagram.
- *Identification of actors*.   Who does what, that is, which users are allocated which tasks and competences in the context of the problem domain. Output: actor diagram, competence scheme, privilege concept.
- *Context description*.   What does the environment where the system under development will later be running look like? Output: an infrastructure model which describes hardware, software, network, and middleware technology and architecture.

Aims

◆ *Use case identification.* What is the definition of the use cases that the system is supposed to support? A named list of use cases provides a first orientation about the requirements. If possible, each use case is briefly explained with one sentence or a couple of keywords. Output: use case overview.

Focal points, priorities

◆ *Priorities.* Focal points are defined and priorities assigned. Which problems are most urgent to be solved, which ones can wait? Output: framework concept.

Alternative solutions

◆ *Alternative solutions.* Possible solution approaches are elaborated and confronted. Which alternatives are conceivable? For very urgent problems, the question of possible instant measures arises. Output: presentation of alternative solutions.

Recommendation

◆ *Recommendation.* Solution alternatives are evaluated (on the basis of previously defined criteria); if necessary, a profitability analysis is carried out. Output: recommendation.

◆ *Further requirements.* To conclude, the further requirements for the recommended alternative – or the one requested by the customer – is planned. Output: recommendation for further requirements.

Results of preliminary study

- ◆ List of contact partners
- ◆ List of information sources
- ◆ Conference protocols
- ◆ Description of the current (is-) state
- ◆ Presentation of alternative solutions
  - – Instant measures
  - – Profitability analysis
  - – Evaluation, prioritization
  - – Recommendation
- ◆ Task description
- ◆ Framework concept
- ◆ Context diagram/actor model
- ◆ Business process model
- ◆ Infrastructure model
- ◆ List of interfaces
- ◆ Batch program descriptions
- ◆ Set structure study
- ◆ Structural and procedural organization
- ◆ Potential RAD workshop
  - – Exemplary use cases
  - – Demo version or prototype

All points combine to make a preliminary study which is elaborated before the project proper begins. Whether a preliminary study is carried out at all, and into how much detail it goes, depends on the size and importance of the project, and the risks it entails for the customer and contractor. There may be cases where the task reveals itself as larger than originally thought. In such a case, consideration should be given to splitting the project into individual sub-projects. The question might also arise as to whether the problem could be solved by using standard products instead of a proprietary software development. If the decision is to produce tailored software, the proper software development project begins.

Preliminary study

Make or buy?

Rapid Analysis and Design   *P2*

Prior to the first proper development cycle, a two- to four-week RAD (Rapid Analysis and Design) workshop may be organized, to analyze the fundamental requirements for the general framework. During this time, developers, users, and clients work closely together and carry out a rapid analysis and a first prototyping. Developers build their systems of terms and contexts for the application's environment, while users get a first idea of the forthcoming developments. Moreover, ways and structures of communication for the subsequent project work are explored and, as far as possible, formalized.

The most important business processes and use cases are cursorily analyzed and immediately implemented in an exemplary way, that is, first application fragments are realized. The workshop ends with a joint evaluation and critical review of the achieved results. If the project domain covers several independent application areas (for example technical departments), separate RAD workshops may have to be carried out for each of these fields.

Business Process Modeling   *P3*

Only in exceptional cases does the system to be developed come right out of the blue. Usually, it will be integrated into an existing application area, or the area will be extended by the new system. To clarify how the new system can be optimally integrated, business processes in the surroundings of the new system need to be analyzed and modeled.

Out of the blue

Usually, business process modeling covers not only EDP-relevant process elements, but also (and mainly) includes organizational aspects. Therefore, in many enterprises, different departments are responsible for the two. The organization department analyzes and implements the processes in the enterprise

Workflow

as a whole, also ensuring their completeness, while the EDP department is concerned with providing the data processing tools for the subset of EDP-relevant processes.

System environment

To achieve an efficient and sensible integration of the new application system, the points of contact with surrounding processes need to be clarified. The system under development must take the resulting facts into consideration. If needed, existing surrounding processes need to be adapted and/or optimized.

Although business process modeling is often the starting point for the development of an EDP system, business organizers and software engineers work with different models and at different tasks. The weakness of object-oriented methods in modeling behavioral aspects of systems is one of the reasons why they work with different models in spite of – or because of – object-oriented development. Specifically, the modeling of business processes of enterprises has long been only marginally considered in object-oriented notations.

UML

UML has substantially remedied the situation. With new and extended concepts, UML goes far beyond the possibilities contained in the original methods of the three UML initiators: Booch, Rumbaugh, and Jacobson.

Nevertheless, the available means of UML still do not reach the expressive power and universality of event-driven process chains and tools such as the ARIS tool set (see Oestereich, 1998, Scheer, 1994 and Scheer *et al.*, 1997).

One new feature of UML, that is, a diagram type not to be found in this form in the old methods of the 'Amigos,' is the activity diagram (see below).

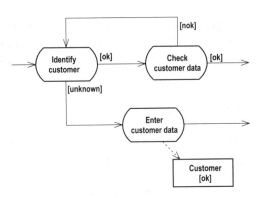

They combine approaches from several other techniques: Jim Odell's event diagrams, state diagrams, and Petri nets. Activity diagrams can also be used in a somewhat fuzzy and conceptional way, as in a detailed specification involving implementational aspects.

◆ Extended Activity Diagrams

Basic elements of these diagrams are again activities and transactions. Results are shown in the form of object states, that is, as rectangles. The production of results is represented by dashed arrows pointing toward the result. If an activity presumes specific results, we will use a dashed arrow that points toward the activity. Dashed arrows may be equipped with cardinality indications if the set of created or needed results needs to be defined precisely.

In addition or as alternatives to start and end states, (gray) filled upright diamonds are used to denote reference points, milestones, or transaction points (commits).

Synchronization bars can be equipped with {and}, {xor}, and other constraints to express that either all or only one of the preceding activities needs to be carried out. Moreover, transitions can be marked as {optional}. The subsequent activity can, but does not necessarily need to be carried out. If it is performed, it will be considered in a subsequent synchronization.

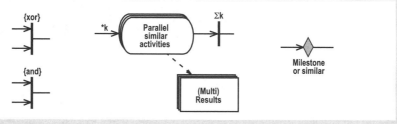

If several similar activities can be performed in parallel, these activities are represented by overlapping overlaid symbols, similar to multi-objects. The same method is used to denote multi-results. For an exact description of parallel activities, cardinalities can be specified, even by using symbolic variable names (such as i, j, k, and so on). These are referred to again at the synchronization bars (synchronization of parallel activity paths, denoted by a Σ sign).

These variables can also be used for the construction of loops. Manipulation (incrementation) of loop counters may occur at reference points or activities. Conditions (in square brackets) and branches (decision points, shown as empty horizontal diamonds) are represented as in normal activity diagrams.

Activity diagrams describe processes by means of activities which can be active sequentially or in parallel and for which branching and synchronization can be defined. Activities can in turn be split into sub-activities. So-called swim lanes (or responsibility lanes) allow simple assignments to be represented, for example to an organizational structure.

Activity diagram ⇒ *p. 252*

Activity diagrams are mainly suitable for description and modeling of business processes, but special conventions are needed in order to model transactions, renewed submissions, turn-around times, and the like. Representation of organizational structures and modeling of role concepts and privileges can only be handled in trivial situations. As soon as complexity reaches a realistic degree, the elements of activity diagrams become unwieldy.

A1 *Use-Case Analysis*

Use Cases ⇒ p. 207

The individual software-relevant working processes are analyzed and described in so-called use cases. Use cases are not only employed for describing the desired requirements (or the current state), but also for introducing the software developers into the special subject of the application. Terminology and language of the application world must be explored.

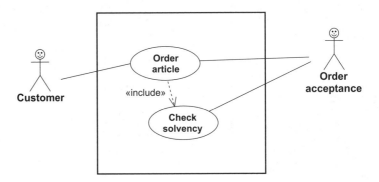

A use case diagram describes the relationships between a set of use cases and the actors involved. A use case is the description of the typical interaction between the user and the system, that is, it represents the external system behavior in a limited working situation from the user's point of view.

Is and should-be descriptions

If use cases are employed for describing the is-state, they need to be followed up by the development of projections of the future system, which formulate and illustrate what working processes within the system to be developed will look like. For each is-case, a desired case is elaborated. Usually, however, only use cases for a desired description are constructed.

Context diagram Example ⇒ p. 102

At the highest level of the use case model, only fundamental use cases are to be seen; here, the focus is on the application context. Therefore, this level is also referred to as the context diagram.

Actor diagram Example ⇒ pp. 102 ff.

In the context diagram, the system limits are emphasized, and it is shown which actors interact with the system and which external events can affect the system.

Use-cases are elaborated together with users and domain experts, or validated and verified by the latter.

Dialog design

One important possibility of validating the requirements is the creation of application prototypes, that is, of application fragments which satisfy a specific requirement aspect, but are not completely functional. In many cases, these are dialog models. Most development tools with dialog editors or generators

- **Pre- and post-conditions (triggers, results)**
  Expected state of the system before or after the use case is run through.
- **Non-functional requirements**
  Qualitative assertions, special response time requirements, frequency estimates, development priorities, and so on.
- **Process**
  Description of the typical process, if needed, subdivided into numbered individual points.
- **Variations**
  Variations of and exceptions to the scenario and description of the alternative scenario for such cases.
- **Rules**
  Business rules, technical dependencies, validity and validation rules, and so on, which are of importance in the framework of the scenario.
- **Services**
  List of operations and, if needed, objects, which are required in the framework of the scenario (used as a transition towards the class design).
- **Contact partners, meetings**
- **Open points**
- **Dialog blueprints or patterns**
- **Diagrams**
- **...**

also provide simple test and process functions. These are useful and usually also sufficient for exploration and validation of the requirements.

Besides dialog designs, form and report designs, calculation rules, and the like can also be used for this purpose. The tools used for creating these explorative prototypes need not necessarily be the same as those that will be used in the final system. Sample dialogs also serve as illustrations of the use cases.

Report and form design

During the use case analysis, synonyms are recognized and resolved. It should also be noted that all use cases are at the same level of abstraction and detail. The challenge for the software engineers is to stick to a given level of detail and maybe even fuzziness, that is, to view the application world in breadth without getting caught in detail studies and other pitfalls. As long as it makes sense, similar use cases can be collected together.

The terms and language of the application world are further reconstructed or explored by the system analysts and noted in a glossary. As far as

Abstraction level

possible, the technical language of the subject area is used, rather than computer jargon.

Unique and
well-defined terms

During analysis with use cases, a multitude of terms from the application world appears which is only in rare cases completely understood and memorized by the system analysts. Frequently, also terms within the application area are either unclear or mean different things to different people. An incorrectly understood application domain can, under certain circumstances, lead to a correctly functioning (verified) system; only it will probably be the wrong system. Clarification of terminology is therefore an elementary part in the validation of system requirements. (Are we developing the right system?) Creation of a technical dictionary will certainly be helpful.

Verify

Validate

CRC cards ⇒ p. 124

To obtain a most comprehensive overview of the terms of the application domain, it is, for example, possible to organize brainstorming sessions with so-called CRC (Class Responsibilities Collaborators) cards. CRC cards can also be used as a structuring and modeling aid. While use cases serve to analyze the behavior, CRC cards help to clarify the structure.

Use cases:
identify behavior

CRC cards:
identify structure

It is a good idea to have the use cases elaborated by staff familiar with the technicalities of the application domain. Abstraction and modeling capacities, however, are more important. Thus, if possible, good system analysts are to be preferred to domain experts.

Provided you are charged with the requirement analysis, try to get familiar with the application domain. Work together with experts in the application area. Try to emulate their tasks and activities and place yourself in their position – where are the decisive challenges and focal points of activity? Always continue to ask why this or that is done in a certain way, and not differently. Also, do all the potential users work in the same way?

Existing information
systems and models

Another source of information is provided by existing information systems, even if these are designed for a different goal. Do descriptions of these systems exist? If data models or class models exist, they are a precious source. Maybe they can be partly re-employed. At least they provide some ideas. How are these information systems judged by the users?

Obviously, a previously elaborated preliminary study also belongs to the fundamental project documents.

Study documentation
and special literature

If there is specialized literature on the application domain, you should ask the local experts which literature they can recommend. In certain cases, there are also standard works that can be found on practically every desk – and your desk should be the next one.

As well as looking and listening, working in the field, and studying existing documentation, an efficient requirement analysis also includes asking well-aimed, well-prepared, and well-structured questions. For this purpose, interviews may be carried out systematically, supported, if required, by previously prepared questionnaires.

Interviews

Terms and objects of the application domain are recorded, and their properties are assimilated together with the way users handle these objects. The same is done with activities, events, and processes in the application domain.

Helpful questions for requirement analysis

- ◆ Which (material and immaterial) objects are used in the application domain (for example forms, contracts, folders, persons, places, equipment, other systems, and so on)?

Objects

- ◆ What are the properties of these objects; how are they built ('a … consists of …' and the like)? What are their structures, how are they put together?

Properties

- ◆ How do users typically handle these objects (enter, remove, and so on)?
- ◆ What do future users expect from the system to be developed? Is the possible performance viewed realistically? What are the pressing issues? Do they have the same expectations and requirements of the system as the requestor (management, for example)?
- ◆ How do employees communicate with each other, that is, who must talk or write to whom in order to process the current tasks? Are there any (periodic) meetings or rituals?

Communication

- ◆ Which objects are used by whom? Do users have different views of the properties of the objects? Which roles and functions can be associated with users and objects? Look out for insufficient terms of description.

Roles

- ◆ What kind of working instructions exist or can be identified? For many tasks there are schemes which are followed as a standard. Sometimes, users are not aware of this. Such processing schemes and working instructions must then be formulated or represented explicitly. Which official and informal agreements exist between users and/or departments? Which concepts, principles, guidelines, and instructions do they follow?

Work processes

- ◆ How are users organized? Which organizational units are affected by the project? What authority, know-how, and type of behavior do users have? Who is responsible for what?

Organization, rights, responsibilities

- ◆ When do different events occur? How are activities initiated (if or when, after, before, …)? Are there any periodical requests, interruptions, orders, and so on? Who triggers the events? Who reacts to them? In which context

Events

do these events occur? Which events need to be memorized (stored)? For how long? By whom? Are there any historical events that must be considered? Are the events data-related, time-related, or user-related?

Conditions
- Which general conditions must be recognized (needs to, always has, is not allowed to, ...)? Are the conditions constant or what is their meaning in time? Who defines the conditions?
- Are the events and activities exceptions or are they standard cases?
- Which undesirable events can occur? What should be the reaction to such events?
- Which processes function well from the point of view of the people involved? Where are future (short-term, medium-term, or long-term) changes to be expected? Are there bottlenecks? Which activities are important, which are less important?

A2   *Architecture and SDE Evaluation*

In many object-oriented projects, new technological ground is entered. This has not only related to object technology, but generally to today's rapid technological development. Perhaps a new database is employed, or a new programming language, new development tools, new communication middleware, a different application architecture, particular quality and other non-functional requirements, or perhaps special existing legacy systems are to be integrated – whatever happens, all side conditions the project team is not familiar with pose risks to the project.

One strategy to minimize these risks is to analyze them as early as possible. This means, for example, gaining experience with the aid of a prototype focused on these risks. Depending on the risks, a 'database prototype', a 'legacy integration prototype', or a general technological prototype is developed.

This prototyping is not only used to study the risks, but also to eliminate identified weaknesses as far as possible, or at least to describe measures needed for their elimination.

Remove obstacles

The results of prototyping are model solutions, development guidelines, work-arounds, and an architecture model which describes the fundamental structure of the software to be developed, such as the layers and units into which the application is divided and their interconnection.

Architecture model
Example ⇒ p. 112

The architecture model influences project planning, project organization, and the general proceedings. With the increase of judgment possibilities and the decrease of development risks, cost estimates can become more precise and secure.

Effects on planning,
organization,
proceeding,
cost estimate

System and application architectures must be supported by the software development environment and therefore need to be integrated in the analysis.

The application architecture is continuously developed during the subsequent phases and activities, in particular during the iterative and incremental development phase; this is, however, no longer explicitly mentioned in the following discussion.

Project Planning, Project Organization, and Cost Estimates

A3

For project management, the results and assessments of the preliminary studies potentially represent the basis for planning further proceedings. Maybe the existing information is sufficient to elaborate the first rough project plan and to determine the order of the cost. If this is so, this activity can be anticipated.

Iteration planning

If the system needs to be developed at a fixed price, the information available at this point may still be insufficient. A precise requirement description is probably only provided by the use cases elaborated during the use case analysis (A1). In order to give a better estimate of existing technological risks it may also be sensible to carry out an architecture prototyping (A2).

Fixed price?

A1 ⇒ p. 62
A2 ⇒ p. 66

Project duration

Required staff

Cost estimate ⇒ p. 80

Project organization

The first rough project plan gives information on how long the project will probably last, which dependencies exist at the highest planning level, where the critical path lies, and how many project staff will be needed. More about cost estimates can be found later in this chapter.

The project organization describes tasks, roles, qualifications, and responsibility areas within the project. Tasks keep changing during the course of a project. Some are only relevant in specific periods, others become more or less important in the course of time. This also affects cooperation between collaborators. Thus, project organization is not static, but a continuous flow.

Therefore, it is of utmost importance to plan it pro-actively, and not leave it to chance or to the influence of current events. Project organization is directly dependent on the process model, which describes the chronological and substantial sequence of activities and outcomes, and which must be optimally supported by the organization.

Restructuring at transition to iterative project phase

At the end of the requirement analysis, enough information is available to describe the organization which will begin the project and to determine at which points in time organizational changes will become necessary. During the phases of requirement analysis and the subsequent problem domain analysis, the organization evolves only slowly, merely changing the extent and importance of individual tasks and roles.

See C3 ⇒ p. 72

At transition time from problem domain analysis to component development, however, a significant restructuring takes place. With component development, the iterative and incremental process begins. Moreover, different teams work in parallel. Thus, results and tasks of the teams need to be centrally coordinated, and cross-sectional, that is, cross-component tasks must be integrated.

Later, at the transition towards test, migration, and certification, another clear change in organizational focuses takes place.

Compromise

It must be noted that the organization cannot be abstractly geared towards the project plan and the chronological dependencies. Very decisive factors are qualification and skills of the existing or expected staff, which will not be ideal. Necessary qualifications and experience will be lacking in certain points, or be insufficient, or only partially available or at the wrong time.

In such cases, the organization should be adapted accordingly, that is, tasks and roles are specified and combined in such a way that they can be covered by suitable people. If appropriate people are available at the wrong time, it should be checked whether the process should not be modified to suit them. Also, staff personal preferences and ambitions should be considered. Here, the question arises as to how the project management gets to know about qualifications and ambitions of the project collaborators.

PROBLEM DOMAIN ANALYSIS

The following activity diagram provides an overview of the processes in the problem domain analysis phase. Activities in this diagram are coded (P1, P2, and so on) and can be linked to their relevant section using the marginal codes. Problem domain analysis includes those activities which consider, abstract, and turn into solution approaches the outcomes obtained from the requirement analysis phase, but which cannot yet be used for reasonable iterative and incremental proceedings.

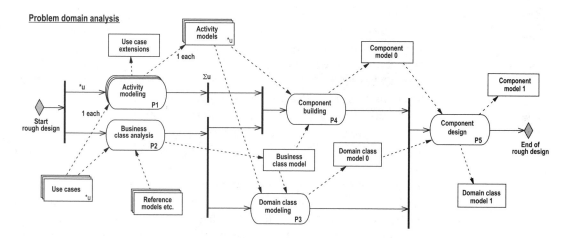

Problem domain analysis activities are used to sorting and structuring requirements, and to identifying and describing development units (components) needed for a sensible further application development.

Activity Modeling   P1

The previously defined use cases describe typical processes and actors' interaction, and are each subdivided into a number of individual activities. Now, for each use case, the corresponding activity diagrams are created. To begin with, each partial step from a use case can be understood as an activity. In contrast to use cases, activity diagrams provide a better description of dependencies, parallel processes, decision and branching points, and so on. Activity diagrams are essentially a more detailed representation.

Example ⇒ p. 128

In the framework of this activity modeling, it usually becomes necessary to tailor the activities differently from what was originally stated in the use case. Some need to be subdivided into further activities, in others, new relationships and dependencies are detected. Activities should cause a significant change of state, otherwise, their contents can probably be incorporated into other activities. A unified and powerful nomenclature and the comparable levels of abstraction and detail help to identify identical and similar activities from different use cases, that is, they help to recognize and eliminate model redundancies.

P2

Business Class Modeling

Identification of business objects

Here, a first class model is created which contains exclusively or pre-eminently elementary terms in form of classes; it is also known as the *analysis model*. The main elementary terms from a user's point of view are interpreted as business objects; the identified responsibilities are a rough outline of the first interface designs of these business objects; and the identified cooperation with other business objects leads to the first draft associative relationships.

Example ⇒ p. 128

Coarse class model and interfaces

Identification of business objects or classes means specification of the most important classes of the future class model and their relationships with each other. Details and subtleties are ignored at this stage. A business class describes an object, a concept, a place, or a person from real business life with a degree of detail that can also be understood by technical departments and managers.

The basis of business class modeling are the use cases, their enclosures (dialog designs, forms), the technical dictionary, CRC cards, and potentially existing reference models (for example ER models of the previous system). Class analysis or business class modeling do not yet mean complete modeling of the application domain, but are intended to provide an early structural overview of the application domain.

P3

Domain Class Modeling

Domain classes are technically motivated classes which represent a concept of the application domain. Thus, a domain class model is a normal class diagram which represents the technical structures of the problem domain; it is also known as the design model. It can be created on the basis of the business model, subdividing the business classes into more detailed units.

Example ⇒ pp. 139 ff.

Domain classes are as far as possible described by means of the attributes, operations, constraints, and relationships identified so far. The emphasis of this modeling process, however, does not rely as much on extensive detailing of the classes with respect to their properties as on an overall consistent abstraction level.

Identifying Components and Subsystems

P4

On the basis of the activity diagrams and the business model, it is now possible to tailor the components or subsystems. Components are mostly understood as smaller units, for example in the sense of Java Beans. A subsystem is a larger unit composed of several individual components. Therefore, a subsystem is a special form of a component.

Component, subsystem

The subdivision of the models is mainly technically motivated, that is, technically related model elements are now also formally united. At this point, it is not yet mandatory to build components; it is sufficient simply to group the model elements. As a first step, packages may be used. Besides the consideration of technical aspects, care should be taken to ensure that dependencies and interfaces between the individual components or packages are minimized. The result is a first component model (or a package model).

Packages ⇒ p. 217
Component ⇒ p. 272

Example ⇒ p. 130

Component Design

P5

On the one hand, the processed component model is now reviewed to incorporate the conclusions of the domain class modeling. Possibly, the domain class model suggests different component boundaries. While the first component model was mainly behavior-driven, that is, created on the basis of activity models, the new model also takes the static structures of the problem domain, that is, the domain class model, into account.

See ⇒ p. 130,
⇒ p. 133, ⇒ p. 155

On the other hand, the domain class model too is reviewed. All activities of the activity models and the interfaces identified in the component model are now mapped onto the domain class model. Activities mostly result in operations which are to be realized, for example, by process control classes or the like, provided the system to be developed has a process control. Other operations can be associated to exactly one domain class.

Architecture

MVC (Model View Controller) ⇒ p. 114

At this point, we realize that the development process is architecture-dependent, and that it can hardly be described in a generally valid way.

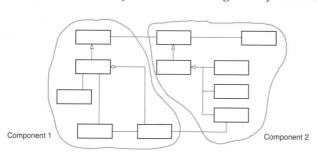

Component 1   Component 2

ITERATIVE-INCREMENTAL COMPONENT DEVELOPMENT

With component development, the application development enters its iterative and incremental phase. Enough information has been collected and structured to develop the application in an evolutionary, that is, growing way.

Generally speaking, one could obviously proceed incrementally and iteratively from the very beginning. The only problem is that this would happen in a largely unplanned manner, without the possibility of systematically ensuring that all requirements are implemented in a sensible order, and without being able to estimate cost and duration with reasonable precision.

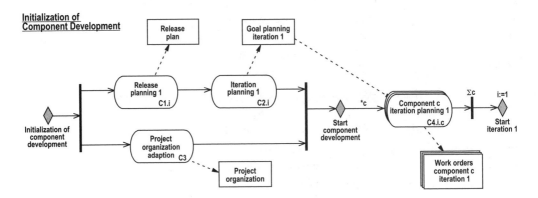

For a systematic evolutionary development, the first iteration needs to be preceded by several preliminary activities. These are summarized in the following diagram showing the initialization of component development. The iterative development process as such is shown later in this section.

C3   *Adapting the Project Organization*

Project organization
⇒ p. 79

As already mentioned under the heading of project organization in the section on requirement analysis, the transition to the iterative development phase requires the project organization to be restructured in order to meet the requirements of this phase.

At this point, the process model allows parallel development, in other words, distribution of the work across a set of partial projects or teams. A sensible subdivision into parallel development processes can be carried out alongside the component borders. The individual subsystems can be developed in teams working in parallel. This is also the point where the corresponding teams should be constituted.

To ensure that subsystems and components result in a common application, the results of the teams must be periodically combined together. Furthermore, there are still development activities which cannot be performed in parallel because they are cross-section tasks or because cross-component outcomes are to be produced.

Both directions, the cross-section one and the component-specific one, need to be considered and coordinated in the project organization.

Release Planning   *C1.i*

After initial analysis and the problem domain analysis, the evolution iteration can now be planned. All requirements must be sensibly distributed across the envisaged iterations. For this purpose, one must know the number of iterations planned, how long they are supposed to last, and which subsystems and components are to be developed when or in which sequence of priorities and dependencies.

This planning can actually be based on the use cases. Use cases which

♦ cover a large part of the total requirements,
♦ are seen as priority by the customer, or
♦ relate to a special risk domain

should be implemented first.

Use cases which refer to a large intersection of common activities need to   *Grouping use cases*
be implemented together, in order to implement the individual activities with regard to a maximum number of application contexts and to reduce coordination efforts. This increases the universality and robustness of the implemented solutions.

The release plan must specify which requirements need to be implemented and when. If needed, the implementation can also be viewed in several steps. Possible implementation steps could be, for example:

♦ *Coarse implementation.* More than 2/3 of the activities of a process are tentatively implemented, that is, they can be simulated.
♦ *Detailed implementation.* All activities are present in their implementations, but not in a completely finished form.
♦ *Complete implementation.* Complete coverage and realization of all activities.

Coordination of release plan

The difficulty lies in finding objective criteria for determining completeness. As far as possible, differentiated assertions should be made, such as 'only implement dialog', 'including all plausibility checks', or 'completely implemented persistence', and so on.

Release planning must be coordinated with all the people involved, that is, externally with the client (requestor, departments, users), and internally. Externally, the plan needs to be considered reasonable; internally, that is, by the developers, it must be seen as feasible.

Depending on system size and environment, one iteration should be envisaged to take a development time of about 1–3 months.

Since a review takes place at the end of each iteration, to assess the level of achievement of the set goals, additional cost is created by pre- and post-paration and execution of the reviews. On the other hand, they provide precious information for controlling the project. Cost is also created at the client's side. Frequently, departments and future users are only available to a limited extent because they need to get on with their daily work.

The development process can be relaxed at this point by not having a review with the customer after each iteration, and having one or two iterations with internal reviews only, after an iteration with customer (external) review.

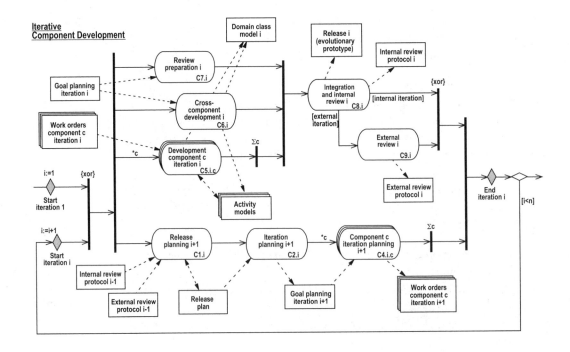

Experience shows that the development project should include about 4–7 iterations with external reviews to develop the complete system. These figures give only a rough orientation and depend, among others, on the following parameters:

- *System size.* Object-oriented pilot projects and large-scale projects may lie outside the above-mentioned limits.
- *Development basis.* Programming environment, modeling tools, generators, class libraries, application frameworks, and so on.
- *Environment.* Interfaces with other systems, and so on.
- *Number and productivity of developers.*

From the second iteration onward, the protocols of the preceding internal and external reviews need to be taken into account in order to correct the overall planning accordingly; that is, new findings and requirements need to be considered, deficits and errors remedied, and so on. Therefore, in each current iteration, the release planning for the iterations to follow must be updated.

Iteration Planning   C2.i

On the basis of the release planning, the first iteration is now concretely prepared. Concrete iteration goals are to be set up which, as far as possible, should be objectively measurable and assessable at the end of the iteration.

The goal is subdivided into an external and an internal part. Both parts are agreed with the involved party (customer, developers). The internal iteration goal agreed upon with the developers is more comprehensive and includes interface agreements as far as possible. Interfaces are contracts between interface providers and users.

Interfaces ⇒ p. 240

Design by contract

During a current iteration, planning is already carried out for the subsequent iteration.

Component-Specific Iteration Planning   C4.i.c

Here, goal planning for an iteration is transferred to the concrete requirements of each application component. The goal specification contains contracts in the form of interface agreements. At this point, detailed plans need to be set up as to how the agreed contracts can be implemented. The outcome of this planning activity is a set of work orders. Work orders indicate (at least):

Work orders

- Start and end date.
- Planned staff-related cost for implementation (in the order of 2–10 staff days total).
- Persons involved, one of which is responsible for the result.
- Description of the result to be achieved.

During a current iteration, the work orders for the subsequent iteration are drafted.

C5.i.k

Component-Specific Development

This heading brings together all activities that need to be carried out in a component-specific manner, that is, the stepwise realization of subsystems and components according to the specific iteration goals. Details of what has to be done are given in the issued work orders.

For example, design ⇒ pp. 50 ff.

Each iteration consists of analysis, design, realization, and test of a number of partial functionalities.

Depending on the given application architecture, dialogs are developed, process controls, classes, and controllers are designed and implemented, interfaces with other components are realized, previous systems are encapsulated or integrated, and so on. In cross-component issues, cooperation with other development units takes place.

C6.i

Cross-Component Development

Not all results to be developed are component-specific. Cross-component developments include, for example, macro-level process control, the design of a unique, consistent domain class model, the development of database schemes, and so on.

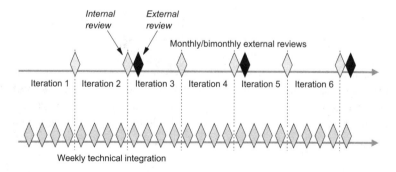

Above all, however, they include cross-sectional tasks, such as further development of application architecture, frameworks, generic services (control and integration of authorization system, standard software interfaces, and so on) and base classes (such as period of time, currency, and so on) if this is not done anyway by a separate architecture group.

People working on cross-sectional tasks also often assume the role of mentors and coaches, and ensure observation of development standards and guidelines, identification and application of design patterns, handling of general implementation problems, enforcing re-use, and so on.

Review Preparation   *C7.i*

Each iteration ends with a review which also triggers consolidation and further development in the subsequent iterations. An external review (that is, with the customer) should take place regularly, but not necessarily after each iteration.

To prepare internal and external reviews, test situations, data, and cases need to be set up which should be capable of testing and measuring the achievement of the iteration goals as precisely as possible. This should not be done by the developers themselves who at this point would not be able to recognize a forest if they saw a thousand trees, but by a separate unit internal to the project. It might also be useful to have customer's representatives working together on this task.

For the external review, the review preparation staff should picture themselves in the position of the customer. What does the technical department expect as a result of this iteration?

Besides the demanding preparation of the reviews, the review preparation staff has the task of organizing the reviews, that is, of booking facilities, inviting participants, moderating and protocoling the reviews, and so on.

Iteration Reviews   *C8.i*
                                                               C9.i

Before an iteration can be checked as to whether it has achieved its goals, the working results of the individual teams need to be integrated, and a new release must be created. Depending on the project and development environment, integration is carried out in very short periods of time, for example daily or weekly. In release planning, however, the only integrations to be taken into account are those which are part of an internal or external review.

Fixed integration frequency

The integration immediately preceding the end of an iteration is of greater importance and usually requires more effort, because this is the state of the project used to assess the developers.

Subsequently, the results of the reviews are made available to all parties involved. For the individual developers, they result in correction and modification orders and, potentially, new requirements. These facts need to be taken into consideration in release and iteration planning.

SYSTEM INTRODUCTION

Certification

Partial certification

If components or subsystems are completely finished before others, they can already be certified. Thus, besides the final certification, one can have anticipated partial certifications for selected system components. The precondition is that these system components can be tested and certified independently of the other parts that are still missing. Provided that such system parts can be sensibly introduced individually and independently of other parts, a stepwise introduction of the system can be put into practice.

Certification and introduction of a system or parts of a system entails a multitude of individual activities in which both customer and contractor participate. Thus, certification needs to be prepared in time; test cases and test data must be conceived and created; data takeover and migration from previous systems must be prepared; the system needs to be transferred from the development environment to the test and certification environment, and finally to the production environment; an operational concept is needed; fallback solutions need to be developed; users must be trained, and so on.

PROJECT MANAGEMENT

Problems and challenges in projects, in other words, their boundary conditions and obstacles, are nearly always the same:

Boundary conditions

- The available project budget is moderate, but above all, it is limited.
- Expectations are too high.
- You don't even want to think of the deadlines to be kept.
- The exact goals are still rather fuzzy.
- Availability of staff, hardware, and software is based on vague promises.

It is therefore important to counteract these drawbacks with a project management system that carries out financial control, takes on responsibility for planning and control, coordinates the technical tasks, and provides guidelines for the staff involved. If the project management or the customer are unable to take on these tasks as part of their responsibilities, external consultants need to be called in.

Localizing and following tasks systematically

The following are the tasks present at the beginning of a project:

- Estimation or verification of the necessary costs, subdivision into surveyable individual tasks, and creation of time and work schedules.
- Identification of critical areas and factors that need special attention.
- Selection and provision of the necessary infrastructure.
- Specification of internal and external decision, report, and information paths, in particular with the customer.

Since project management has many interfaces and contact points, the information flow between all parties involved is of the utmost importance. If communication is not supported and guaranteed, the perception and decision space of the project leader is bound to narrow down as well.

Cost Estimate

Empirical values are required

Cost can reasonably be estimated only when the extent of the project is roughly known. This means that the essential use cases and environment conditions must be determined first. Without this information, the extent can only be guessed. This is not a feature of object-oriented projects, but it applies in general. If your customer is of a different opinion, and you do not wish to run a risk, you have no alternative but to set the cost as high as possible.

The process model introduced here takes the determination of estimation basis and factors into account. It provides various points where estimates can be repeated or verified. Such estimates can be carried out on the basis of use cases, identified dialogs, activity models, the business model, and the domain model. During iterative proceeding, the progress can be measured after each iteration. Depending on these factors, project control can be adapted and estimates corrected.

Each iteration yields a defined product. After each iteration, the deviation from the original estimate can be determined, and the estimate can be corrected accordingly. The experience gained most recently can also be used as part of a new, improved estimate.

You will therefore not need to complete your first project before being able to produce a well thought-through estimate; the necessary information becomes available during the current project.

A well-founded cost estimate presumes that empirical values have already been collected and that these can be transferred to another project, taking different border conditions into account where necessary. The following data should be available:

◆ Number and implementation cost of use cases.
◆ Number and implementation cost of activities, together with the average number of activities per use case.
◆ Number of dialog views (individual windows, notebook pages, and the like), in consideration of their complexity which can be deducted from:
   – Number of display fields
   – Number of simple input fields
   – Number of joining elements (selection lists, ...)
   – Number of event-triggering elements (buttons, menu items, ...).
◆ Number of business classes, number of domain classes, number of domain classes per business class, complexity of domain classes (number of attributes, operations, and relations).

- Number and complexity of components (number of included classes, external interfaces, and dependencies).
- Number and weight of the elements to be generated automatically.

In addition, the following questions are of interest too:

- How does the number of found classes develop during the course of the project?
- How does the number of found operations, attributes, and constraints develop (absolute and relative to the number or classes)?
- How does the number of re-used classes develop and, if needed, the cost of their adaptation?
- How does the number of relationships (association, aggregation, inheritance) develop with respect to the individual classes?

Some of these key figures can also be determined with regard to individual people. Other important issues are:

- Number of team members.
- Availability of team members.
- Productivity factors of the team members.

If you have these key figures from previous projects, and the general environment conditions have not changed radically (for example, through new development tools), you may dare to produce an estimate for a new project.

Team size, availability, and productivity factors need to be determined for the new team. The more team members share a common project history, the smoother their cooperation. They have a similar empirical background. New members in the envisaged team constellation raise the communication effort needed for the project, that is, they lower the productivity factors of all members. Another rule is: the larger the team, the smaller the individual productivity. Experience shows that the productivity factors of individual collaborators in an enterprise often vary by a factor of 1 to 10 (although their salaries don't), whereas differences of the order of 1 to 25 have been seen to occur between members of different organizations.

Productivity factors

Since the number of classes or lines of code produced per unit of time cannot be a yardstick, the estimate of staff productivity remains subjective (in Booch (1994), Grady Booch admits that even the number of pizza boxes at the workplace is not a reliable measurement). In order to obtain more precise figures, time must be seen in relation to the given requirements, that is,

Measuring pizza boxes and code lines per time unit

◆ **Estimating GUI Client Size with Widget Points**   *Hartmut Krasemann*

Estimating the size of a system prior to its construction enables the engineer to predict the amount of work needed, assuming he knows his productivity. This holds for any engineering discipline, it is by no means unique to software engineering.

The LOC size measure is distinct to an environment

Productivity is defined as size over effort. Measuring the effort of a task is easy, we just count the number of working hours spent on it. Measuring the size is more difficult. The widely used size measure for software, lines of code (or LOC), is intrinsic: it depends heavily on the engineering environment. Thus size in LOC can only be compared with respect to a distinct engineering environment shared by similar projects.

Consequently, productivity measurements in LOC/h are constrained to a single environment as well, although an alternative engineering environment might gain real productivity by a factor. The same program written in a Java or Smalltalk environment might need as little as a fifth of the lines of code compared with the Cobol environment. Thus, for the purpose of productivity measurements across different environments, we need a software size measure valid in these different environments. The LOC size measure becomes meaningless.

Function points are an alternative, but hard to count

A meaningful size measure must be extrinsic, that is, independent of the production environment. The best known extrinsic size measure is that of function points, invented at IBM (Albrecht, 1979).

Function points are popular, they are supported by a large user group, the IFPUG (www.ifpug.org), but they are not ubiquitous. Why is this so? Well, at the heart of a function point measurement there is a count of the end user business functions of a data processing program. Unfortunately, functions of different programs are by no means comparable, therefore they must be made comparable by classifying each function, giving it a weight, and finally making an adjustment for technical complexity. Weighted functions are measured by function points. This is a linear measure, that is, function points can simply be added and compared. The IFPUG has developed a scheme for counting function points and advises consultation for the first applications of function point measurement.

The limitations of a Function Point measurement are twofold:

◆ *Subjectivity.*   The conversion from a function to function points is done by a weight factor which is subject to personal judgement and therefore possibly biased. This is one reason why the IFPUG advises consultancy.
◆ *I/O intensive.*   Function points can only be applied to data processing applications, they do not help to measure heavily computational software. The complexity of the interfaces must outweigh the algorithmic complexity.

Widget points can easily be counted

Of these limitations, subjectivity is the most severe (and dangerous). However, most modern applications have a graphical user interface (GUI) with almost standardized interaction elements:

complexity and potential risks must be taken into account. The more a team member resorts to existing solutions, that is, practices re-use, the better.

Besides the key figures of the development team, the key figures of extent and complexity of the new task need to be determined. On the basis of previous projects, you will probably be able to directly rate the new project only with respect to its size. To make a more precise assessment, you need a preliminary study. The number and extent of the most important classes and objects can

◆ **Estimating GUI Client Size with Widget Points**

the widgets. Widgets can be counted easily, let us call their sum the 'widget point' count of a program. For a finished program, widgets can even be counted automatically. Their count is not weighted, therefore it is bias free, no consultancy is needed. Widget Points of different programs are directly comparable. In the box 'Counting Widget Points' (page 84) we give a detailed account of how to count widget points.

The limitations of a widget point measurement are twofold, too:

- ◆ *GUI only*.   Widget point counting can only be done on a GUI. Therefore, it is restricted to programs, which have a GUI.
- ◆ *I/O intensive*.   Again, the complexity of the interfaces must outweigh the algorithmic complexity. This is typically true for information systems.

Thus, widget point counting can be applied to most modern client–server information systems, independent of the business area. It provides us with an extrinsic size measure, independent of the development environment, and one that is easily derived, even automatically. Widget points written per hour define a new measure for productivity.

Results
We have measured the size of four projects at debis and one project at IC&C, using widget points. The measured systems are fat clients, written in Smalltalk, in Java, and in C++. In a fifth Smalltalk project at debis we compared the widget point estimate with a traditional estimate of the program size.

We found the following results:

1. One widget point compares to two function points.
2. The lines of code written per hour are essentially independent of the programming language, they only vary slightly with project size and programmer skills.
3. The productivity relation between Smalltalk and C++ fits into the productivity pattern published in the Programming Language Tables of Capers Jones (www.spr.com/library/0langtbl.htm), for example the productivity of programming in Smalltalk is four times higher than that of programming in C++.
4. The productivity in Java is slightly less than but quite close to Smalltalk.

Application of the results
Widget points can be used to evaluate the programming environment. An automatic widget point measurement of the program after project completion is done within a day by one person. Combined with the effort spent, it gives the productivity of that project in widget points/h.

Widget points can be used to estimate the required effort in advance. This can be done (i) after all the screens are defined, or (ii) based on an estimate of the number of widgets in all the screens. In the latter case, of course, additional uncertainty creeps in.

Widget points open the chance for contracts based on the amount of functionality instead of a vague definition of a 'complete' system.

During system lifetime the change request process must cope not only with new and changed requirements but with the financial consequences, too. Here, things can be eased by contracting an amount of changed functionality measured by widget points.

already be estimated after a first analysis of the application domain. If you have carried out a more or less equally detailed study for a previous project, you can calculate the factor between the first estimate and actual value and transfer it to your new first assessment.

You should also try to derive relationships from your empirical values. Why do some classes require more effort than others? Why do some classes get stable very quickly, while others need to be continuously modified over a long

Assess complexity of classes

◆ **Counting Widget Points**   *Hartmut Krasemann*

The widget points of an application are just the sum of all widgets used in the graphical user interface (GUI) of the application. The number of widgets is an extrinsic measure of the functionality of an application since the widget types which appear in a window do not depend on the implementation environment.

Nevertheless, in trying to count widgets, a few questions arise:

1. What exactly is a widget?
2. Do we count every instance of a widget?
3. How can we automate counting?

What exactly is a widget?
The simple answer is 'everything which can be seen in a window,' to the level of elements that have to be specified by the GUI programmer. This definition works because GUI programming environments all use the same level of abstraction. The most important widgets are input widgets of any type, buttons, labels and lists, plus all items of menus.

A more detailed account is:

◆ *Input.*   InputField, ComboBox, MenuButton, RadioButton, ActionButton, CheckBox, TextEditor.
◆ *Description.*   Label, Divider, Group, Window.
◆ *Composite.*   List, Slider, Table, Column, NoteBook.
◆ *Menu.*   MenuItem.

For example, the widgets of the following window are to be counted:

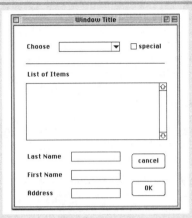

We have (1) the window, (2) its title (a label), (3–10) eight labels, including those of the action buttons and the check box, (11–15) a combo box with a choice of four items (not to be seen), (16) the check box, (17) the list, (18–20) three input fields and (21–22) two action buttons, (23) a divider line.

This window has 23 widget points.

Do we count every instance of a widget?
The user interface is made up of several different interacting windows, let there be *n* different windows. Two windows are different, if their specifications differ, that is they are not defined and opened by the same code. In almost all cases their static layout differs, too. We count all *n* different windows.

Any of these *n* windows may open several times in the course of a user interaction presenting different data. We do not count these

period of time? Try to develop a feel for which classes will probably become complex (number of dependency relationships, subclasses, operations, attributes, and so on). Roughly determine the complexity of a class.

If the existing data allow conclusions to be drawn about a dependency between complexity factors and invested costs, you can use estimated complexity factors to determine the expected cost of the new project.

Assess subtasks
It is in fact more advantageous (or safer) not to estimate the total extent, but to assess several subtasks and have as many (qualified) people as possible

◆ Counting Widget Points

dynamic repetitions.Each of the *n* windows contains a number of widgets, of these some may be of the same type. We count each single widget in each window.

Alternatively, we can imagine that each of the *n* windows is specified by a declarative window specification. This specification contains only widget symbols qualified by strings and numbers. No repetition of widgets can be specified. Then counting widgets is equivalent to counting the occurrences of all widget symbols in all window specifications.

How can we automate counting?
Different programming environments may create widgets in different ways. One example is a procedure call at window creation time to instantiate a widget, another example is a declarative window specification as described above, which is interpreted at window building time.

Counting is particularly easy in an environment where every window is defined by a specification. Here we identify the widget symbols of a window specification and count those across the window specifications of the program. If the specification language allows us to specify repetition, we have to determine how often and which subsets are reused. This process is easily automated. Note that only the widget symbols are counted, not the other parts of the specification (numbers, strings).

In environments that rely on procedural construction of a window, the specification of a window is usually scattered over a procedure hierarchy. Therefore it requires more thought to find all program locations which specify a single window. One best determines (i) all program locations where windows are defined and opened, (ii) which procedures are called and how often for opening a window, and (iii) how many widgets each procedure constructs, eventually taking further procedure calls into account. This process can be automated, too.

Automatic counting should be validated carefully. This is best done by counting a fairly complex example window by hand and automatically as well, and comparing the results.

Experiences
Initial results (see the box 'Estimating GUI Client Size with Widget Points') indicate that:

1. Widget points are useful to determine the functionality of a GUI client independent of the implementation environment.
2. One widget point corresponds to two function points.
3. Widget points can be counted automatically, and as easy as lines of code. An automatic count is done within a day. A count by hand may take a few days.

A measurement of Widget Points and effort spent in different projects yielded the productivity for different programming environments. The productivity numbers obtained are consistent with those given in the Programming Language Tables by Capers Jones (www.spr.com/library/0langtbl.htm).

contribute to the estimate. The subtasks chosen for assessment must be neither too big nor too small; experience shows that they should ideally lie between one staff week and one staff month. The smaller the individual packages, the higher the relative total, because idle times and other overheads included are counted to a disproportionally high extent.

The number of estimators makes the average result more reliable, but if significant deviations of individual results occur, the cause should be sought. Frequently, different boundary conditions are applied; then you need to discuss

Let several people estimate

which of these should be taken into account for the estimate. Another cause might be that some estimators have overlooked some facts or – and this is why the discussion is so important – have found new facts which had been overlooked until now in the task description submitted for assessment. If in doubt, you should always use the higher values for a comparable situation.

The total cost achieved through this procedure is now adjusted with the productivity key figures of the team, and you have a first, empirically founded cost estimate. Costs should be re-estimated periodically during the project. The precision of the estimate grows with the progress of the project.

It is difficult to tell general, experience-based values and set grids for the factors mentioned above. For commercial applications, such as those commonly employed in insurance companies, banks, and so on, the following figures are possible:

300–600	Entries in special dictionary
20–100	Use cases
5–20	Activities per use case
100–500	Domain classes
about 1 to 12	Proportion between classes and operations

These do not include the classes of ready-made frameworks and class libraries. The operations do not include primitive operations or standard operations generated by a modeling tool (such as reading an attribute). A subdivision into several partial projects is generally sensible for projects with more than 500 classes.

'What does a class cost?'

At this point, you might look for some hints of likely costs. It would, however, be somewhat unprofessional to band figures about or even use them for calculations without adequately considering the actual circumstances and boundary conditions.

The first object-oriented projects are usually developed at a higher cost than traditionally developed projects, which is perfectly normal when switching to a new method and tool. After the third true project, however, it becomes possible to cut costs. A functioning and well-established object-oriented development methodology and environment is likely to be able to manage with 20–50% of the cost of a traditional development. Frequently, the cost does not decrease simply because of the ensuing requirements of a higher performance and quality for the developed products.

Enforcing Re-Use

There are two main types of re-use:

♦ direct re-use by inheritance and delegation, and
♦ project-transcendent re-use by design patterns, frameworks, business objects, interfaces, components, and the like.

This section primarily discusses the most important aspects of project-transcendent re-use.

Before classes can be re-used, they first need to be used. This means that *First use, then re-use* application developers develop usable business classes, and architecture experts build on these to develop re-usable business classes or components.

The principal aim should be project-transcendent re-usability. A company-wide re-usability cannot, however, be achieved at a justifiable cost – such an enterprise would be highly likely to be a Sisphean task because it is not always possible (within a finite time) to completely cover all requirements in a contradiction-free manner. As far as possible, classes which contain very similar things, but cannot or must not be united, should be given different names, so that the name already indicates their special meaning or role.

The essential beneficial aspects of re-use are: *Benefits*

♦ Slightly lower implementation cost (after a higher initial cost).
♦ Significantly reduced maintenance cost.
♦ Significantly higher reliability.
♦ Model and educational effect.
♦ Multiplication of the efforts of the best people.

There are, however, fundamental problems with re-use, in particular in *Version management* version management: different versions of frameworks used in different applications and projects cannot be avoided. This is obviously a general problem which has nothing special to do with object-oriented concepts. The common solution is that old applications initially keep old frameworks. When applications are developed further or are updated, they should be adapted to the current versions of the frameworks.

In order to practice re-use efficiently, a fundamental ruling is required from management. Re-use does not come of its own accord, but must be pursued purposefully, and this takes time and generates costs. Preconditions for efficient re-use are a supreme mastery of the technology, creation of a re-use culture in the enterprise (motivation), and the proper organizational conditions.

Different approaches

To enforce re-use, several organizational approaches have been tried out, for example, the creation of a re-use team which compiles a class catalog. This approach usually fails because only paper ('closetware') is produced. Another approach is the creation of a repository – which often means creation of a system that causes expenses because it must be constantly maintained, without, however, creating much benefit because of its lack of reference to reality. A similar approach is to designate a central class manager or administrator, which is practically the offline-version of the repository. Here too, only rarely does a benefit develop because the reference to project practice is too weak.

Forming native elites

Currently, the most promising approach is the creation of an architecture group that sees itself as a service and consulting group for the projects. This group should include only the best people and thus form an elite. However, its members should also do normal project work at defined intervals. A healthy mixture between the two poles can ensure that the architecture group is sufficiently high caliber, but still keeps its feet on the ground.

Frameworks

Requirements for general frameworks and re-usable classes originate from the application projects. These requirements originate in the normal evolution of an application and may – if they are new – not be satisfied immediately. On the other hand, frameworks developed for re-use go through their own, independent evolution process. At regular intervals, new versions appear with new features which (only) then can be used by the projects.

Experience shows that about three to five people should work together on a framework.

Motivation of individuals and teams for re-use is an important aspect for the creation of a re-use culture. Financial incentives are problematic; questions arise with regard to measurability and determination of benefits, to association between performance and individuals, to distribution of remuneration between the originator of the re-usable classes on the one hand, and the re-user on the other hand, and so forth. In practice, financial incentives can easily be felt to be unfair.

Non-fully quantifiable incentives seem to be more advantageous, the most important aspect being social prestige.

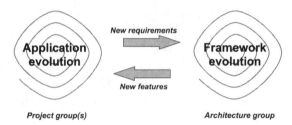

Project group(s)   *Architecture group*

Internal Developers' Conferences

One possibility of broadening the know-how about re-usability within an enterprise is offered by internal developers' conferences. These conferences should be a forum for project-transcendent exchange of knowledge and experience. They should be organized periodically and build on lectures of internal and external speakers. Internal speakers can talk about experiences, experiments, tools, and so on, with regard to specific projects or in a general way, and introduce new standards, procedures, or other technological and methodological novelties. External speakers can bring in stimuli from the outside world about similar subjects.

Internal developers' conferences motivate participating and organizing staff, broaden the know-how, create mutual understanding, improve cooperation between colleagues and teams, and are on the whole less expensive than external training courses.

Prototyping, Testing, Quality Assurance

Following the object-oriented way integrates different approaches to quality assurance. One important element is prototyping. Mainly during the phase of analysis, *explorative prototyping* is used to clarify area-specific and other requirements. It may also be possible to evaluate alternative solutions. In the subsequent design phase, *experimental prototyping* can be used to verify the usability of the modeled solutions. The relevant criteria are quality, performance, and general implementability.

Explorative prototyping Example ⇒ p. 81

Experimental prototyping

Both prototyping approaches build only to a certain extent on re-usable prototypes. However, since object-oriented procedures supports evolutionary development, the final product can also emerge stepwise in the framework of *evolutionary prototyping*. In large-scale projects, and also in a first object-oriented project, you should assume in your planning that you may well have to trash the first one or two of these intermediate products.

One-way prototypes

Thus, prototyping alone already offers various possibilities of quality assurance. On the other hand, this way of proceeding does not in itself guarantee quality. It is the project management's task to systematically exploit the existing possibilities of validation and verification.

You should always ensure that, before each prototyping, the aspects to be clarified or tested are explicitly formulated and documented, and that (and how) the results of the prototyping are protocoled. Furthermore, you should make sure that the results flow back into the work, and take adequate measures to check that this is done.

Planning prototyping

- Prior to prototyping, a description is to be produced which specifies what is to be clarified and in which form.
- During prototyping, a list is to be kept of detected errors, misunderstandings, suggestions, and so on.
- For each point on this list, the people involved must agree on how urgently the discovery is to be taken into account, who will be responsible for further clarification, if needed, and for implementation, by when the implementation should be completed and how a successful implementation is going to be checked.
- Prototyping results specified in this way are then handed over to the responsible staff in the form of work orders (either verbally or in writing, depending on their size).
- The project management or another team member is charged with the responsibility of monitoring these work orders both formally and with regard to the agreed schedules.

Test cases
The situations simulated in prototyping may yield test data or processes as a by-product. Where specific processes and data are to be considered serious tests, this should be explicitly stated, and they should be documented. On the basis of these test cases, the final product and also intermediate products can be checked at a later stage (even by third parties). Moreover, they help create a *Certification criteria* consensus on certification criteria between users and developers.

The developers and designers test protoypes and products with a knowledge of their internals (white box test), whereas the quality assurance people are qualified to perform a black box test.

Systematic and controled prototyping protects you from nasty surprises and ensures the success of your project. Particularly in the early phases, involvement of future users is important to avoid misunderstandings and misjudgments. Users get an early idea of the consequences of fundamental design decisions. This ensures basic acceptance of the final product.

Watch out for conflicts of interest
However, as the project leader, you should also make sure that prototyping does not pointlessly degenerate or becomes worn out through conflicts of interest. The question of prototyping 'What needs to be clarified?' becomes more important the more the interests of the participants differ. Especially when different departments or application groups are to receive a common project, each party will try to bring their own specific interests to the foreground. If it appears that major contrasts exist and a consensus is far from *Highest decision instance* being reached, a decision needs to be made by a higher entity (management, steering committee, or others). This decision must then be supported by all parties.

All system requirements, and specifically later ones which stem from prototyping or environmental modifications, should be tagged with (agreed) priorities. If the priorities are not clear, later acceptance may be compromised. Priorities derive from expected benefits or value, suspected technical problems, and cost. Thus, the highest priority is given to requirements with the highest benefit and the lowest cost.

Training Concept

Staff qualification determines cost and quality of the software. Attentive and systematic training is a precondition for starting with object technology. Object-oriented software development is not easier than conventional development, and the demands on developers are definitely higher.

These demands are not only of an intellectual nature; social, linguistic, and ontological dimensions need to be considered as well. Developers who for years on end have worked in bureaucratic structures and have focused exclusively on their own terminals do not fail because of intellectual demands, but because of their inability to understand and practice software development as a social and communicative process. Teamwork and communication skills are slow-growth individual features that cannot be learned in a seminar.

To these social requirements, we now need to add the requirements for understanding the object-oriented thinking process. The real innovation of object-orientation is not the individual methodological concepts, but the totally different perception of application development. Only through this new perception do different system models emerge – not by application of an object-oriented method or an object-orientation-labeled tool.

Imparting the object-oriented view

In the training of new object-oriented developers, you must calculate certain losses: depending on given qualifications and commitment, up to 30% of trainees do not master programming languages to a sufficient degree. Although, in comparison to C++, and even to Java, Smalltalk is a significantly easier language to learn (having no hybrid properties), a higher rate of success may seem to occur in C++ or Java training. This is partly due to the fact that you can still write programs in hybrid languages even when you have not fully understood the object-oriented concepts. In Smalltalk training, even partial ignorance becomes more evident.

Programming language training

Training in Smalltalk is therefore recommended, even if then C++ or a similar language is used for development. Hard-boiled procedural programmers need first to be *untaught* in order to create free space in their brains ready to accommodate the new perspective. Experience shows that developers

3–6 months practice

can work productively after about three months of object-oriented practice, and that after six months, they have gained enough confidence to work mostly on their own. This means that during the first three months, additional costs arise for mentoring and the ensuing environmental difficulties. Critical application domains and collaboration in architecture groups certainly require at least twelve months of practical experience.

Fundamental requirements (not included in the cost) are knowledge and experience in hardware and software (PC, operating system, graphical user interfaces, mouse, and so on), as well as knowledge of the following elementary concepts: type concept, abstract data types, modules, information hiding.

Another important factor, besides the adoption of the object-oriented view and the theoretical and practical training in the development language, is familiarization with frameworks and the like. This part too must not be underrated; thus, it is relatively easy to learn the Smalltalk language. But to be able to develop in Smalltalk, the class libraries and frameworks belonging to the system need to be known (this also applies to C++ and Java). The fundamental structure of the libraries must be studied and a basic orientation capacity in the existing classes must be achieved.

Getting to know the class library

A small part of the staff charged with this task will be overstrained with the degree of abstraction present in the frameworks. Therefore, effort and costs to be invested in the training should not be underestimated.

Tasks and Roles

As with traditional software development, object-orientation entails strong division of labor and specialization. Which roles and specializations are sensible depends on the type of enterprise and the framework of your software development. You may wish to call in a competent advisor. The following keywords give a rough overview:

- Project management, project planning, project control, project organization, project staffing, project office.
- Users.
- Organizers, product planners (with power of veto).
- Domain experts.
- Architecture experts, project advisors (with power of veto).
- Analysts.
- Designers, coders.
- Database and tool experts.
- System administration, version management, technical integration.

- Interface and legacy system experts.
- Batch developers.
- Dialog experts.
- Coaches, mentors, object-orientation trainers (when introducing object-orientation).
- Application supervisors, user training.
- Workshop moderators, team trainers.
- Quality assurance, test, certification, and migration experts.
- Application installers.

The architecture group or an OTC (Object Technology Center) should not be set up immediately, but only after the first project. If, however, an architecture group needs to be established from the very beginning, then only a small one should be established. Members of the architecture group need periodical participation in project work in order not to deviate from project reality. Project work of the architecture group people should reasonably not take place in slices (hours, half days, and so on), but in blocks (several uninterrupted weeks).

A coach or mentor is neither a productive project worker nor a spare project worker.

Team Work, Social Competence

Top performances of development teams can only be controlled or induced to a limited extent. The most important aspect is to inspire the whole team for a common goal, to create a vision for which everybody feels responsible.

Creating visions

All team members must be able to identify exactly where their specific tasks, challenges, and possibilities of participation lie. A possible basis is the assignment of responsibilities for specific subject areas. The responsibilities obviously change during the course of the project; at the project's start, they are necessarily structured more roughly than at later points in time.

If possible, do without employing your authority, or giving orders or rewards to break resistance. Concentrate on the fact that your employees are both able and willing to reach a useful solution and will take responsibility for this. Your task is to commit everyone to the right goal! Specify the goals, but leave people the possibility of choosing their own way of getting there. Obviously, the goals must correspond adequately to the capabilities of the responsible person. Assign goals in relation to persons, and not globally to the team.

If obvious problems occur with reaching the goals, do not step in and act yourself, but together with the people concerned, try to find the causes and help with their elimination. If the same problems occur again, then it is your fault as a project manager. Either aims and motivation have not filtered down to the team, or people have been overstrained or employed in the wrong place. If team members lack qualifications, you need to 'return' them (to another project?) or otherwise 'keep them busy.'

Team culture must always be characterized by mutual understanding and openness, also towards individual weaknesses. Coach your team members, but never take over the main substance of their work and responsibility without asking. We learn from our errors when we have to sort them out ourselves, not when we are forcibly shown what we may well perceive as only an alleged cause.

The satisfaction of having achieved something, but also of having coped with error on one's own, is much higher with this satisfaction-related approach. But do not always quote errors or brilliant feats of the past – canned food tastes stale. All staff should periodically have the chance to present the results of their own work. This fosters mutual understanding and motivation.

Besides being able to handle power and authority, it is obviously decisive to measure and evaluate the performance of the team and the individual members, and to pass the results back to them. Thus, project control serves not only for monitoring and detection of weak points, but also for motivation.

Model Power and Self-Organization

Model monopoly

When you charge a team with elaborating a solution for a given problem, a model monopoly may well emerge within the team. This occurs when one person is ahead of the others through preparation of a solution approach. Even if this approach is initially only introduced: its perspective and terminology become the default. Each discussion of another, competing model will then take place in the language of the monopolizing model (*see* Pasch, 1989).

This can be exploited if one wants to enforce a specific solution. You just give the inventor of that idea the chance to establish it. The result, however, is in most cases the work of an individual.

Rivaling convergently for ideas

The alternative: everybody involved enters the discussion at the same level and processes the model together. You, as project manager, are responsible for creating or assuring this initial symmetry. Try to commit your team to a co-operative working style. Team members will then work together on one model, no longer fighting for model power, but investing all their energies into a common model. They compete for the best ideas, but their thinking actively focuses on converging into the same model. The result is then likely to be more than the sum of the individual efforts! In any case more than that of an individual person.

The phenomenon of model power is also an example of how a group organizes itself. The organizational structure and, for example, a hierarchical position of the individual members can be predefined, but there is always an informal organizational structure that will emerge. The informal structures in a project are the most efficient ones; they are the vehicle for exchanging the most important information. They must, therefore, be respected by the project management. An external intervention in this naturally grown structure can impair the stability of the group.

Self-organization

Informal organization

SUGGESTED READING

1. A Goldberg, A., K. S. Rubin, K. S. (1995) *Succeeding with Objects, Design Frameworks for Project Management*. Addison-Wesley.
2. Booch, G. (1994) *Object-Oriented Analysis and Design with Applications*, 2nd edn., Benjamin/Cummings.
3. Rumbaugh, J., Blaha, M., Premerlani, W., Eddy, F., Lorenson, W. (1991) *Object-Oriented Modelling and Design*. Prentice Hall.
4. Jacobson, I., Christerson, M., Jonsson, P., Övergaard, G. (1992) *Object-Oriented Software Engineering, A Use Case Driver Approach*. Addison-Wesley.
5. Wirfs-Brock, R., Wilkerson, B., Wiener, L. (1990) *Designing Object-Oriented Software*. Prentice Hall.
6. Meyer, B. (1988) *Object-Oriented Software Construction*. Prentice Hall.
7. Szyperski, C. (1997) *Component Software, Beyond Object-Oriented Programming*. Addison-Wesley (ACM Press), Harlow.
8. Sims, O. (1994) *Business Objects: Delivering Cooperative Objects for Client-Server*. McGraw-Hill, New York.
9. Rational Software: *The Objectory Process*. www.rational.com/uml.
10. Graham, I., Henderson-Sellers, B., Younessi, H. (1997) *The OPEN Process Specification*. Addison-Wesley (ACM Press), Harlow.
11. DeMarco, T. (1992) *Controlling Software Projects, Management Measurements and Estimation*. Prentice Hall, 1992.
12. Metzger, P. W. (1998) *Managing Programming People, A Personnel View*. Prentice Hall.
13. DeMarco, T., Lister, T. (1997) *Peopleware, Productive Projects and Teams*. Dorset House.

Part II

Example

*The root of all confusions
is the puzzling word 'object'.*

Ludwig Wittgenstein, *Philosophical Grammar*

The following two chapters illustrate object-oriented analysis and design with the Unified Modeling Language, with the aid of an example.

Chapter 4

Analysis

It is not precision that counts,
but the fertility of the concepts.

Werner Heisenberg

This chapter demonstrates and discusses object-oriented analysis with the aid of an example, and shows the application of the individual methodological concepts. Their detailed description in Part III, Fundamentals, is referred to using page cross-references.

Task Description

In a car rental company, all customer-related business processes are to be supported by a coherent, unique information system. Currently, some business processes are not at all or only insufficiently supported by electronic data processing. For the remaining ones, there are various specialized systems. Several systems are needed to be able to handle all sides of customer service.

The new system to be developed should provide all functions directly related to handling customers and other business partners (for example suppliers). These include customer information, management of core data (addresses, bank details, and so on), reservations, vehicle rental, and customer billing.

Inbound areas and those that touch business partners only remotely, such as internal accounting, tariff and product planning, vehicle transfer and disposition, are not part of the system.

AIMS

This chapter illustrates and explains object-oriented analysis with the aid of one coherent example. The UML elements and concepts used in this description are, however, only rudimentarily explained. The emphasis lies on the demonstration of their application. A detailed description of the individual concepts can be found in Part III, Fundamentals (see page cross-references throughout this chapter).

The basic concept behind this example is described in the box above. The example was originally developed for training purposes and does not stem from a real project. Readers who have developed such a system are kindly asked to overlook simplifications and inaccuracies where they occur.

USE CASE ANALYSIS

Fundamentals
⇒ *p. 174*

A use case describes the interaction between users and an application system needed to carry out a working operation. The following applies to the size of a use case: a use case should describe what a user does with an application system (for example a reservation system) to conclude a business event (for example, the reservation of a Ferrari for Mr Agnelli) within a business process.

A process should be subdivided into several use cases if it is clearly interrupted at a given moment, or if clearly identifiable parts are handled by different people.

CONTACT PARTNERS FOR THE ANALYSIS. In order to begin with the analysis of the application domain, the contact partners need to be defined by searching and finding the application domain experts. Frequently, but not always, these are also the future users.

Domain experts

When proceeding in the project, it is sensible to differentiate the contact partners in terms of whether they are novice users, expert users, application domain experts, or responsible management staff, and whether or not they have decision-making power (and if so, how much) within the agreement of requirements and use cases.

The quality of the analysis results is highly influenced by the domain experts, which is why communication with these people is initially a priority. The users need to support these results; otherwise, the finished application system will have to fight against resistances.

Discussion with users and domain experts can be carried out independently – this allows for a comparison of the presented and recognized facts. In case of deviations, further data needs to be gathered. If required, all people involved need to meet and discuss the issues together, to reach a consensus or clarify the contradictions. The individual contact partners for specific problems are also noted down in the use cases.

For the example used in this book, the following contact partners can be identified:

*Introduction
Example ⇒ p. 100*

- Customer service (central phone operator)
  - Information
  - Reservation
- Customer service (branch office)
  - Vehicle hand-over
  - Vehicle return
- Service personnel (branch office, vehicle check)
- Branch office management
- Phone service management
- Managing clerks, vehicle transfer staff, accounting staff (if required)

WORKING MATERIAL AND OBJECTS. Analysis of the application domain also includes collection and study of working material and other tangible objects, such as forms, schedules, correspondence, workplace descriptions, and so on. In addition, the obvious working objects are to be identified or named.

These are, for example:

- Customer data
- Contracts
- Invoices
- Reservation confirmations
- Vehicle return protocols
- Garage protocols
- Vehicle documentation
- Mobile accessories
  (children's seats, roof racks)
- Fixed accessories
  (air conditioning, tow bar, sun roof)
- Vehicle keys
- Customer files
- Parking lots
- Tariff descriptions
- Contract conditions
- And so forth

Identifying Use Cases and Actors

The use cases contemplated in the car rental example are shown in the diagram below. Here, the actors are the interested party, that is, the customers, and staff for reservation, vehicle hand-over, and vehicle return.

The interested parties are different from the customer because they remain anonymous, that is, their personal data are not registered. Also, the fact that the customer need not necessarily be one person is not taken into account at this stage. For example, a customer may be an enterprise whose secretarial office has reserved a car for an employee (who will actually drive the rented car).

Business use case
System use case

Fundamentals
⇒ *p. 180*

BUSINESS AND SYSTEM USE CASES.   In business use cases, the actors are all roles involved in the business process, while in system use cases, they are limited to those entering directly into contact with the application system. Usually, customers do not enter into direct contact with the application system, but in business use cases, they are nevertheless noted down. If customers were able to reserve their car directly at self-service terminals, they would enter into direct contact with the application system and would therefore also be included in system use cases.

In the further course of the analysis, it is of interest whether there are other actors who interact with the system infrequently or in a less obvious

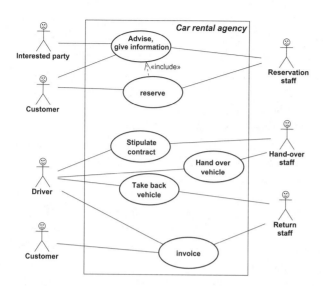

way. Furthermore, identifying individual tasks and privileges for the actors may also be useful. Depending on the environment and complexity of the application to be developed, sophisticated access concepts and schemes might be needed. Other systems, instead, might do completely without a differentiation of roles and actors.

The following diagram shows a hierarchical structure of actors (inheritance relationships). Actors are stereotyped classes. In this example, the tasks for which the actors need to have access rights are listed in a relatively free form in the classes.

Actors ⇒ p. 178
Stereotype ⇒ p. 213

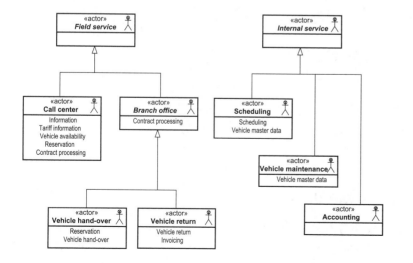

Users describe their jobs

In the description of their tasks and activities, users are induced by the system analyst's questions to look at their work from a different, less every-day perspective. They are required to report both on (interesting and eventful) peculiarities and exceptions, as well as routine matters of course.

Process modeling
Activity diagrams

If you find a multitude of use cases, and your modeling tool provides the possibility of drawing different kinds of relationships between the use cases, you might be tempted by the idea of subdividing the use cases functionally. If you try to do this, you are potentially on your way to model processes by means of use cases, and you will very probably come up against a brick wall, because use cases are unfit for this purpose. Better possibilities are provided by activity diagrams – more about this later.

«include»
«extend»

Functional
decomposition

Component building

In specific cases, the use of relationships between use cases may be sensible, eventually even with a distinction between «include» and «extend»; a functional decomposition should, however, be avoided. It is on the other hand practical to group use cases on the basis of their technical status, for example with the aid of packages. This is the first step towards component building or modularization.

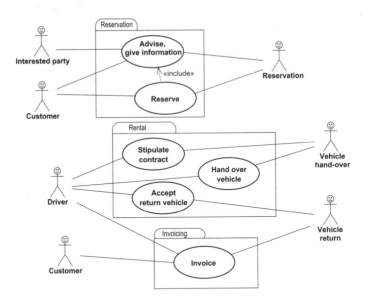

Describing Use Cases

Representing the use cases in the diagram by ellipses was the first step; now, the use cases are identified. The next step is to describe them in more detail.

Describing the use cases is the main task of use cases analysis.

Two simple examples:

CRC ⇒ p. 124

> **Uc1.2 Vehicle reservation by phone**
>
> Objects involved: *customer, booking staff.*
>
> A customer calls to reserve a car. Reservation and customer data are accepted by the booking clerk and entered into the reservation system. The customer is given the reservation number.

> **Uc2.2 Vehicle hand-over**
>
> Objects involved: *customer, customer service person.*
>
> A customer would like to collect the reserved car (⇒Uc2.1 Contract stipulation) at the branch office. The customer service clerk takes the corresponding agreement from the customer's file, checks whether all contract items are present (as well as the vehicle, other items such as a roof rack), amends the agreement if needed, hands vehicle documents and keys over to the customer, names the current parking lot, and if necessary instructs the customer on how to use specific contract items.

Several more use cases could be formulated for the car rental example: vehicle return, cancellation of reservations, modification of reservations, fully booked (if all vehicles from selected category unavailable, go to next best category), late return, return after accident/damage/loss.

Use cases are textual descriptions of sections of the business process model. They outline the basic course of a business event, but may be detailed in such a way that they describe how users actually handle the application to be developed. For this, a use case can be subdivided into further smaller sections, and possible exceptions and deviations from the standard course can be protocoled.

At a later stage, use cases can also be further analyzed or detailed by means of sequence and activity diagrams. Staff in the application area sometimes have difficulties in describing their activity in an abstract or generalised way. In any case, they should not always be expected to. It is much easier for them to describe their work with the aid of concrete examples.

Sequence diagram ⇒ p. 262

Summarizing or protocoling the scenarios presented by the users in full length or even in direct speech – more or less as shown on page 109 – would obviously involve a lot of work.

◆ Mind Maps

Now you are spending the whole day with the future users, looking over their shoulders, asking questions, discussing, and making notes with lots of question marks. Later, maybe even in a break, you are back at your desk, sitting there alone and trying to sort thoughts and notes, remembering, and clarifying the questions. One technique to allow you to give free rein to your thoughts is the so-called mind maps.

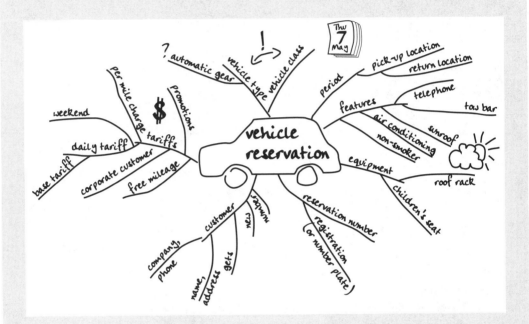

As we all know, our brain consists of two halves. The left hemisphere is associated with more rational aspects. Left-brain thinking can be described with the keywords linearity, precision, order, and structure. Right-brain thinking is associated more with creativity, associations, fantasy, wholeness, chaos, and so on.

To use our brain potential efficiently, both brain aspects need to be activated and stimulated. The better we succeed in mobilizing both aspects at the same time, the stronger our thinking power is likely to be. To incite the right hemisphere to more activity, we can use stimulation techniques which, by the way, are generally suited to fix and sort unstructured flowing thoughts. These techniques are quite handy especially for requirement analysis.

So, what will stimulate our right hemisphere? First of all, it is useful to counteract our automatic logical thinking. When we look at a blank sheet of paper in portrait orientation, we view the upper left corner and think in lines that run from left to right. The ordering and sorting requirements of our left hemisphere are satisfied, but the right hemisphere is hardly stimulated – it is getting bored!

Now, if you rotate the paper to landscape orientation, you are inclined to look more towards the center. The horizontal lines are too long to be perceived as such at a single

◆ Mind Maps

glance. We tend to think more from the middle out. This does not stop our left-brain thinking, but the mechanism is broken. There is something unusual about the sheet of paper; this stimulates our creativity.

A further trick consists in not producing completely formulated sentences, but in working only with keywords. Therefore not 'Our brain consists of a left and a right hemisphere,' but only 'brain hemispheres.' The missing information will nevertheless not get lost! Our creative hemisphere knows the association fields that surround these keywords in the respective context and restores them. The right hemisphere is stimulated and encouraged to produce associations. Reduction to keywords has the additional advantage of

recalling quickly more extensive thoughts, facts, and the like.

Try to use small illustrations, drawn abbreviations, symbols, pictograms, colors (colored pens!) and variations and degrees in your form of writing: main concepts in upper case, sub-items in lower case. You need not be a great artist; everyone can draw a simple symbol.

More about this subject can be found in the literature (for example in Beyer, 1993). Make use of these sketches only to gather your associations and do without subsequent elaboration (believe it or not, specific mind map editors are already available …).

Possibilities for developing this technique can be found everywhere: just read a news item or a similar text and then jot down its contents as a mind map.

When the customer comes back and returns the key and the papers, I load the customer data in and check the correspondence that goes with the contract, that is, the items that belong to it and the terms, schedules, and such like, which were agreed. When everything is confirmed, I fill in the return protocol, enter mileage, fuel level, and other notes if needed, and process the invoice.

Instead, it is usually sufficient to note down such statements by keywords and in a compressed form:

Uc2.2   Vehicle return

Customer returns vehicle, keys, and documents.
Consult contract: are items returned completely and have schedules and other conditions been adhered to?
Fill in return protocol: mileage, fuel level, notes.
Then process invoice.

In our examples, use cases are mostly formulated quite concisely. The amount of detail in the description depends on the actual project situation and the complexity of the domain section under observation. The aim of the use cases is not an airtight and perfect description – it is sufficient to reach a depth of detail that provides all people involved in the project with a quick and

*Recommended
level of detail*

understandable access to the application domain and the integration of the future application (also at later moments in time).

It is really a matter of opinion at which level of detail the use cases should be elaborated, that is, how many use cases finally come up in a project. Jacobson *et al*. would expect about 20 use cases for a project of the order of 10 staff years (without variations and abstract cases), while Fowler and Scott (1997) talk about 100 use cases for a project of the same size. My own project experience puts the value approximately halfway between the two extremes.

Primarily, use cases are a means for determination of requirements and a rough outline of the future outbound system behavior. Use cases are less suitable for specification of detailed business rules, program sequences, dependencies, or abstraction of such facts.

*Is- and should-be
scenarios*

The aim is to produce use cases that describe the should-be state. Since users usually describe the is-state, possibly enriched with critical remarks and suggestions for improvement, it might be necessary to record both is- and should-be use cases. The is-descriptions are, for example, converted into should-be scenarios together with the domain experts and the organization people. Example Uc2.2 shown earlier is an is-scenario. Its should-be variation might, for example, look like this:

Uc2.2   Vehicle return

Actors
Customer, customer service staff.

Trigger
Customer comes in and wishes to return vehicle.

Process

1. *Find contract*
    A search dialog is used to find the contract. The vehicle registration number is entered, and the current contract for this vehicle is sought.

2. *Check adherence to contract terms*
    In the contract file, the return checklist page is opened and the return of all items listed here is checked (vehicle, keys, documents). Additionally required information is entered (have terms and conditions been satisfied; is there any damage?)

3. *Acquire invoicing data*
    In the contract file, the invoice data page is opened and all data required is entered (mileage, fuel level, additional notes).

4. *Create invoice*
    The invoice creation action is initiated. The invoice is displayed.

Subsequently, the invoice printing action is triggered, which results in the invoice being printed on the standard printer. The customer is given one copy of the invoice.

5. The contract is closed.

Variations

1.1 Instead of the vehicle registration, the contract number is used for the search.

1.2 The customer file is sought via a different search dialog.

1.2.1 For this purpose, name, customer number, or one or more other attributes of the customer are entered.

1.2.2 Subsequently, the contract page is opened in the customer file, and the current contract is selected from a list.

1.3 Several current contracts are found.

1.3.1 The required contract is selected from a selection list.

1.... The vehicle has been damaged.

2.1 The vehicle has been damaged.

2.1.1 In addition, the damage report page is selected, and information on the damage is entered.

2.2 An accident is signaled.

2.2.1 ...

2.3 Tolerance limit of return deadline exceeded.

2.3.1 ...

2.4 Total break-down/loss of vehicle.

2.4.1 ...

Dialogs

Search dialog for contracts.
Search dialog for customers.
Contract file with following pages: return checklist, invoice data, damage report.

Open issues

What if the customer has lost the vehicle documents?

*Customer file
Example ⇒ p. 122*

Use cases are usually illustrated with dialog designs, sometimes also with form designs and sample printouts. On the one hand, they contain text which accurately describes the process; on the other, they include the dialogs required for this process (directly on screen or as printed samples). The future handling of the system is simulated (on paper or with prototypes). More about dialog design (explorative prototypes) on page 119.

*Explorative prototypes
⇒ p. 119*

Uc1.1 Customer service by phone

Actors

Interested party, call center staff.

Trigger

Interested party calls for information.

Process

1. *Price information*
    Interested party asks specific questions. Corresponding data is entered in the information dialog. In particular, rental period, vehicle type and equipment. Further mandatory fields are prompted. Where possible, important fields are preset to sensible default values. After triggering the tariff calculation action, tariff data and prices are displayed.

2. If needed, step 1 is repeated with alternative data.

3. By triggering the new action, the information dialog is reset to its initial state.

Variations

1.1 Instead of an interested party, an existing customer calls.

1.1.1 The customer search dialog is used to find the customer file. For this purpose, name, customer number, or one or more other attributes of the customer are entered.

1.1.2 The information dialog is started via the context menu of the customer file. This is identical to the one mentioned under item 1, but takes special customer tariffs and discounts into account. Dialog fields are preset to the stored special preferences of the customer.

3.1 Instead of New, the availability check action is initiated. Proceed with ⇒Uc 1.2 Reservation

Uc1.2 Reservation by phone

Actors

Interested party or customer, call center staff.

Trigger

Interested party or customer calls to reserve a car.

Process

1. *Enter customer requirements*
    Customer names reservation requirements. Corresponding data is entered in reservation dialog, in particular rental period, vehicle type and equipment.

2. *Identify customer*
    Customer search dialog is used to find customer file. For this purpose, name, customer number, or one or more other attributes of customer are entered. Basic customer data is checked and confirmed by customer.

3. *Reserve vehicle*
    After activating the Reserve button, the system checks availability of the required vehicle and stores the reservation. The reservation number is displayed.

Variations

1.1   Requests made in ⇒Uc1.1 Customer service by phone are taken up automatically.

2.1   *New customer*
      The customer is new.

2.1.1 Therefore a new customer record is created. ⇒Uc ...

3.1   *Change to customer data*
      Part of the customer data is no longer up-to-date.

3.1.1 Customer record is amended accordingly.

3.2   *Reservation denied*
      Reservation denied by the system because of customer solvency problems.

3.2.1 The situation is discussed with the customer. The content of the conversation is written down in a brief note which is added to the customer file.

The following use case is kept very brief on purpose, to show how use cases can be formulated using keywords. At a later stage, they can be refined step by step.

Uc2   Stipulate contract and hand over vehicle

Actors
      Customer, service staff.

Trigger
      Customer wishes to pick up reserved vehicle.

Process

1.   *Identify reservation*

2.   *Stipulate contract*

3.   *Hand over vehicle*

*Introduction
Example ⇒ p. 100*

*Use cases
⇒ pp. 100 ff.*

CLARIFICATION OF SYSTEM REQUIREMENTS.   Another part of the analysis is to clarify the hardware and software requirements for the application to be developed, in particular, to estimate the amount of data to be processed and stored. Such information can often be acquired together with the use cases. In the quoted example, the data is:

- 100 rental stations with a total of 170 terminals
- 500 rentals/day
- 600 reservations/day
- 50 cancellations/day
- 70 reservation changes/day
- 10 incorrect pick-ups/day
- 20 incorrect returns/day
- 210 rental contracts/day for > 1 day
- 60% corporate customers, 23% first customers
- 850 vehicles available in 3 categories (student, standard, de luxe)

APPLICATION ARCHITECTURE

*What needs to be
designed?*

System requirements also include the architecture to be implemented, the development tools, standards to be met, and so on. Before beginning the first design activities, it is necessary to specify the architecture of the future applications. It determines which kinds of classes and, as a result, which interfaces need to be designed. A well thought-through, clean application architecture also helps to achieve:

- a sensible division of labor and a clear overview,
- long-term flexibility in system development, and
- a higher degree of re-usability.

Packages ⇒ p. 217

In this context, application architecture means the way in which the individual subsystems and components are structured internally. In the literature and in application development enterprises, we can find many, partly very similar application architectures. The architecture outlined here by way of example reflects today's common demands on such architectures. These include the separation of presentation layer and domain class layer, as well as work flow control.

   This is not a book on application architectures; therefore, without further discussion, one possible application architecture is provided as an example.

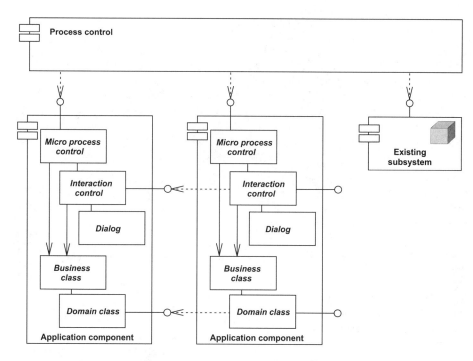

The figure shown above illustrates the principal structure of the application to be developed. The individual internal components are explained in the following paragraphs.

- **Dialogs** (view, presentation).   Dialogs are the interface with the users. They take care of presentation of information and accept input. The entire system–user communication is initially processed by the dialog control classes. They ensure an adequate representation and formatting of information, but do not process or change the contents of the data. User input is also not processed substantially, but only formally.

  A dialog is composed of different individual parts. On the one hand, these are the elements displayed on the monitor, that is, input fields, selection buttons, and one or more windows in which the dialog takes place. On the other hand, these are invisible elements: usually, there will be a controller which directly controls the presentation and the dialog. The controller generates and initializes the display elements, shows or hides them, highlights them, and so on. Moreover, it directly processes the user input. For example, it will ensure that after the tab or enter key has been pressed, the cursor jumps to the next field. Other input that

◆ **Model View Controller (MVC)** *Arne Wallrabe*

MVC is a design pattern originating from Smalltalk which has been modified a number of times and, as an architectural principle, has to be seen as a standard. The basic idea behind MVC is the separation of domain-specific semantics from its presentation. With the MVC principle, applications are subdivided into three parts:

- *Model.* Model is the term for the component which holds the actual technical knowledge. Therefore, Model classes are also called technical classes or domain classes.
- *View.* View is the component used to define the representation of information on a screen or in a window.
- *Controller.* This is the component that controls interaction with the user. It processes, for example, mouse events and other user input.

None of the three components, model, view, and controller, can function on its own; they all need to support each other mutually. The cooperation of the three components, however, must not stop the model remaining as far as possible independent from the other two components. This allows model classes to be designed and implemented independently of their representation, and on the other hand, there may exist several different views for one model without necessarily entailing changes to the model.

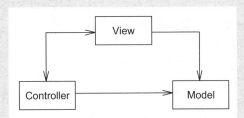

The illustration shows the relationships between model, view, and controller. While view and controller know each other and communicate in both directions, their relation with the model is one-way. View and controller know their model, but not vice versa. Its actual implementation is as simple as the MVC principle looks complicated at first sight.

needs not be processed directly, such as pressing the OK button, is forwarded to the interaction control.

Dialog control is usually neither directly programmed nor designed in detail, but generated by means of commercial dialog editors (GUI builders).

- **Interaction control** (controller, technical process control). The classes of this layer receive the events forwarded by the dialog control. Contents- and domain-specifically, this layer too processes display or input information only as far as it is needed to determine and influence the context of the current processing situation. Interaction control governs and assures the communication between the dialog and domain objects involved, and neutralizes their dependencies. It ensures that dialogs are displayed and removed, that error and status messages of domain objects and process control are forwarded to the dialog control, and so forth.

Thus, interaction control is responsible for all technical and formal aspects and contexts, while all domain-specific issues are cared for and managed by the domain (or business) classes.

◆ **Process control** (technical process control).   Processes are sub-units of a workflow. Process control initiates, monitors, and controls processing of a business event from a domain-specific point of view. All technical and formal aspects are cared for by the interaction control. If the task is, for example, to create a new contract, the process control initiates a corresponding interaction with the user. The process control creates, for example, a new (empty) contract and instructs the interaction control to execute the corresponding dialogs for processing of these domain objects.

Control of domain-specific context

Process control within components is also called micro-process control, because components provide services for partial processes, whereas the cross-component control governs the processes overall.

◆ **Business and domain classes** (model).   These classes represent the actual application domain, the technical view of the application world. They contain and encapsulate the attributes, operations. and constraints of the application world. All domain-specific relationships are reflected in the domain objects. They ensure their own internal consistency and correct relationships with other domain objects. However, they do not know anything about the presentation of their data and operations in the dialog layer, and they do not know in which elaboration contexts (of process and interaction control) they are situated. A business class is a collection of a set of domain classes with the aim of providing them with a common interface.

Responsibility for substantial and domain-specific consistency

TECHNICAL DICTIONARY

While we are getting acquainted with the application domain and develop scenarios, we permanently encounter technical terms of the application domain. These are collected in a technical dictionary or glossary and are carefully and precisely described.

Helpful questions ⇒ p. 65

On the one hand, this is important to minimize communication problems between developers and users. Often one side quite naturally uses specific terms and carelessly assumes that the other side has exactly the same understanding of these terms.

On the other hand, the same terms are used and interpreted differently even by users and domain experts from within the application domain. As naïve

◆ **Language Consolidation**

Object-oriented analysis is the unfolding and reconstruction of the conceptual world of the application domain by information technology. This is a multi-facetted and error-prone social process which mostly takes place via linguistic actions, that is, via every-day language. Use cases, scenarios, CRC cards, and the like, are techniques aimed at transforming this analysis into a methodological and systematic process.

Nevertheless, the basic problem still remains that different people can talk for a long time about the same object, maybe even using the same terms, and yet have more or less divergent views of that same thing.

Many fundamental assumptions and facts will be withheld from the IT people in this process, because for people from the application area, they are so self-evident and common that they seldom speak about them explicitly. They are much more inclined to talk about exceptions and special cases, and even these are often seen from only one perspective.

Developers and domain experts communicate mainly via natural language and therefore generally not very precisely. The following rules will help you gain more confidence (*see* Irion, 1995).

Try to use active instead of passive formulations

Passive formulations distract and hide the responsible parties. Instead of 'The contract is stipulated.' you should write more clearly 'The branch office stipulates a contract with the customer.' or 'The branch office's customer service attendant hands the customer a copy of the rental contract.'

Do not use synonyms, homonyms, or tautologies

If you encounter such terms, try to use a non-equivocal term. Do not use synonyms for pure linguistic embellishment, but feel free to point out possible synonyms. Example: instead of 'branch' it is preferable to speak about 'branch office' if you mean that one, or of 'branching' if you want to talk about two alternative ways of proceeding.

Instead of 'legal contract' it is sufficient to say 'contract' because a contract is by definition a legal agreement. Mixing up this kind of

Supplier
Employee
Customer

as it may sound, this concerns even seemingly simple concepts such as customer and address. For example, it may turn out that suppliers and employees too may be customers, that customers can be either enterprises or private persons, and so on. Different people in the application domain may look at the objects denoted by these terms from very different points of view and see completely different distinctions, responsibilities, roles, and attributes.

Thus, the definition of terms in a technical dictionary helps developers become familiar with the application domain and calls for confrontation of different interpretations. In many cases, different interpretations can be clarified without contradictions. There may, however, be terms that cannot be unified, and their different and contradictory interpretations are possibly justified. In such cases, the contradictions can at least be documented in the technical dictionary.

formulation may give rise to potential misinterpretations.

Use verbs instead of nouns that are not technical terms

In the formulation 'The customer is sent a message about …' ('message' used as a common language term) the term 'message' is not a technical term but a hidden process. Alternative formulations could be 'The customer service attendant informs the customer that …' or 'The customer service attendant notifies the customer about the fact …'

Do not use terms in the plural except where strictly necessary

Formulate your assertions in the singular if a thing occurs only individually in a context. Thus, for example 'The customer returns the vehicle.' instead of 'Customers return vehicles.' Further example: the term 'kind of business partner' means the classification, whereas 'kinds of business partners' means possible expressions, such as supplier, customer, corporate customer, interested party, employee, cooperation partner, and so on.

Try to use qualified terms

Qualification is a restrictive feature and specifies a term; it is usually placed in front of the original term: 'quality check list' instead of 'check list.'

Do not confuse information and information vehicle

Example: 'customer file/record' and 'customer.'

Be aware of possible misunderstandings with ambiguous terms

It makes no sense and only leads to misunderstandings if terms that are factually incorrect but unequivocal are replaced: the 'glove box' may still be called 'glove box' because no misunderstanding will arise, although only in very rare cases is it used to hold gloves. 'Storage compartment' or something similar would create ambiguity. If a term is really so ambiguous that it might lead to errors in communication, try to find a term that conveys the meaning better and without risks of misunderstanding.

Which facts should be considered in the technical dictionary? Besides the actual definition and description, these include:

- structure, components, subdivision;
- conditions, events, expected/undesirable events;
- life cycle: construction and destruction moments;
- hints regarding language consolidation;
- data types, forms of representation, constraints, roles, operations;
- relationships with other objects;
- set specifications/set grid;
- privileges, responsibilities;
- take-over of data from existing systems, and the like;
- significance, importance for specific persons, business goals, and so on;
- synonyms, related terms.

Language consolidation

Two examples, (address and invoice), can be seen below. Further conceivable entries in the technical dictionary might be: Customer, Condition, Tariff, Invoice addressee, Invoice position, Individual invoice, Monthly invoice, Collective invoice, Partial invoice, Vehicle type, Mobile accessories, Rental object, Fixed accessories, Equipment feature, Rental periods, Transfer, Contract, Availability, and so on.

See Design
⇒ *p. 147*

Address

An address belongs to an enterprise or to a person, where either may have several addresses. Addresses may have special meanings:

♦ Invoice address
♦ Registered office address
♦ Private address
♦ Holiday address

Addresses can be differently structured and have different contents. The following variations need to be distinguished:

♦ Street address (Street, Town, ZIP)
♦ P.O.B. address (P.O.Box, Town, ZIP)
♦ Corporate customer address (Town, ZIP)
♦ Foreign country address (free text)

Domestic addresses can be checked against street and ZIP code lists.

Invoice

Each invoice derives from a contract.

There are single, monthly, partial, and collective invoices, […].

Invoices may only be created by […, if […].

Per branch office, the average number of invoices created per month is […].

An invoice consists of an invoice addressee, a date, an invoice number, a customer number, the invoice positions that list the individual contract items.

Each position contains a description, a quantity, a per-unit and a total amount (position sum).

The invoice contains a total sum (sum of all positions).

[…]

EXPLORATIVE PROTOTYPES

Explorative prototypes are in most cases sequences of dialog designs which illustrate previously elaborated use cases. Dialog designs are executable dialogs in which data can be entered, but which do not include all features of a finished application, such as help functions, error handling, database storage, performance, robustness, an undo functionality, and so on. Use cases describe concrete user actions, including potential exceptions and special cases.

Dialog designs, formula designs

Explorative prototyping is used for analysis. It is a medium for communicating with future users about the planned application system. Frequently, explorative prototypes are dialog designs. They can, however, also be evaluations, printing samples, form designs, simulations, or calculation rules. The latter could be, for example, realized as spread sheets and reviewed together with experts from the application domain.

First, it has to be established which dialogs are needed and on the basis of which use cases they are required. Sometimes, doubts can arise as to whether in a specific situation one or several dialogs are needed, or whether in two different situations the same dialog might be used. In such cases, the requirements must be carefully compared. If in doubt, it might be better to opt for the simpler solution, that is, the one with fewer dialogs. Potentially, this may lead to conflict at a later stage, which suggests a different structure is required. But at least you will know why.

Explorative dialog prototypes show users and specialists actual aspects of the future system. Depending on the users' power of abstraction and imagination and their experience with software systems, you may also get some critical reactions on the dialog designs, such as 'this field needs to be shifted further up, and that one is far too small.' You as a system analyst, however, might be glad to have identified the dialogs at all, and do not really wish to hear these comments at this stage.

In such situations, it may be helpful not to show dialog designs, but to discuss brief textual descriptions which in a few keywords summarize the most important functions of the dialogs.

Customer search	‣ *Input of various search terms, such as customer number, name, phone, place* ‣ *Start search* ‣ *Select customer* ‣ *Delete all search terms*
Customer file	‣ *Display; processing of customer attributes, if required* ‣ *Customer number, name, addresses, phone numbers, and so on* ‣ *List of all reservations, contracts, invoices, damages, and so on, with corresponding branching possibilities* ‣ *Store modifications*

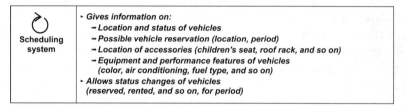

Dialog specification
⇒ *p. 136*

In a similar way, you can also describe existing marginal systems and interfaces. This does not make precise interface specifications superfluous, but for a first sketch of the surroundings of the new application, this form of description can be very useful.

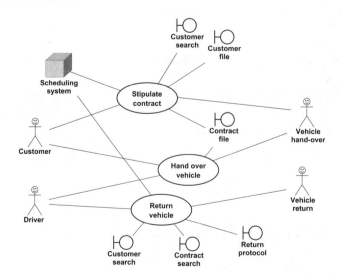

In use case diagrams, the individual use cases can be assigned the dialogs they require. The same process also applies to external systems, as shown in the illustration below.

The use case *stipulate contract* concerns the actor *vehicle hand-over* staff, and requires use of the scheduling system and the *customer search* and *customer file* dialogs.

Work with use cases and CRC cards (*see* next section ⇒ p. 152) open the application domain up to the development team, in the same way as putting together the technical dictionary (which, however, can also be used as a fine-tuning tool). All knowledge on the application domain acquired by means of these tools can now be found in the explorative prototypes.

The information acquired about the application domain is used by the development team as a basis for the design of dialog sequences. Thus, dialog designs become part of the use cases, since all processes described in the use cases need to be supported by the application system to be developed. All situations described in the use cases can be simulated dialog by dialog with the future users and, as a rule, lead to many more conclusions and questions.

See use case ⇒ p. 108

Illustration of use cases

Now finally, with their future tool in front of them as a sample, users will wish to assess and criticize it concretely. They have their every-day work before their eyes and try to find out how they can cope with it using the new tool. Users' statements frequently point out a lack of specific attributes (data fields) or actions (*'And where is the monthly turnaround?'*, *'The customer has a P.O. Box – do I enter it in the street field?'*, *'How can I change the invoice address?'*).

All questions, objections, suggestions, ideas, and so on that are brought forward by the users and cannot be immediately clarified, need to be protocoled and subsequently evaluated. Thus, when the session is later repeated with new designs, the planned solutions of the previous session's problems will be discussed.

Users' questions, objections, suggestions

Dialog designs can be drawn simply on a piece of paper, but it is better to show them directly on screen. With modern GUI builders, the effort is relatively little. The layout should be relatively detailed and near to the final version. Data fields may remain empty or filled with hard-wired sample values. Buttons and similar dialog elements may remain without any special functionality, but the expected outcomes should be explained.

Paper or screen?

Prototyping workshops should be well-prepared:

Preparing dialog workshops

◆ Each workshop has a clearly defined subject or deals with a specific aspect previously communicated to all participants. Users should, if possible, contribute sample material (contracts, forms, and so on).

◆ Arising questions should be protocoled, together with the person(s) responsible for clarification of how to handle this problem. A copy of the protocol is later given to each participant.

'But the customer has a P.O. Box ...'

Before the dialog designs are discussed with the users, they should be discussed inside the development team, in order to present the user workshop with a relatively mature version of the designs. It is usually not sufficient to show the identified attributes in a window and add a triad of buttons (such as STORE, CANCEL, HELP). Dialogs cannot be viewed as separate parts, but must be understood as components of a scenario, or a process. The process as a whole must be practical and sensible for the users.

Validation

Prototyping workshops make everybody involved more convinced that the right system is being developed. Misdevelopments are identified at an early stage and can still be corrected at a relatively low cost.

TOOLS-MATERIALS IMAGE. When the dialogs are looked at individually, it may be helpful to view them as users' tools for processing materials. This also influences language use: instead of customer dialog or customer form, we find the *customer file* and, in the same way, the *invoice file* and the *contract file*. Instead of a selection list, we talk about *customer search* or *contract search*. And when a customer has been selected and one of the related contracts has been opened to generate an invoice mostly automatically, the tool is, for example, called *invoice creation*.

Customer file, customer search, invoicing

Later, when a finished invoice is to be processed (the customer/contract relation was established by the invoice creation tool), this is done by invoice processing. Finally, the invoice is placed into the *out basket*.

If you think this is cheap and mere renaming of things that otherwise would not change, just try it out. At first, the change might feel difficult,

◆ Tools–Materials Aspects

One abstraction possibility in software development consists in looking at the roles of the objects and perform projections. Budde *et al.* (1991) and Kilberth *et al.* (1993) suggest that the objects of the application domain should be seen as tools and materials. Tools are those that can modify and process materials, such as copiers, stamps, editors, and accounting programs. Materials are working objects, that is, objects that can be processed by tools: books, copies, cheques, contracts, postings, and so on.

An object can be imagined as being both a tool and a material. A printer is usually used as a tool, but if the configuration of a printer is modified in an appropriate dialog, then in this context it is an object to be worked on, a material. This example shows that an object can be viewed under different aspects. Therefore, we not only differentiate between tools and materials, but in addition we define aspect classes. Only the aspect under which the objects are viewed makes them become tools or materials. The application of this image can be very helpful in modeling.

Possible aspect classes might be, for example, *printable*, *editable*, and *copiable*. The aspect class is the neutral interface between tool and material, that is, it usually represents an interface class. All materials and tools that want to enter an aspect or working relationship must provide the properties and interfaces required by the corresponding aspect class. It is via the *printable* aspect class that letter and printer get together.

Frequently used aspect classes are, for example, printable, editable, storable, listable.

Tools are usually designed for an isolated working process, while working objects can be processed in multiple ways, that is, by different tools. This also defines the relationship between tool, material, and aspect classes in relation to each other.

because the old terms are well-established and run-in. But as soon as you have mastered the new tool-material image, you will note that you now look at things differently, that is, that you perceive them differently and therefore arrive at different working results.

In the old language world, dialog forms were only viewed as a way of presentation – they were all forms, although the data in the forms could be structured quite differently. In the new language world, we find tools that have their own, data-independent existence and that have specific semantics attributed to them: they are searching and processing tools, out baskets, printers, and so forth. The terms are not only more pictorial and metaphorical, but also clearer. You would not want to extend a search tool with the functionality of a processing tool, simply because this does not fit into the search tool concept.

An example: every Christmas, the car rental agency in our example sends Christmas cards to their best customers. Branch office managers are to be given the possibility in the application system to tick every customer who should receive a card.

Therefore, a specific field was included in the processing form. However, the branch office managers complained about ticking off the card field was too

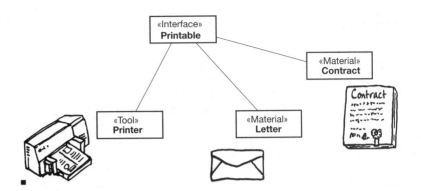

labour-intensive (having to navigate in each individual processing form). What they wanted was a list of names to tick off.

A customer list already exists in the system; it is used to select customers, amongst other functions. This list is extended by a new tick box and the turn-around figure (to determine the 'best' customers).

Christmas and golf tournament

If you see this dialog as a customer search tool, this solution immediately creates discomfort, because customers are no longer sought and selected, but also processed. The uneasiness derives from the fact that a special case has been added. The next special cases can already be foreseen: exceptionally good customers receive Christmas presents; the list should show whether customers have already received a Christmas card last year; moreover, for the annual customers' golf tournament, there should be check boxes for the invitations (has been invited, has confirmed, has participated), and so forth.

You soon get to an overloaded, clumsy, and no longer extendible form. Error correction too is becoming increasingly expensive. And all this only because of Christmas and a golf tournament.

Screwdrivers and nails

If you perceive dialogs as tools, you notice that a screwdriver is being (mis)used for knocking in nails. Alternatively, one would develop a customer action planning tool in addition to the customer search.

CRC CARDS

Classes Responsibilities, Collaborators

CRC is the abbreviation of *Class–Responsibilities–Collaborators*. CRC cards are filing cards on which a class, its responsibilities, and other collaborators are noted. The primary application area of CRC cards is structuring and detailing concepts of the application domain, often emerging from a specific use case.

One CRC card is created for each of the terms occurring in a use case. The term is entered as a class name. On the left-hand side of the card, the obvious responsibilities are noted, where responsibility includes the attributes and operations available for an object. On the right-hand side, terms are noted with which the objects of this class cooperate to fulfill their tasks. Then, similarly to the metaplan technique, the cards are attached to a pinboard or a magnetic board. Magnetic whiteboards are ideal because it is not only possible to arrange the cards, but also to use appropriate felt-tip pens to draw lines between the cards and wipe them out again.

Reservation	
Required vehicle type	Customer
Rental period from to	List of vehicle types
Required accessories	List of equipment features
Pick-up branch office	
Return branch office	

Uc1.2 ⇒ pp. 104 ff.

CRC workshops usually have 3–10 participants: domain experts, users, and developers. One person coordinates the entire process, that is, receives suggestions from the group, monitors the discussion, and tries to create a consensus. Another person supports the coordinator and takes on the practical work of writing the cards and attaching them to the pinboard.

You begin with indisputable and immediately concretely describable classes and add less precisely definable classes at a later stage. Thus, the vague classes are inserted into a fairly stable context. If you notice that, in one of the classes, responsibilities or collaborators have been overlooked, they are added.

Begin with indisputable classes

During this process, you usually arrive at the weak points of the classes early on. Their actual significance and their properties are compared and adjusted. It is often difficult to assign responsibilities to one card or the other. Discussions about this sometimes lead to further contradictions and questions, so that you move increasingly more deeply into the details. Often the question arises whether something is a responsibility or a collaborator. In case of doubt, you should decide on collaborator and open a new card for the term. If at a later stage it turns out that the card does not receive any further entries, you should remove it and enter the term on the original card as a responsibility.

In this way, the problem domain is covered step by step. When the cards have become unclear because of too many corrections, they should be replaced with new ones by the assistant.

Quantitative and qualitative analysis of the application domain

CRC cards are used to pursue two goals: on the one hand, they are a collective-type technique which quantitatively opens the conceptual and relational world and as such are a means for elaborating the technical dictionary. The fact that many people are involved and bring in their specific views of the application domain has the effect that new responsibilities, collaborators, and classes continue to appear during the process. On the other hand, the discussions on the different views allow the ideas backed by the individual participants to be checked for their validity. The task of the moderating person is to ensure that this discussion is carried out in a structured and concentrated manner. It should not continuously jump from one special subject to the other, but deal with the individual subjects one after the other. Moreover, it should be ensured that all subject areas are discussed at more or less the same level of detail.

AVOID DATA-HEAVY CARDS. A further aspect that needs considering: the participants should not only collect attributes and see the classes exclusively as containers of data. This would generate a data model: the responsibilities turn into attributes, the collaborators into relations, and entities are described instead of classes. Thus, if you deal, for example, with the CRC card 'Invoice' you should not only note invoice position, invoice date, invoice addressee, and discuss that an invoice always belongs to a customer and a customer can have many invoices, and so on. Try also thinking of how the invoice is put together. Where does the data come from? How does the data get into the invoice? The invoice positions are, for example, taken over from a contract. The invoice number should be generated automatically. The invoice address should be modifiable; it does not always correspond to the address of the customer's employee who reserved the car or who actually drove it. Thus, responsibilities of an invoice would also be:

- generation of invoice numbers;
- taking over contract positions (as invoice positions);
- modification of invoice addresses.

DEVELOPMENT TEAM-INTERNAL CRC DISCUSSIONS. CRC cards can also be used again later in detailed discussions. They can also be suitably employed in clarification of questions inside the development team. The subject of such rounds is usually no longer the qualitative and quantitative opening of the conceptual world of the application domain, but the problem of mapping complex requirements to the fine-grain design. In most cases, actual scenarios at the level of message exchange between objects are simulated and discussed.

Example ⇒ p. 158

Here, sequence diagrams should be used in addition to the CRC cards. Thus, on one side we find a pinboard with the classes as CRC cards, and on the other side a whiteboard or a flipchart with the message exchange between concrete objects. Working with sequence diagrams is shown at a later point in the text.

ROLES.   During the last stage in the discussion of CRC cards, it turns out that there are classes whose objects assume different roles in different situations. Depending on the situation, a customer in the car rental agency example might be in the role of invoice addressee, driver, reserver, and so on. Roles are not meant to be the actors of the use cases, although similarities can occur.   *Actors* ⇒ *p. 102*

Wherever such a role becomes evident, it should be noted because it improves the understanding of relations in general and of the current situation in particular. Either you create a new card, or you put the role directly before the denomination of a collaborator: thus, instead of customer, for example, *invoice_addressee=customer* or the like. The role specification becomes indispensable when two different collaborators of the same class are noted on the card, for example *insurant=customer* and *beneficiary=customer*. If you indicated only the class without the roles, you would look in vain for the CRC cards of the classes *insurant* and *beneficiary*, since the corresponding class is in both cases *customer*.

In addition to the role specifications for collaborators, the possible roles of a class should be noted on the CRC card of the class itself, for example directly below the class name. This shows at a glance in which roles objects of that class can appear. In the car rental agency example, customers, staff, vehicle, and invoices can, for example, appear in the following roles:

- ◆ **Customer**
  Interested party; reserving, renting, returning a car; new customer; customer service staff; driver; invoice addressee
- ◆ **Staff**
  Call center, customer desk, reservation, hand-over, accounting, car checking, scheduling, or transferring staff; customer
- ◆ **Vehicle**
  available, serviced, to be scheduled, rented, replacement
- ◆ **Invoice**
  Partial invoice, monthly invoice, open invoice

Sometimes, roles also give hints on stated and status values, as shown by the above list for 'vehicle.'

IDENTIFYING BUSINESS CLASSES

Understandable for managers and technical departments

A business class describes an object, a concept, a place, or a person from real business life in a degree of detail that can also be understood by technical departments and managers (contract, invoice, and so on). For the practical implementation, business classes are aggregations of fundamental domain classes reduced to purely technically motivated properties (invoice positions, address, and so on) to which everything else is delegated. Typically, they mostly define interfaces.

Interfaces

Identification of business classes means elaboration of the most important classes of the future class model. Details and subtleties are for the moment neglected. During the design process, each business class is further subdivided and will lead to something like 3 to 20 domain classes.

Business classes: summaries of fundamental classes

Candidates for business classes are, for example: customer, reservation, contract, vehicle, tariff, and invoice. At the level of these business classes, the first obvious relationships can be modeled, as shown in the following illustration.

See Development Process ⇒ p. 69

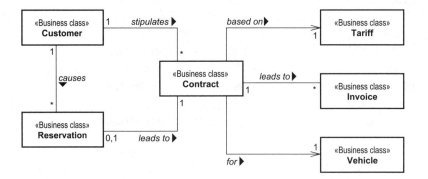

ACTIVITY MODELING

Use cases describe requirements to the system with a view to its outbound behavior. Thus, it seems sensible, for a detailed description of the processes the system is supposed to support, to elaborate activity models on the basis of such use cases. The illustration on the next page shows the path from identification of the use cases via their textual description to activity diagrams.

See Development Process ⇒ p. 69

With this step, the system analyst can make the transition from analysis to design. On the one hand, the activity diagrams derived from the use cases

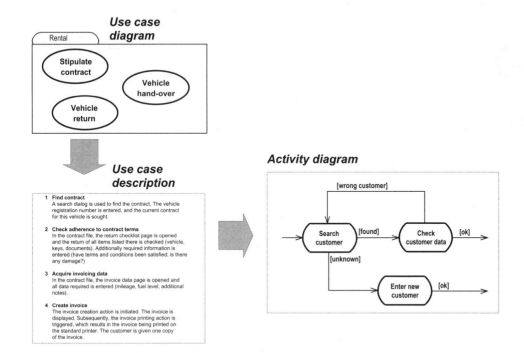

represent a further concretization of the requirements; on the other hand, this is the starting point for shaping the possibilities of **how** the system is to satisfy these requirements.

The activity diagram on the next page is based on the requirements of use case *Uc3.1 Vehicle return*. There are two different starting points. Either, a customer is selected first and then the required contract is selected from the set of current contracts of that customer, or the required contract is selected directly, for example via its contract number.

Uc3.1 Vehicle return
⇒ *p. 108*

The *select contract* activity occurs twice; in one case, it needs a customer object (in order to determine the customer's set of contracts). In the other case, no further dependencies exist.

The *vehicle return* activity is an action which must be initiated in the vehicle scheduling system. It is intended to ensure that the vehicle is now available and can be rented again.

In the following illustration, the described process is represented in two versions as an activity diagram. The diagram on the left-hand side only includes activities and transitions between these activities. The diagram on the right-hand side contains additional information.

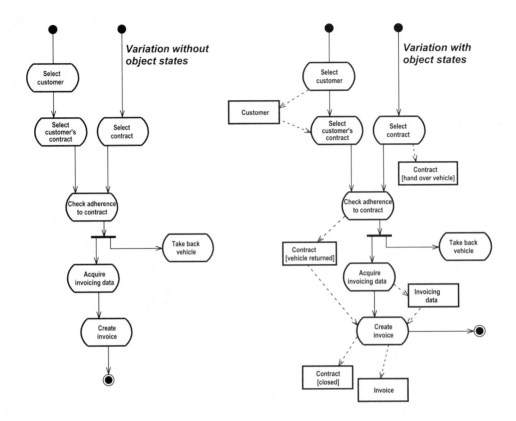

Each activity must produce a significant change of state; otherwise it might have no right to exist. Activity diagrams allow object states to be noted in addition to the activities. The right-hand side activity diagram contains the same facts as the left-hand side one, but in addition, object states are noted. Visual clarity does suffer a bit, but the expressive power, that is, the semantic content is significantly higher.

COMPONENT BUILDING

See Development Process ⇒ pp. 70 ff.

On the previous pages, we already mentioned component boundaries and interfaces. Thus, use cases were grouped with the aid of packages, and business classes identified as roughly structured component-like units. Interfaces with external systems have also been mentioned in the context of use cases.

The description regarding application architectures also shows how subsystems are mainly structured in the present example. The activity diagram of the previous section now opens for the first time the possibility for defining component boundaries on the basis of the system behavior identified up to now.

An important criterion for component building is minimizing interfaces and dependencies between components. In the following illustrations, the previous activity diagram is taken up once again. Each activity is now uniquely assigned to a component. In many cases, this assignment can be easily decided from a technical point of view. In cases of doubt, however, minimization of interfaces takes precedence.

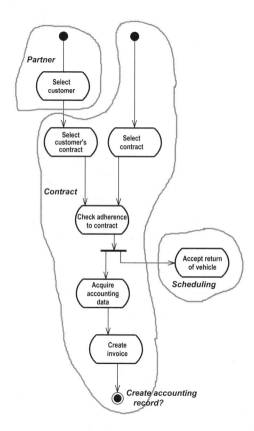

The activity diagram shown on the next page is now subdivided into four responsibility zones (so-called swim lanes), which represent the possible component structure. It shows a total of three simple interfaces:

1. between partner and contract,
2. between contract and the external scheduling system, and
3. between contract and accounting.

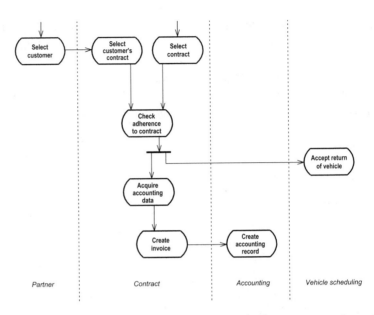

It is sufficient to note which activity belongs to which component. A graphical representation or modeling as shown in the activity diagram is not necessary or even not practical. The activity diagram shown on the previous page is instead intended to indicate the way of how components can be cut: just take printouts of activity diagrams and use a pen to circle groups of activities that belong to a common component.

Once the activities have been assigned in this way, dependencies between components can be derived. The result is a component diagram such as the one shown below.

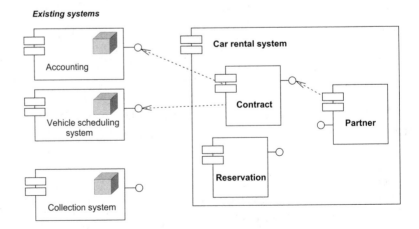

Chapter 5

Design

Logic is not a theory but a reflection of the world.

Ludwig Wittgenstein, *Tractatus logico-philosophicus*

Building on the example of the Analysis chapter, the process of object-oriented design is discussed, and the application of the individual methodological concepts is shown.

COMPONENT DESIGN

See ⇒ p. 130

At the end of the previous chapter, we demonstrated how components could be identified and defined with the aid of activity models. On this basis, we can now derive the first component interfaces.

Fundamentals
Components ⇒ p. 272
Interfaces ⇒ p. 202

Wherever the flow of activity passes a component boundary, it becomes necessary that the component from which the flow of activity starts calls a service of the component which hosts the subsequent activity. The following illustration shows the principle.

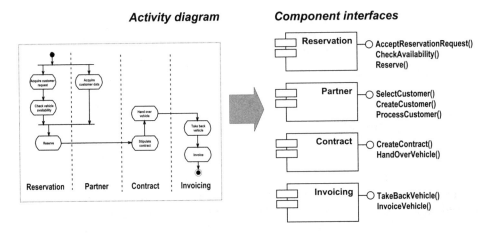

Activity diagram *Component interfaces*

Each interface is described by one or (if required) a number of interface classes:

«interface» CustomerBehavior
selectCustomer():Customer createCustomer():Customer processCustomer(Customer):Customer

«interface» ContractBehavior
selectConract():Contract selectContract(Customer):Contract createContract():Contract handOverVehicle(Contract):Contract

Activity models in the sense of a behavioral and process view of the system are by themselves not sufficient to identify all interfaces. A further basis is the domain class model, which represents the technical structures that also pass component boundaries.

In a first approach, here too component boundaries can be drawn on the basis of technical relationships. As with activity-driven component formation, minimization of interfaces must also be considered. The following illustration outlines the delimitation of components in the domain class model.

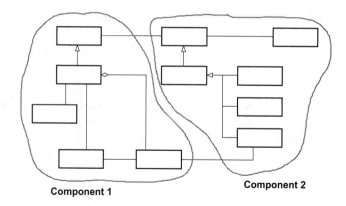

Component 1   Component 2

The previous chapter's section on application architecture (page 112) introduced the basic interfaces of the subsystems. These are:

◆ Interfaces concerned with processes and behavior such as, for example, *SelectCustomer*.
◆ Interfaces between domain classes, for example the association between customer and contract (*customer has n contracts*).
◆ Interfaces at dialog level. If, for example, the name and address of the customer are shown in the contract dialog, then name and address are dialog elements which are implemented in the partner component and imported by the contract component into the contract file implemented in the contract component.

The association of dialog components to use cases and activities can be used to identify interfaces and relationships between dialogs.

Identification of interfaces is only a first step. A more important step is to specify the interfaces in detail. This can be done with the aid of interface classes. For the various types of categories of component interfaces (processes, dialogs, structural relationships), separate (and, where necessary, stereotyped) interface classes should be created.

Application Frameworks

The architecture described in Chapter 4, Analysis, is used as consistently as possible for the whole application development. Reasonably enough, the fundamental relationships of the model, and the required infrastructure, such as communication between layers, their structure, and so on, are defined in a so-

Application architecture ⇒ p. 112

called framework. Frameworks usually provide a multitude of abstract classes from which the concrete classes for the current application layer are derived. Thus, frameworks are, among other things, abstract implementations of the application architecture.

Abstract architecture implementation

A peculiarity of such frameworks is the transfer of the vertical relationships, that is, the control of the fundamental interfaces, into the framework. Communication between layers occurs as far as possible via the classes of the framework. Classes built on top of the framework communicate if possible only within their own layer. When using the framework, the old saying applies: '*Don't call the framework, the framework will call you*' (that is, reversal of control).

Don't call the framework …

SPECIFYING DIALOGS

In a systematic process of application development, in particular in major projects, it does not necessarily make sense to devise ('draw') dialogs completely and immediately any time they are needed. Dialogs are elements with which users are confronted directly; thus, their quality is decisive for positive acceptance of the software and consequently for the whole success of the project.

Dialog contexts

In complex applications, individual dialogs mostly occur in a multitude of contexts. To prevent users from being presented with a separate, different dialog for each processing context, and also in view of the development and maintenance cost, the general aim is to employ dialogs as universally as possible in different contexts.

The simplest contexts are, for example, creating, editing, and viewing data. Usually, a single dialog is sufficient for this purpose. With more complex dependencies in data creation, so-called assistant dialogs have proved a good solution, while in other cases, users are given more freedom.

As well as these trivial dialog contexts, such as creation and modification of data, there are further, mostly domain-related contexts which often also correspond to possible states of their elementary domain objects, such as reservation, contract, invoiced contract, and so on.

Dialogs, activities, subsystems, components

Dialog contexts are the activities of the activity diagrams (or the use cases from which the activity diagrams originate). To view these relationships systematically and be able to deduct requirements from them, it is helpful to associate the identified dialog components to the activities in question. Identification of dialogs has already been shown at use-case level (page 121). This refinement of use cases into activity models is now matched by the

See ⇒ p. 121

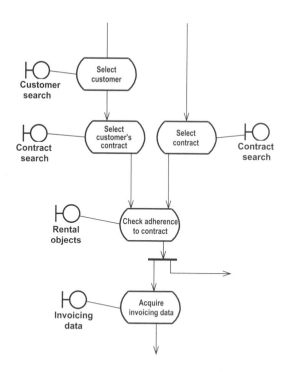

refinement of dialogs into dialog components. Since the activities are already associated to concrete subsystems or components, the association of dialog components to activities implicitly entails an association of dialog components to subsystems.

When dialogs are supposed to be employed in highly different contexts, the design can only be finalized after all working contexts are known. Otherwise, a dialog is made up for the current environment, and is extended and modified accordingly when it is to be employed in another situation. This may, however, make part of the previously invested effort null and void.

DIALOG COMPONENTS. Therefore, it would appear to be best initially only to specify the dialog requirements. This may again happen at two levels. On the one hand, the individual fields and dialog elements need to be specified, for example length and type of the input field *street*. On the other hand, dialog elements can be combined into groups, for example *street*, *place*, and *ZIP* into an *address* group. Such groups can also be called dialog components; they are the smallest technically reasonable combination of individual dialog elements.

Here is a simple scheme for the specification of dialogs:

Dialog specification

Syntax	Meaning	Example
M	mandatory field	ZIP: M
M {condition}	conditional mandatory field	ZIP: M {length(name) > 0}
L=min–max	range of positions to input	name: L=3-40
[default setting]	default setting	name: ['A.N. Other']
D {condition}	conditional fields disable	date: D {date<today}
H {condition}	conditional hide	pobox: H {type<>POBaddress}
T=type	type of dialog element	maritalStatus: T=ComboBox
C(n) {condition} = error	field check, error as text, error code or the like	dateFrom: C(1) {dateFrom>dateTo}= 'negative period'
B=text	short info text (bubble help)	ZIP: B='ZIP code'
I=text	long info text	ZIP: I='Enter a valid ZIP code'
S={set of values}	predefined set of values, calculation/selection prescription or the like	sex: S={'male', 'female', '??'} sex: S={select entry from TypeOfEntry where type='Sex'}
E=event	triggered event	okayButton: E=ReleaseContract
E {condition}= event	conditional event	date: E {date isValid}=EnterDate

Here is an example for the *contractStatus* field (see the dialog shown in the screenshot on page 122 where, however, it was only used for requirement specification and communication with the users; therefore it was not fully elaborated, for example, the contract status is not yet shown as a *ComboBox*):

```
contractStatus:
    M, T=ComboBox,
    S={#reserved, vehHandedOver, vehReturned},
    C(1) {factRentedUntil isEmpty and contractStatus=
    vehReturned}= Please enter return date&time first
```

Depending on programming language and development environment, these definitions should be made directly at this point. It should also be possible to print out an appropriate documentation, so that the information does not get buried somewhere in the depth of the code or the tools, but is present explicitly and extracted from the surrounding code.

Dialog components encapsulate a set of individual dialog elements and provide a uniform external interface. Uniform, because all dialog components should provide a homogeneous interface. Besides operations for reading and setting field contents, default settings, and other properties, dialog components should also provide services which enable users of the component to make themselves dependent, for example, of events (forwarding event, *addActionListener()*, and the like). Component interfaces can be described by means of interface classes.

Java Beans

Interface classes

It should be noted that a large number of formal checks and consistency conditions can already be assured by the dialogs – but only to provide user-friendly and easy-to-handle dialogs. The responsibility for consistency of data and states is ultimately with the domain objects, in which all constraints must be implemented so that they never get into an undefined state. Within dialogs, instead, admitting incomplete and contradictory data is unavoidable, at least temporarily.

Constraints

In addition to the constraints required by the domain classes, dialogs can enforce further restrictions to guide users in a more directive, that is, restrictive fashion.

Dialog components should be composed of elements that show complex dependencies and relationships with each other. For example, the contract status depends on the specifications made for the rental period. To the outside, components should appear self-sufficient and have simple interfaces.

Interfaces

Design by contract

IDENTIFYING DOMAIN CLASSES AND RELATIONSHIPS

IDENTIFYING CLASSES.   Let us assume that in the first development iteration of the application to be developed, the *business partner* domain is to be designed. In the technical dictionary and the use cases, the following terms were used in this domain:

- business partner,
- customer,
- customer file,
- contact partner,
- supplier,
- supplier file,
- enterprise,

- private person,
- bank account,
- telecommunication connections (in short: phone number),
- address,
- employees.

How do I find classes? To begin with, all listed terms are interpreted as classes.

The terms *enterprise* and *private person* do not exist on their own, but only in connection with the terms *business partner*, *customer*, *supplier*, *contact partner*, and *employee* ('*A customer is an enterprise or a private person*').

The term *business partner* is a generic term for *customer*, *supplier*, *contact partner*, and *employee*.

A more detailed analysis of the address shows that there are several different types of addresses:

Technical dictionary
⇒ *p. 115*
- Street address: address with street, city, and ZIP,
- P.O.B. address: address with P.O.B., city, and ZIP,
- Corporate address: corporate address consisting of city and ZIP,
- Foreign country address: no uniform structure.

IDENTIFYING RELATIONSHIPS. After having identified the classes, we are now going to analyze their relationships with each other, that is, their associations, aggregations, and inheritance relationships.

The following discussion contains several examples which violate important design rules. They are intended to show the difficulties that may arise, and how things should not be done. The corresponding illustrations all contain a sad smiley to show that the solution is problematic.

Business Partners and their Roles

As already mentioned in the previous section, *business partner* is a generic term for *customer*, *supplier*, *contact partner*, and *employee*. Furthermore, the terms *enterprise* and *private person* do not exist on their own, but only in connection with a business partner. A customer (as a specialization of the business partner) can be either a private person or an enterprise. The attempt to represent these facts with the aid of inheritance relationships would lead to the following class diagram:

Multiple inheritance
⇒ *p. 226* This model is, however, unsatisfactory: on the one hand, it requires multiple inheritance (even with an exclusive OR); on the other hand, contact partners

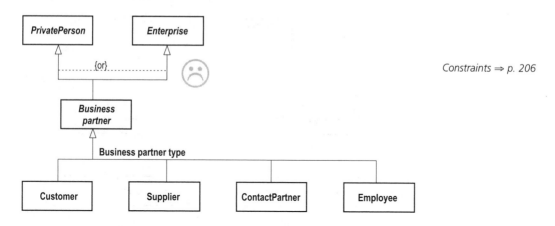

Constraints ⇒ p. 206

and employees, although business partners, are always private persons, never enterprises.

The following illustration shows an approach which allows customers and suppliers to be private persons or enterprises. Contact partners and employees, however, are always private persons.

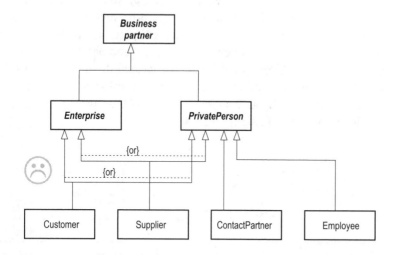

For *customer* and *supplier*, there still remains the problem of multiple inheritance. To avoid this, one might think of the following solution which, however, in less trivial cases might quickly lead to a combinatorial explosion of possibilities. Furthermore, the properties to be assigned to the terms *enterpriseCustomer* and *privateCustomer* will supposedly be more or less the same.

Combinatorial explosion of inheritance relationships

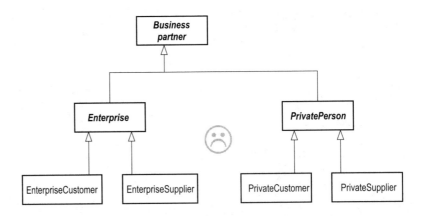

Composition ⇒ p. 245

The following illustration shows a solution in which *private person* and *enterprise* are each a part (composition) of a concrete business partner. The model takes into account the fact that customer and supplier are either a private person or an enterprise, but never both at the same time. *Contact partner* and *employee*, instead, have always exactly one person object.

This variation covers the requirements, but would probably become complicated when detailed further. Since enterprise and private person are not connected with the abstract class business partner, but with its concrete instances, communication between enterprise and person data and the concrete business partners would have to be located there. This means that the required operations – although similar or identical – would have to be main-

Redundance?

tained redundantly in four concrete business partner instances. This should be avoided for reasons of quality and cost.

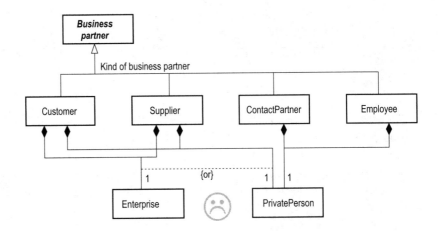

OCL ⇒ p. 276

The OR constraint between the composition relations between enterprise and private person can also be described by means of OCL expressions. The OR constraint shown above is only a short notation; OCL expressions are usually more precise and therefore preferable. The illustration below shows the corresponding section once again, this time with OCL expressions.

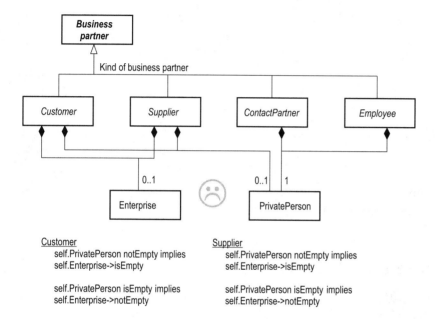

Customer
    self.PrivatePerson notEmpty implies
    self.Enterprise->isEmpty

    self.PrivatePerson isEmpty implies
    self.Enterprise->notEmpty

Supplier
    self.PrivatePerson notEmpty implies
    self.Enterprise->isEmpty

    self.PrivatePerson isEmpty implies
    self.Enterprise->notEmpty

Constraints ⇒ p. 206

Two constraints each are needed. The first one prevents a customer referring to a private person while simultaneously referring to an enterprise. The second one requires the same if no private person is referred to. Without the second constraint, it would be possible for a customer to be neither an enterprise nor a private person.

In the following solution, again an OR constraint between two composition relations is used. Therefore, we will show once again, how this can be converted into the corresponding OCL expressions.

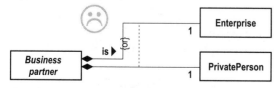

The following diagram now shows the previously announced better solution. Private person and enterprise have a composition relation with the

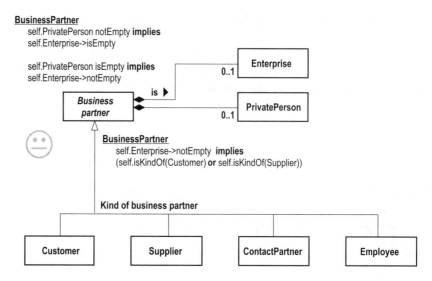

business partner. The exception that contact partners and employees are not enterprises is noted as a constraint. This solution covers the requirements, but unfortunately contains a large number of constraints.

A Critical Check of Inheritance

Employee and supplier can be customers

See Analysis ⇒ p. 115

At first sight, the specialization by kind of business partner appears obvious and plausible. A look at the requirements, however, puts this into question. Thus, for example, it was found that suppliers and employees too can be customers. An object can, however, not simply change its class membership (for example from supplier to customer). Moreover, this would not match the fact, because the concrete business partner is not alternating between being once a supplier and then a customer, but can be both at the same time. An object can, however, not be simultaneously an instance of two classes.

Specialization vs. role assignment

The real problem lies in the fact that the kind of view used in modeling is not entirely correct. Business partners cannot be specialized into customers, suppliers, and so on. Instead, customer, supplier, and so on, are possible properties of a business partner. In specific situations, some of these properties come to the fore, for example the customer properties when renting a vehicle.

Business partner roles

Customer, supplier, employee, and *contact partner* are therefore no business partner classes, but business partner roles. A role defines a special perspective of an object, and is a property of the viewer, not of the viewed. The perspective, that is, the role, initially changes things only for the person viewing or using the object. In our example, it is the car rental agency, or the

◆ Delegation

Delegation is a mechanism in which an object does not interpret a message completely on its own, but forwards the message to another object. Thus, it can also be used as an alternative to inheritance.

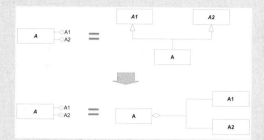

Delegation allows objects to use existing properties of other classes or to provide additional properties. In other words, a class can extend (propagate) its properties by delegation. The effects of inheritance can, for example, be emulated with the means of aggregation, which makes delegation a valid mechanism for prevention of multiple inheritance. Properties which in an inheritance relation would have to be located in the superclass, are evacuated into a separate class which can then be incorporated again via an aggregation relation.

The figure shows the class *A* which provides the interfaces *A1* and *A2*, in the first case directly via multiple inheritance, in the second case indirectly via a delegation mechanism to be implemented.

In Smalltalk, delegation can very easily and globally be achieved by overwriting the method *does-Not-Understand:*, while in C++ and Java the implementation effort is substantial (*see* Gamma *et al.* (1996), p. 22, p. 367 and Halter (1996). An argument against global delegation is that it may have difficulty in controlling side effects and causes runtime losses. It is in any case more advantageous to model delegation and to use code generation to implement it as direct delegation only.

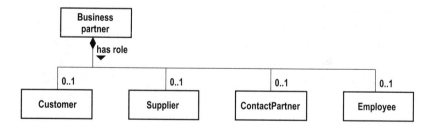

users of the software to be developed, who perceive business partners in specific situations in a specific role such as supplier or customer. The above class diagram takes these reflections into account.

Yet another – and in connection with our business partner roles the last – variation is based on the actor–role pattern. The design problem discussed here is a classical application for this design pattern. In Smalltalk, its implementation is relatively easy and requires only a few lines of instructions (overwriting of the *messageNotUnderstand:* method). In languages without dynamic type binding and without classes accessible at runtime (such as C++ and Java), it requires a little more effort.

Actor–role pattern

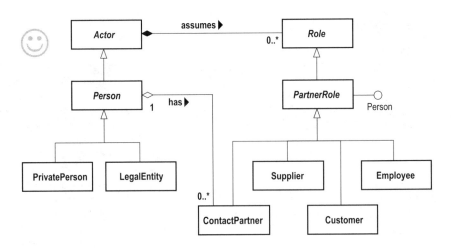

A special feature of this design pattern is that the different partner roles (*customer, supplier, employee, contact partner,* and so on) can forward (propagate) messages to the person to whom they belong. This means that, for example, suppliers can be treated in the same way as an object of the *Person* class. All messages that cannot be directly interpreted by a partner role object (the name of the person, the date of birth of a private person, and so on) are forwarded to the person object (for example a private person) and answered by the latter. The *Partner role* class provides the interface of *Person*, which in the diagram is symbolized by the interface lollipop.

Interface lollipop
⇒ *p. 204*

The above diagram also shows a relationship between *Person* and *contact partner*. Contact partners are needed in particular for legal entities. Frequently, there are also several contact partners (for special domains, and the like) in one enterprise. However, we can also conceive contact partners for private persons, if for example the husband or wife of the actual hirer and driver makes the vehicle reservations.

To prevent a person from being able to refer to itself as contact partner, the following OCL constraint needs to be noted:

```
ContactPartner
    self.Person <> self.Actor
```

DOMAIN CLASS MODELING: BUSINESS PARTNER

Composition ⇒ *p. 245*

Next, we can integrate the classes bank account, phone number, and address into the class model. This is slightly easier: each of the objects of the three classes is part of a business partner. Each kind of business partner may have an

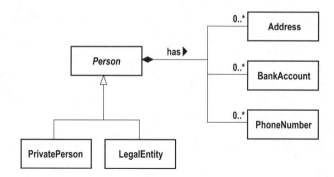

arbitrary number of them (0..*). All three are perceived as existence-dependent on their respective business partner; that is, we are dealing with composition relations.

Address

As mentioned earlier, there are four kinds of addresses: street addresses, post box addresses, corporate addresses, and foreign country addresses. The following paragraphs intend to refine the address domain of the class model. The basis for our discussion is the model outlined in the following illustration. It is composed of the four concrete kinds of address and two abstract classes *Address* and *Domestic address*.

Identifying classes ⇒ *p. 139*

Technical dictionary ⇒ *p. 115*

This model shows a hierarchical structure of the different kinds of address which, at first sight, looks plausible. The question is, however, whether this solution can be adequately implemented. *Adequate* in this context means that the implementation cost is reasonable and that the solution is sufficiently

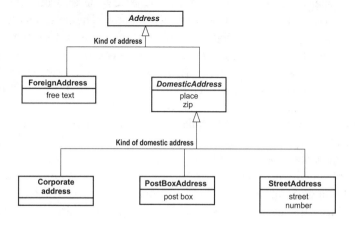

| Street | Miller Road | | P. O. Box | 652 541 | |
| City, ZIP | San Francisco, CA | 94114 | City, ZIP | San Francisco, CA | 94132 |

Adress type
- ⦿ Street adress   ○ Corporate adress
- ○ P.O.B. adress   ○ Foreign country

Adress type
- ○ Street adress   ○ Corporate adress
- ⦿ P.O.B. adress   ○ Foreign country

	Ida-Virumaa
City, ZIP	San Francisco, CA	94114	EE2033 Alajoe
	Vallavalitsus Uuskula
	Estonia

Adress type
- ○ Street adress   ⦿ Corporate adress
- ○ P.O.B. adress   ○ Foreign country

Adress type
- ○ Street adress   ○ Corporate adress
- ○ P.O.B. adress   ⦿ Foreign country

robust and flexible. To clarify this, it is helpful not only to look at the data side, but also to consider the behavior of such objects and to take their representation into account.

The above illustration shows the four dialog variations. The kind of address is selected by means of radio buttons. Depending on the activated option, specific address fields are shown or hidden. Users can change the type of an address at any time.

As long as the address dialog is not terminated, the kind can always be switched. The contents of the fields – even if they are currently hidden – are preserved. As soon as the dialog is exited, however, only the data of the current kind of address is taken over.

Dynamic classification

Returning to the present class model, the change of kind of address means that the class membership of the address object would need to change – which is not envisaged in Java and C++, and is not common practice in Smalltalk. Precisely speaking, with each change of kind, a new address would need to be created, that is, a new object with its own identity. The previous old object could be destroyed. Address objects are part of a business partner, so that with each change of object the aggregation relation between *business partner* and *address* would need to be updated. These consideration already show that in order to implement the class model, much effort needs to go into the details.

Delegation ⇒ p. 145

The following illustration shows a solution whose particular feature is an interface class which is used to hide the internal structure. The solution is based on the *Façade* design pattern, with borrowings from the *Status* pattern.

Interfaces ⇒ p. 202
Design patterns ⇒ p. 44
Packages ⇒ p. 217

The advantage of this solution is that the owner of an address is always only confronted with one class and one interface. Delegation of the actual attributes and operations is hidden; four interfaces are reduced into one. This also reduces the dependencies between the classes (address and business

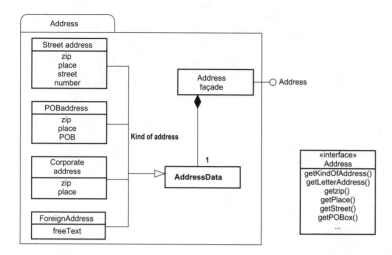

partner). Internally, the address is structured very pragmatically, that is, the attributes *city* and *zip* for domestic and other addresses are not factorized out because this would (as we have seen on pages 147 ff.) produce abstract classes with only one or two attributes. The operation *getLetterAddress()* returns a complete multi-line string containing all important components of the address as required, for example, for printing letters, mailshots, and so on.

Since in a running system a large number of addresses is to be expected, their structure should not be too complicated. On the other hand, the internal structure is well protected by the interfaces, so that modifications and maintenance of the internal representation pose no problems.

Depending on the premises, other solutions may be sensible too. Here, we have merely discussed one possible version.

Configurable sets of values

Configurable sets of values are sets of values that are uniquely defined across the entire application and usually appear as constant to their users, but can in fact be configured. They are employed at all points where data input is restricted by a predefined set of possible values. Typically, such sets of values appear in drop-down list boxes.

Examples are sex (male, female), marital status (single, married, divorced, widowed), type of phone number (phone, fax, mobile), type of address (private, business, holiday, and so on).

In class modeling, such sets of values are not noted via associations or the like, but as attributes with a corresponding type. A particular feature is that

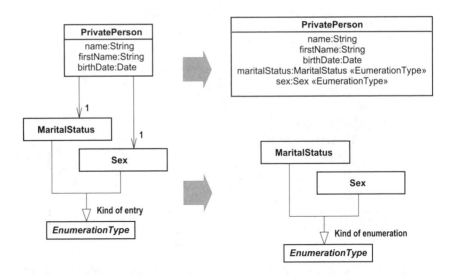

these associations would be directed and of cardinality 1. Thus, if these sets of values were principally noted as associations, the class models would become overloaded and unclear. This can be avoided, because the semantic information is relatively small, and such relations are not interesting from a modeling point of view. Therefore, it is more sensible to note them as attributes.

These attributes are often also called type entries, system values, and the like. Since this is a special kind of attribute, it is sensible to define a stereotype which describes this particular context of usage, for example «*TypeEnumeration*».

Stereotype
«TypeEnumeration»

DOMAIN CLASS MODELING:
RESERVATION AND CONTRACT

In the previous steps (iterations), we took a closer look at partner roles and addresses. In the following sections we will now analyze and design the actual rental and contract in more detail. First, we consider reservation, then contract and invoice, making use of the previously modeled partner roles.

Reservation

A reservation is made by a customer. A customer may have any number of reservations, but a reservation always belongs to one customer. A customer is a business partner with whom a contract has already been stipulated once.

Reservations can, however, also be made by interested parties, that is, persons who wish to become customers. We will not for the moment consider this possibility; for simplicity sake we will only consider customers. At a later stage, for example in the next iteration, clarification is needed at this point. To ensure that the interested party does not get lost, the *Interested party* class has already been created and put next to the customer in the diagram, as a sort of bookmark.

Not all at once

In particular, the *Reservation* class also includes the reservation period. Since this is an important information for understanding the model, this attribute is already captured and shown in the diagram.

Show important attributes

Reservations are, however, not made for a concrete vehicle, but only for a vehicle type. The car rental agency needs to ensure that a sufficient number of vehicles of the reserved types is available at any time. Only when the contract is stipulated is the customer assigned a physical vehicle.

The same applies to equipment, such as children's seats, roof racks, and the like, and to special accessories, such as air conditioning, car phone, and so on.

The illustration represents the described facts in the form of a class diagram. It should be noted that vehicle type, equipment, and special accessories are referenced only one-way. The instances of, for example, the *Vehicle type* class have no knowledge about the reservations they are going to be used for. This is not necessary. The use cases focus on reservation and contract; these are the objects the users essentially work with. Vehicle type, for example, represents only a predefined set of values from which the users select during a reservation to make the reservation actual. There is no use case that envisages an independent use of the vehicle type.

One could at most imagine the question of reservation of a specific vehicle type, but then again, the main focus still lies on reservation. In such a case, one would simply search the set of reservations for specific, referenced vehicle types.

Vehicle Rental Contract

Next, we will look at the rental contract and the surrounding classes. First of all, we note that a rental contract may originate from a reservation; this is, however, not mandatory.

The contract is stipulated for the rental of a specific vehicle and for specific accessories. For pieces of equipment such as children's seats, roof racks, and so on, this means in practice that they must be uniquely identifiable, for example by means of an inventory number.

Since the contract does not assume a reservation, and the rental data may deviate from the original reservation data, several attributes of the reservation will also be contained in the rental contract. Deviations occur, for example, when a customer decides to return the vehicle earlier than originally reserved.

Moreover, the contract may specify a vehicle that does not correspond to the reserved type, for example when the rental company gives the customer a better vehicle for the same price because the reserved type is currently not available.

Potentially, there might be the possibility of factoring out common features of *reservation* and *rental contract* and of generalizing or delegating them. However, to be able to make this kind of design decision in a serious manner, additional data on the environment of the two classes, in particular of the contract, is required. This problem should therefore be studied at a later stage.

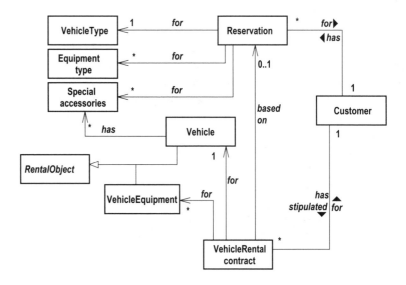

For vehicle and equipment, however, a generalization (rental object) has been stated. How well this will hold, will become evident during the course of model detailing; the abstraction does, however, suggest itself and appears quite plausible.

Vehicle Hand-Over and Return

In the contract, the authorized or envisaged drivers are specified (there may be more than one driver). Their driving licenses are checked at vehicle hand-over time, at the latest. Driver and customer do not need to match. For example, the customer is an enterprise and the driver an employee of this enterprise. Or two private persons drive together, but only one of them appears as the customer.

During vehicle hand-over, a hand-over protocol is drawn up which describes the hand-over state of the vehicle (existing damages, mileage, and so on). When the vehicle is returned, a corresponding return protocol is made. The difference, for example in mileage, is then taken as a basis for invoicing.

In the protocols, composition relations were used, because the protocols are existence-dependent on the contract. If the vehicle was involved in an accident, an additional accident protocol must be drawn up, which is considered part of the return protocol.

Similarly to the reservation, the rental contract includes the agreed rental period. The hand-over and return protocols are then used to record the actual hand-over and return times.

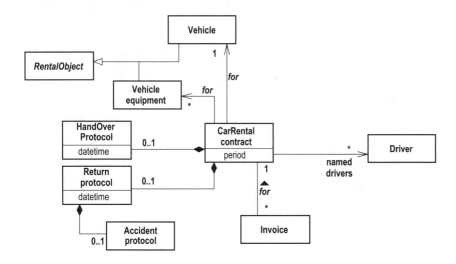

OCL ⇒ p. 276

Appropriate constraints need to be noted, which ensure factual consistency with regard to these times, for example that the return time does not fall prior to the hand-over time and that no return protocol should exist without a previous hand-over protocol. It also needs noting that, together with the hand-over protocol, the drivers need to be defined. The following OCL expressions describe these constraints.

```
VehicleRentalContract
    self.HandoverProtocol->isEmpty implies
        self.ReturnProtocol->isEmpty
VehicleRentalContract
    self.HandoverProtocol->notEmpty implies
    self.authorDriver->notEmpty
VehicleRentalContract
    self.ReturnProtocol->notEmpty implies
        self.HandoverProtocol.datetime <
        self.ReturnProtocol.datetime
```

The first two constraints refer to pure existence-dependencies; a model variation with which these constraints can be circumvented is shown in the following illustration.

The return protocol is now directly existence-dependent on the hand-over protocol. Thus, the rental contract can only navigate indirectly to the return protocol. For later invoicing, navigation also becomes more expensive. In the implementation, in particular with regard to object loading strategies (persistence), this variation could turn out to be disadvantageous. Here, a design decision needs to be made at a later stage, carefully considering all different points of view.

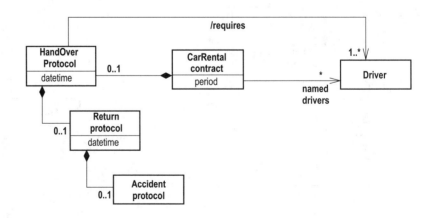

Between the hand-over protocol and the drivers we now find a derived association. Since it requires a multiplicity of 1..*, the assignment of at least one driver is required at the latest when the hand-over protocol is drawn up. The derived association can be calculated from the relation hand-over protocol – rental contract – driver. The derivation prescription is similar to the constraint shown earlier for this fact; this means that the model has not become any simpler. The derived association will therefore be omitted in the course of further proceedings.

DELIMITING COMPONENTS

In the model processed so far we can now check or specify the component boundaries. On the one hand, it must be ensured that technically related classes stay together and that interfaces between the components are kept as simple as possible. Classes sharing a common superclass will usually be accommodated in the same component; there must be important reasons for deviating from this principle.

Component building
⇒ pp. 130, 134

The *Partner* domain can be delimited with relatively few problems. The protocols are existence-dependent on the contract; this too suggests that the involved components should be bundled into a common component. The

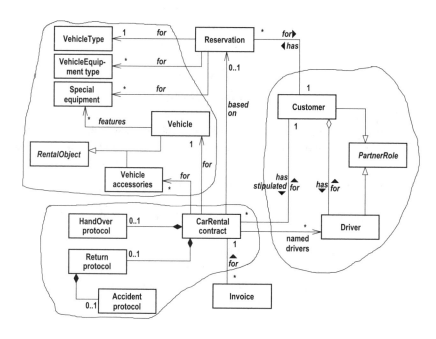

invoicing environment has not yet been looked at in detail, but since an *invoice* component has already been identified during the analysis phase, invoicing can be temporarily added to this component. Similar arguments apply to the reservation.

The rental objects and their types also form a unit because of their technical proximity and the generalization of *rental object*. No corresponding component has been stated so far, so that here a new component has been found. It might initially be called something like *rental objects*. Further detailing will show whether the design decisions made at this point will hold.

SPECIFYING OPERATIONS

Fundamentals
⇒ *p. 198*

Identifying relationships
⇒ *pp. 49 ff.*

Use cases ⇒ *p. 100*

Besides the classes, operations are also specified (where this has not already happened). As with the identification of relationships, special attention must be paid to use cases and scenarios processed during the analysis phase. The interactions between objects described there need to be reflected in the operations. The name of an operation should, if possible, contain an (active) verb form.

Add contract
Uc2.2 ⇒ *p. 105*

Operations for the *business partner* class would be, for example, *addContract*, *addCP* and *removeCP* (CP = contact partner). These operations result from the outcome of the analysis.

Helpful questions for identification of operations:

State diagrams
⇒ *p. 265*

♦ What kind of service is expected from the object (for example, setting of a standard address)?
♦ Which state transitions might apply to the object?
♦ When does the life cycle of an object begin, and when does it end?
♦ For which relations with other objects are add or remove operations required (for example adding a contract)?

- Which information must the object be able to give?
- Which data contents are modifiable? Data changes are carried out via operations which might also take over formal and content check of the data change.

During determination of the operations, you will occasionally gather new insights and a new understanding of relationships between classes. As a consequence, associations, aggregations, and inheritance hierarchies are also adjusted accordingly.

The following items belong to the specification of an operation:

- *Signature.*   Describes name, arguments, and return type of the operation.
- *Precondition* (pre:).   Describes the object state that must be given before execution of the operation.
- *Postcondition* (post:).   Describes the object state given after execution of the operation.
- *Invariance.*   Describes the object state that must be given during execution of the operation.
- *Semantics.*   Describes task and significance of the operation by way of a comment.

Moreover, type checks and special value checks may need to be specified for the arguments. These can be indicated in the invariant part. The following example uses OCL formulations: OCL ⇒ p. 276

```
setStandardaddress(address : Address):Address
  pre:
    (standardaddress.isKindOf(Address)) or
    (standardaddress = null)
  post:
    (standardaddress = address) or
    (standardaddress = null)
  invariant:
    (address.isKindOf(Address)) and
    (self.addresses.includes(address))
  semantics:
    The address passed in <address> becomes the
    standard address of the business partner.
    In case of error, the standard address is
    set to null.
```

The specification of preconditions, postconditions, and invariants helps developers and users of the operation and makes them feel safe. These are, so-to-speak, the business conditions for the cooperation of provider and user. This also facilitates testing of the operation.

If you do without specification of such details, both providers and users will implicitly make assumptions without, however, ensuring that they match. Thus, the above example defines that the *address* argument is not allowed to have a null value. Otherwise, a user might (very naïvely) get the brilliant idea of sending

```
setStandardaddress(null)
```

in order to reset the standard address. Such a reset operation is, however, not permitted by the operation specified above.

SPECIFYING ATTRIBUTES

Attribute fundamentals
⇒ p. 195

Besides the operations, we also need to determine the remaining attributes that have not yet been taken into consideration, that is, we need to take a closer look at the data aspect of the classes. The following questions will help:

- ◆ What does the object have to know (generally, short-time)?
- ◆ Which information must the object be able to give?
- ◆ Which are the attributes used to describe the properties of the object?
- ◆ Where does the information come from? What happens to the information in the course of time?

Customer
customerNo
specialAgreemets
branch
customerGroup
solvency

Standard data
elements

As well as the name, data types, initial values, and constraints are specified too, as far as they are known. Besides the usual, system-defined standard data types such as *Integer*, *Date*, *Boolean*, and so on, additional, user-defined data types should be created: *StaffNumber, CustomerNumber, AccountNumber, Currency, ZIP,* and so on.

The found attributes are now thoroughly examined. It has, for example, to be considered whether some attributes had not better be viewed as independent objects. The *customer* class shown above contains, for example, the attribute *Customer group* – this attribute would be an appropriate candidate. The attribute becomes the class *Customer group*, and *Customer* is assigned a relationship with this class. Attributes and objects differ insofar as attributes have identity of their own and can be accessed only via objects. Objects always have their own independent identity and dispose of operations. The questions regarding our above example are:

Attribute or class?

- Does a customer group have an independent identity of its own?
- Should the customer group only be accessible by the customer or are there other classes which would like to enter into a direct relation with customer groups?
- Does a customer group have to provide special operations of its own that go beyond setting and reading an attribute?
- Is the customer group something that you might handle on its own and that can be used, for example, as a navigation unit?

If the last point applies, we would arrive at the following model:

Consolidate

Having a closer look at the attributes to consolidate the present model also means once again finding common features between the classes, to generalize differences, to recognize dependent and independent properties, and if needed to further generalize the classes. With this abstraction, classes will potentially become usable more universally – both in the current and in future projects.

Find out common features

Here are some more attribute samples of classes discussed on the previous pages.

STREET ADDRESS

Attribute	Type	Initial value	Constraints, ...
zip	ZIP	„00000"	
city	String	„Unknown"	Length = 1..30
city2	String		Length = 0..30
street	String		Length = 1..30
number	String		Length = 0..5

POST BOX ADDRESS

Attribute	Type	Initial value	Constraints, ...
zip	ZIP	„00000"	
place	String	„Unknown"	Length = 1..30
pobox	String		Length = 1..10

PRIVATE PERSON

Attribute	Type	Initial value	Constraints, ...
name	String	„NoName"	Length = 1..40
first_name	String		Length = 0..30
title	String		Length = 0..20
birthday	Date		birthday < today
female	Boolean	false	

EMPLOYEE

Attribute	Type	Initial value	Constraints, ...
staffNo	Integer	Current no.	staffNo = 1..99999
initials	String		Length = 2..4

MODELING ACTIVITIES

Fundamentals
⇒ *p. 252*

Activities are individual steps for data processing or represent part of an algorithm. The following activity diagram shows the processing path for the reservation of a vehicle.

In the upper thread between the splitting and synchronization points, the customer's requirements regarding the reservation are received, and a check is made as to whether a corresponding vehicle is available. If it is not available, the requirements are modified and availability is checked again. In the lower thread, the customer is identified and the relevant data checked. If the customer is not yet known, the corresponding data is entered into the system.

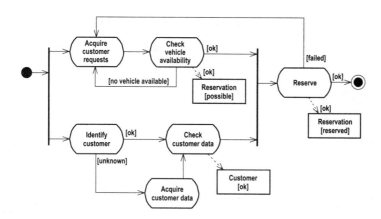

The activity diagram shows that both threads must be gone through. At   *Object state*
their end, there is a customer object with a state of *ok*, and a reservation with
a state of *possible*. No assertion is made about the processing sequence. Thus,
the reservation data can be acquired first, and then the customer identified,
but it can also be the other way round, or it could occur in parallel.

At the end, we find the *Reservation* activity, that is, the customer actually
wishes to reserve a vehicle. If this does not fail, for example due to a change of
availability data, the reservation object finally has a state of *reserved*.

MODELING STATES

If and in what detail states are modeled during the design firstly depends on   *Fundamentals*
whether the behavior of an object is considered as sufficiently significant to be   *⇒ p. 265*
modeled. Objects that have only two to three different states which barely
influence the behavioral possibilities of that object can usually be designed to
a satisfactory degree without modeling.

Messages which an object can only interpret in specific states justify the   *State-dependent*
effort of creating state diagrams only to a certain extent. Often it is sufficient   *messages*
to handle such situations independently of state transitions and the like, for
example by putting constraints on specific attribute values. If, however, a large
part of the messages is state-dependent or more than one or two attributes
determine a state, detailed modeling of the state transitions is recommended.

The following diagram shows the life cycle of a customer. After a customer
object has been created, it is initially not viewed as a true customer, but as a
contact. Name and maybe address of the customer are known, but no transaction has taken place yet. Before a customer or a contact can reserve and rent
a vehicle, a customer file is created – this creates a true customer. If reserva-

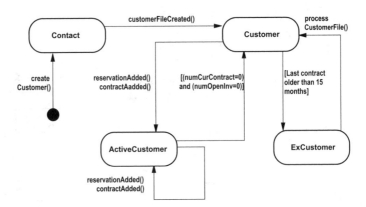

tions, rentals, or invoices are currently open, the customer is viewed as an active customer. Customers that do not appear for a specific period of time become ex-customers – their data is transferred into the archive database.

MODELING OBJECT INTERACTION

Fundamentals

Collaboration diagrams ⇒ *p. 257*

Sequence diagrams ⇒ *p. 262*

Collaboration and sequence diagrams illustrate and detail selected situations which result from stimuli of the dialog layer. Each button triggers an event whose processing can be described by means of a collaboration or sequence diagram. This applies to creation, deletion, and modification of objects or associations, exactly in the same way.

The latter case, namely the creation of a relationship between two objects, will be shown in the following example. The trigger is the creation of a new contact partner for a customer.

This example shows the possible communication between the individual architecture layers. Starting point is the *openFile()* event which is to be used to open the customer file and display it on screen. The message is passed to the appropriate process control.

Before the customer file can be opened, the user needs to select a customer. Therefore, the process control *PcCustomerFile* initiates a further process control *PcSearchCustomer*. The way this works in detail has been omitted for the sake of simplicity. In one form or the other, the user is presented with a search dialog. Its result is the selected customer (*cm*).

Now, the process control *PcCustomerFile* asks for interaction control to open the corresponding customer file. The resulting communication between interaction control and dialog classes is once again omitted for simplicity sake.

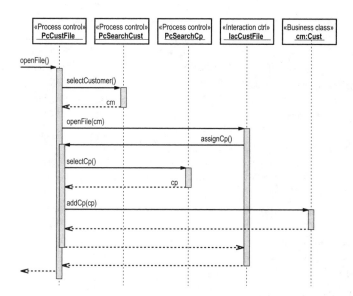

From within the interaction control, the assignment of a contact partner is requested (*cpAssign()*). Here, it may be assumed that the user has, for example, clicked on an appropriate button or selection element.

Now, similarly to the customer selection process, a contact partner is selected. The *PcCustomerFile* process control delegates this to *PcSearchCp*.

Finally, the selected contact partner (*cp*) is associated to the customer, that is, the business class *Customer* is sent the message *addCp(cp)* for adding a new contact partner.

This process is represented above as a sequence diagram. The same could also have been shown in the form of a collaboration diagram.

DATABASE CONNECTION

For storage of persistent objects, object-oriented database systems can be used. The persistent parts are mapped one-to-one in the database. Loading and storing of objects is ususally performed autonomously. Not all object-oriented databases support storing of operations – most are limited to persistent data.

Object-oriented database systems are only just out of nappies, so to speak. With very large data amounts and with sensitive data (think of the millions of records of insurance companies and banks) the risk they might constitute is

Persistent objects
⇒ *p. 44*

Object identity
⇒ *p. 43*

◆ Design Rules and Heuristics

- ◆ Design coherent operations, that is, operations that fulfill only one task.

- ◆ Do without side effects: do not work with global variables and the like in your operations. Pass this kind of information as parameters, instead.

- ◆ A subclass should support all attributes, operations, and relations of its superclasses; suppression of these properties should be avoided.

- ◆ A subclass should not define constraints on inherited properties of its superclass.

- ◆ If inherited operations need to be overwritten, they should be compatible with the behavior of the overwritten ones.

- ◆ Aim for an even distribution of knowledge about the application domain across all classes.

- ◆ Design your concepts to be as general as possible, that is, design with a view to interfaces instead of implementation.

- ◆ Design client–server relationships between classes (cooperation principle).

- ◆ Minimize dependencies between classes.

- ◆ The superclass of an abstract class is itself an abstract class too.

- ◆ Maximize the internal binding of classes. Responsibilities which belong together should be concentrated in one class.

- ◆ Minimize the external dependencies of a class. Keep the number of different contracts (interfaces) with other classes to a minimum.

- ◆ Instead of functional modes, separate operation should be provided.

- ◆ Avoid indirect navigation. Limit the knowledge of classes about their neighboring classes.

- ◆ The code for one operation should not exceed one page; otherwise you better return to Cobol, PL/1, and company.

- ◆ Mind uniform and descriptive names, data types, and parameter orders.

- ◆ Separate domain classes and instance classes (example: class *vehicle* with *serial number*, *owner*, *color*, and class *vehicle type* with *model number*, *length*, *number of doors*, and so on).

- ◆ If in an operation you find switch/case instructions or several consecutive instructions, this is a symptom of procedural thinking (so-called polymorphism phobia).

- ◆ Take extreme values into account (minimum, maximum, nil, nonsense) and plan a robust behavior in all situations. Try to do without artificial or arbitrary limits (for example, a list with max. 14 entries) and try to implement a dynamic behavior.

- ◆ It is never too early to start thinking about undo functions, user-specific configurations, user access right concepts, error handling, and so forth.

- ◆ Take company-specific and general standards into account.

- ◆ Avoid data-heavy and data-driven design. Behavior-driven design has advantages over purely data-driven design. In data-driven design, few central control classes emerge, but a high overall coupling of classes. In behavior-driven design the tasks are more equally divided across the classes, significantly fewer messages are generated, and the classes are coupled more loosely.

♦ **Some Important Naming Conventions**

- ◆ Class names, global variables, and class attributes begin with an upper case letter. In compound words, each word begins with an upper case letter, without insertion of underscores.

- ◆ Attributes, temporary variables, operations, and parameters begin with a lower case letter. In compound words, all subsequent words begin with an upper case letter, without insertion of underscores.

- ◆ Implementation details, in particular type specifications, should not be mentioned in the name of a descriptor.

- ◆ Names with semantic content are to be preferred to names with type specifications (*sizeOfArray* instead of *anInteger*).

- ◆ Names of descriptors should be chosen in such a way that they can be read like a sentence within instructions.

- ◆ Operations which return Boolean as a result should be prefixed with *is* or *has* (*isEmpty*, *hasPrinted*).

- ◆ Names of operations should contain active verb forms and imperatives (*deleteInvoice*, *openCustomerFile*).

- ◆ Comments should consist of complete sentences and follow an active language, naming responsibilities ('Adds the element' instead of 'The element is added').

- ◆ Operations which return the value of an attribute have the same name as the variable (without the prefix *get*).

- ◆ Operations which change the value of an attribute have the same name as the attribute (without the prefix *set*); the parameter describes the expected type.

- ◆ Temporary variable should always be used for one purpose only; otherwise, several variables should be declared.

often avoided, and data is continued to be kept in well-proven relational databases. Existing databases are also often preferred for reasons of cost.

However, as already shown in the section on application architecture, an implementation-neutral database connection can be realized. Some object-oriented development environments provide special tools for connection of SQL databases (so-called mapping tools, persistence object managers, persistence frameworks, and so on).

Application architecture ⇒ pp. 112 ff.

The question remains which database scheme is necessary or sensible in the underlying database when a relational database is to be employed. Three principal alternatives need to be distinguished:

- ◆ *All objects are stored in one single table.* A simple solution. The data record length varies depending on the class of the stored object – the database should support this efficiently. With large amounts of data or numerous associations, a noticeable loss of performance may occur.

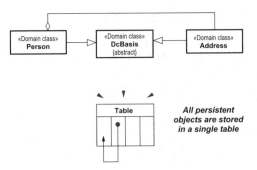

◆ *One table is created for each class.* All data records in a table are the same length, but this does not cause specific requirements for the database. Objects of classes which have superclasses (which is mostly the case) need to collect their data from different tables. Disadvantage of this solution: in order to load an object, data needs to be picked from a (potentially large) number of tables. To simplify this, appropriate database views can be defined, for example:

```
create view Person
  as select tabPerson.*, tabFkBasis.*,
  from      tabPerson, tabFkBasis,
  where     (tabPerson.ObjId = tabFkBasis.ObjId);
```

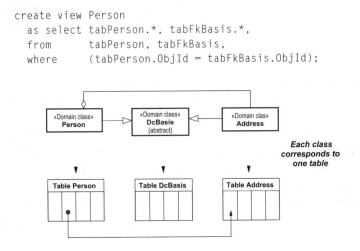

◆ *One table is created for each object type.* This means that an object is stored in one data record. One table is created for each concrete class. To load an object, only one single record needs to be read. Disadvantage: when reading a set of objects belonging to a common subclass or abstract class, partial sets of different tables need to be assembled. For simplification purpose, appropriate database views can be defined.

```
create view BusinessPartner as
  select * from tabPerson
union
  select * from tabCustomer
union
  select * from tabSupplier;
```

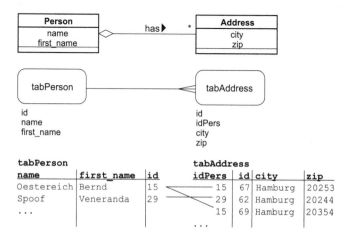

A further disadvantage: attributes of superclasses are strewn across different tables. A change of an attribute definition in an abstract class (which, as experience shows, happens less frequently than in concrete classes) needs to be redundantly maintained in different tables.

This latter variation is implemented frequently. It represents an acceptable compromise between implementation cost and performance.

Associations and aggregations can also be realized with relational databases, as shown by the following illustration. Relationships between objects are mainly expressed via object IDs. In contrast to the relational model, data contents, that is, attribute values, are not used for this purpose.

tabPerson			tabAddress				
name	**first_name**	**id**		**idPers**	**id**	**city**	**zip**
Oestereich	Bernd	15		15	67	Hamburg	20253
Spoof	Veneranda	29		29	62	Hamburg	20244
...				15	69	Hamburg	20354
				...			

Part III

Fundamentals of the Unified Modeling Language

The following chapters explain the individual diagrams and model elements of the Unified Modeling Language in detail.

INTRODUCTION

The Unified Modeling Language (UML) is a language and notation for specification, construction, visualization, and documentation of models of software systems. UML takes the increased demands on today's systems into account, covers a broad spectrum of application domains, and is suitable for concurrent, distributed, time-critical, socially embedded systems and many more.

What is UML?

History ⇒ p. 5

UML in its current version 1.3, which is the basis for this book, can be seen as an industry standard. Almost all tool manufacturers and authors already support UML or have announced their intention to do so. The Object Management Group (OMG) has declared UML as its standard. It was developed under the direction of Grady Booch, Ivar Jacobson, and James Rumbaugh (the 'Amigos') of Rational Software. Many other enterprises, such as for example Digital Equipment, Hewlett-Packard, i-Logix, ICON Computing, MCI Systemhouse, Microsoft, Oracle, Texas Instruments, and Unisys, have actively participated in its development and currently support UML.

Who stands behind UML?

UML is a language and notation for modeling, but it is intentionally not a method. The Amigos do not undervalue the importance of a method, but consider it as something different. A method needs to consider the specific framework and conditions of the application domain, the organizational environment, and much more. UML can serve as a basis for different methods, as it provides a well-defined set of modeling constructs with uniform notation and semantics.

Why is UML not a method?

The method underlying the analysis and design chapters of this book is use case driven, architecture-centered, and evolutionary, with a view to development of interactive business information systems as they can be found in particular in service and commercial enterprises. This also influences the following explanations of UML, which is why some elements, such as distribution diagrams, receive slightly less attention.

Which method is used here?

Focus of Part III

UML includes a multitude of model elements and details. To facilitate getting acquainted with the subject, special and, in practice, less significant elements of the UML are marked as 'advanced UML'. Moreover, to ensure a compact and simplified access, the UML metamodel has been left out of the discussion.

advanced

TYPES OF DIAGRAMS

The following chapters provide detailed explanations of all model elements of UML, ordered by the types of diagram in which the elements are used. Some elements can be part of different diagrams; these are explained in the context of the diagram in which they primarily occur.

The following diagram types are introduced:

Example ⇒ *p. 180*
◆ *Use case diagram*
shows actors, use cases, and their relationships.

Example ⇒ *p. 224*
◆ *Class diagram*
shows classes and their relationships with each other.

◆ *Behavior diagrams*

Example ⇒ *p. 255*
– *Activity diagram*
shows activities, object states, states, state transitions, and events.

Example ⇒ *p. 261*
– *Collaboration diagram*
shows objects and their relationships, including their spatially structured message exchange.

Example ⇒ *p. 264*
– *Sequence diagram*
shows objects and their relationships, including their chronologically structured message exchange.

Example ⇒ *p. 266*
– *State diagram*
shows states, state transitions, and events.

◆ *Implementation diagrams*

Example ⇒ *p. 272*
– *Component diagram*
shows components and their relationships.

Example ⇒ *p. 273*
– *Deployment diagram*
shows components, nodes, and their relationships.

Chapter 6

Use Case Diagrams

This chapter gives a detailed explanation of those elements of the Unified Modeling Language that are needed for the representation of use case diagrams.

USE CASE

Related terms: *scenario*, *script*.

Definition

A use case describes a set of activities of a system from the point of view of its actors, which lead to a perceptible outcome for the actors. A use case is always initiated by an actor. In all other respects, a use case is a complete, indivisible description.

Description

Business processes, business events

A use case is a description of a typical interaction between a user and a system, that is, it represents the external system behavior in a limited working situation from the point of view of the user. It describes requirements for the system, that is, *what* it should do, but not *how* it should do it. A use case can have different variations. A very specific variation of a use case is called a scenario. A use case describes a set of possible scenarios. The context of a use case is usually limited by the actions a user carries out on an application system in one operating cycle in order to process one business event of a business process.

Pay attention to detail

The above definition applies to all use cases, which means that when a use case is subdivided into several smaller ones, care needs to be taken that each of the new use cases satisfies these requirements. Use cases which are not initiated by an actor or do not lead to a perceptible result for the actor are wrong or incomplete. Use cases are not suitable to be used for functional decomposition of a system.

No functional decomposition

A use case describes a typical working process. The process is composed of (usually consecutively numbered) individual steps. These steps are also known as activities. Since the description is purely textual, noting down dependencies between individual steps is a very long-winded task. Often, for example, the sequence of steps present in the use case is typical, but not mandatory. Some steps may even be skipped in specific situations. Such interrelationships can be textually described only with great effort and remain nevertheless hidden in the text.

A graphical representation of such processes is easier to produce and to understand. Therefore, use case diagrams are often detailed and illustrated by behavior diagrams, for example by activity diagrams and, in specific cases, also by sequence, collaboration, or state diagrams. This is mostly done with a view to the design, in other words, to the description or analysis of the necessary internal system behavior resulting from the use case.

Use cases may also be illustrated with dialog designs or prototypes. This is of greater interest for users and technical departments: processes are visualized and thus communicated in a substantially more concrete way, which provides an additional possibility of validating use cases.

The interrelationships between different use cases can be represented in use case diagrams. Activity diagrams too can be employed to cover several use cases at a time.

Notation

A use case is graphically represented by an ellipsis that bears the name of the use case.

For each ellipse, there is a text that describes the use case in more detail. Such texts may be keyword summaries or more extensive descriptions. They may be informal, however, some content-related structuring is recommended.

Uc No.	Name of use case
	Actors: …
	Preconditions: …
	Postconditions: …
	Invariants: …
	Non-functional requirements: …
	Process description: …
	Exceptions, error situations: …
	Variations: …
	Rules: …
	Services:
	Contact partners: …
	Notes/open questions: …
	Dialog samples, references: …
	Diagrams: …

Each use case has a unique name. Use cases may additionally be numbered for quick identification in diagrams and in their textual form. The following list shows a sample structure of a use case:

- *Actors.* Actors (roles) involved in the use case. This corresponds to the relationships between use case and actors noted in use case diagrams. *Actors ⇒ p. 178*
- *Preconditions.* State of the system before the use cases occurs.

- *Postcondition.* State of the system after the use case has been successfully gone through.
- *Invariants.* Conditions which, in the context of the use case, must always be satisfied.
- *Non-functional requirements.* Important constraints for design and implementation, such as platform and environment conditions, qualitative statements, response time requirements, frequency estimates, priorities, and so on.
- *Process description.* Description of the use case, possibly structured into numbered individual items. This is the proper kernel of a use case.
- *Exceptions, error situations.* Description of the exceptions and error situations that may occur in the context of the use case. These are not technical errors, but domain-related errors, such as lack of users' access rights, impossibility of plausible filling in of input fields, and the like.
- *Variations.* Deviations and exceptions from the normal process and description of alternative processes for these cases.
- *Rules.* Business rules, domain-specific dependencies, validity and validation rules, and so on, which are of importance in the framework of the process. Often, activity diagrams are a more suitable alternative for describing such interrelationships.
- *Services.* List of operations and, where required, objects which are needed in the context of the process (used as a transition towards class design).
- *Contact partners, sessions.* List of persons with whom the use case was elaborated or discussed, date and time of such sessions, and so on; if required, list of people still to be talked to, roles and functions assumed by the people involved, and so on.
- *Notes/open questions.* This is, for example, the place for documentation of important design decisions. Sometimes, several competing designs exists for a use case. Therefore, the reasons that led to the decision for one alternative or the other should be briefly protocoled; otherwise, at a later stage, the discussion starts again on whether the other alternative would not have been a better choice.
- *Documents, references, dialog samples or patterns.* Sample dialogs, screen shots, dialog prototypes, printout and form samples, instructions, manuals, and all other material which illustrate the use case, and which were used in discussions with the users and so on, or were somehow part of the context.
- *Diagrams.* Sequence and collaboration diagrams which represent the internal system behavior resulting from or needed for the use case. Class

diagrams which show the static model structure resulting from or corresponding to the use case. Activity and state diagrams which show the system-internal dependencies and state transitions in connection with this use case.

Example

The use case diagram shown later in this section illustrates the parts of the business process *magazine circulation*. The following use cases belong to this process:

Use case diagram
⇒ *p. 108*

Example ⇒ *p. 133*

Uc2 Register marked articles

Process

1. Select magazine copy.
2. Enter title, author(s), keywords, and summary of the article to be registered.
3. Store.

Notes

'Magazine copy' stands for name of magazine and specification of issue number or publication date.

Uc3 Create circulation note

Process

1. Select a magazine from the list of subscribed magazines.
2. Press *Print* button.

Variations

2.a There is only one reader who, at the same time, is the analyzer. A corresponding message is displayed and no circulation note is printed.

Explorative Prototypes

Explorative prototypes are a useful instrument in use case analysis. Often, use case diagrams and descriptions are insufficient to determine, together with the users, which requirements the future system should meet. In many situations, communication is much easier when it can be based on a concrete screen dialog.

See ⇒ *p. 122*

Instead of dialog prototypes, you may also employ forms, sample printouts, and other visual material.

Explorative prototypes illustrate use case descriptions and serve as a basis for communication. Further details can be found in Chapter 4, Analysis, from page 119 onward.

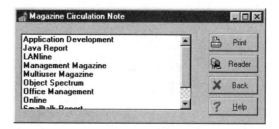

ACTORS

Related terms: *involved party, event, external system, dialog, boundary, control, entity.*

Definition

An actor is a class located outside the system which is involved in the interaction with the system described in a use case. Usually, actors assume a well-defined role in the interaction. An actor is a stereotyped class.

Description

Actors = roles

Actors are, for example, the users of a system. As actors, however, it is not the person involved who is perceived, but the roles they assume in the context of the use case. Thus, if a person appears in several roles (for example customer advice and order reception), several corresponding actors are noted in the use case diagram.

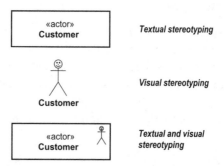

One should not, however, be unduly concerned with the actors; they are above all an instrument to arrive at the use cases.

As well as the actors, it is also possible to list chronological events, dialogs, external systems, and external passive objects (so-called entities), if these are involved in the use case.

Events, external systems

Notation and Example

Actors can be represented in different ways: as textual stereotypes, visual stereotypes, or in a mixed representation (see illustration above).

Further examples ⇒ p. 103

As well as the actors, other involved parties can be noted. For this purpose, the stereotypes illustrated below are predefined in UML.

Stereotypes ⇒ p. 213

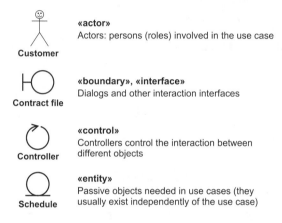

«actor»
Actors: persons (roles) involved in the use case
Customer

«boundary», «interface»
Dialogs and other interaction interfaces
Contract file

«control»
Controllers control the interaction between different objects
Controller

«entity»
Passive objects needed in use cases (they usually exist independently of the use case)
Schedule

Actors describe the roles of the parties involved in the use case. These roles can be generalized or specialized.

The following illustration shows the hierarchical order (generalization and specialization) of actors. In this case, *office clerks* of an insurance company are differentiated into *field service*, *car insurance*, and *home insurance clerks*.

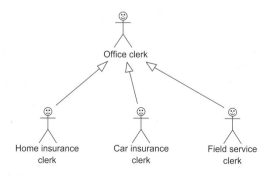

Generalization and specialization are represented in the same way as the corresponding relationships between classes.

Since use cases are employed to record system requirements in the form of typical processes seen from the users point of view, acceptance and comprehension of the symbols and concepts used is decisive. In practice, it might therefore be sensible to use simpler or more intuitive representations, such as the ones shown in the following illustration.

| Actor | External system | Chronological event |

USE CASE DIAGRAM

Definition

A use case diagram shows the relationships between actors and use cases.

Description

Business processes, business events

A use case diagram describes the interaction between a set of use cases and the actors involved in these use cases. It therefore represents both context and structure for the description of how a business event is handled.

A business event is, for example, the written damage report of a home-insured person. The business process (for example Damage claim home insurance) describes the entire process of handling such an event. Potentially, the business process also includes activities which are not directly supported by software or the application to be developed (for example Visit to the premises by a loss adjuster).

Example ⇒ pp. 102 ff.

Explanation of use cases ⇒ p. 174

Use cases usually describe only those activities that are to be supported by the software under development, and their contact points with the environment of this software. All use cases together form a model which describes the requirements to be met by the external behavior of the entire system. What exactly makes a use case a use case is described in detail in the following paragraphs.

It should be noted that use cases do not represent a design approach, and that they do not describe the internal behavior of the system, but are a tool for requirement determination. Use cases should not be used for functional destructuring; they are not process diagrams, data flow charts, nor functional models. *Not process diagrams*

Use cases support communication with future users, the customer, the technical department, and the like. Use cases describe external system behavior, that is, *what* the system is supposed to do. *How* this comes into being, that is, which system design and which implementation contribute to this external system behavior are questions to which use cases provide no answer.

Notation

A use case diagram includes a set of use cases which are represented as individual ellipses, and a set of actors and events that are involved (actors). The use cases are joined by straight lines with the classes involved. A frame around the use cases symbolizes the system boundaries.

Use case diagram

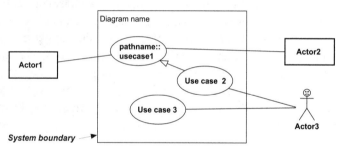

INCLUDE AND EXTEND.   In UML, three types of relationships between use cases are defined: *Include and extend*

- ¨*include*¨, substitutes the ¨*uses*¨ relationship of UML 1.1, and is used to denote that another use case occurs inside a use case. This construct is therefore suited to extract identical sections occurring in several use cases in order to prevent redundancy. *advanced*
- ¨*extend*¨ is used to show that in certain circumstances or at a specific point (the so-called extension point) a use case is extended with another use case.
- *Generalization* (UML 1.3) allows sub use cases to inherit behavior and semantics from super use cases, in analogy with the generalization relationship between classes.

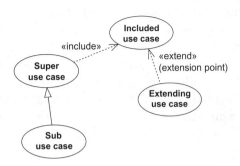

Example

The use case diagram below shows those parts of a *Magazine circulation* business process supported by software within an enterprise. Each incoming magazine is first registered by the library. Subsequently, its content is analyzed by an employee. The articles the analyzer has found to be of interest are entered into the system as summaries. Subsequently, the magazine is circulated among the employees, which is not considered in the use case diagram because it is not to be supported by the system under development. However, magazine circulation requires a circulation note to be produced. This note is attached to the magazine and contains the names of the employees currently reading the magazine. Creation of this note is to be supported by the system. Finally, after the last reader has returned the magazine to the library, it is archived in the library.

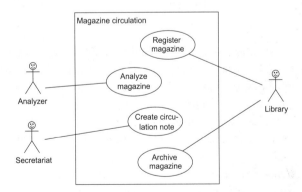

The example shown below illustrates the application of ˙include˙˙ and ˙extend˙, at the same time pointing out the difficulties that this entails.

«include» and «extend»

The example shows the use case *Stipulate contract* which jointly uses the *Identify customer* use case. *Identify customer* is also used in various other contexts and therefore exists as a separate use case. In specific cases, the *Identify customer* use case also employs the use case *Create new customer*, namely every time a customer is not yet included in the customer list and therefore needs to be created.

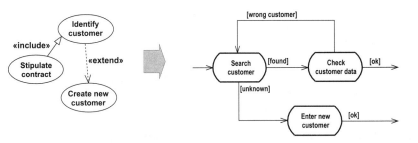

Interrelations between use cases

The use case diagram very generically shows the relations between the three use cases, but describes no details. You can see, for example, that the *Identify customer* use case is extended by the *Create new customer* use case, but you cannot see *how*. The activity diagram on the right-hand side describes this relationship much more concretely.

Activity diagram ⇒ p. 252

The way the individual use cases interrelate, that is, the use-case-transcendent description of processes, could be noted textually within the use case descriptions, but would not be very clear. Activity diagrams convey such relationships visually and therefore in a way which is easier to see.

Thus, ˙include˙˙ and ˙extend˙ can be used to point out connections, but the expressive power of these elements is very weak. Many modelers therefore completely do without ˙include˙˙ and ˙extend˙.

Further use case examples ⇒ pp. 102 ff.

Chapter 7

Class Diagrams (Basic Elements)

This chapter explains the individual basic elements of the Unified Modeling Language for the representation of class diagrams – each of them structured into definition, description, notation, and example.

CLASSES

Related terms: *type*, *object factory*.

Definition

Objects ⇒ p. 193
Attributes ⇒ p. 195
Operations ⇒ p. 198

A class is the definition of the attributes, the operations, and the semantics of a set of objects. All objects in a class correspond to that definition.

Description

Type ⇒ p. 305

Often, the term *type* is used instead of *class*, where it should be noted that *type* is the more general term. A class contains the description of structure and behavior of objects it generates or which can be generated using it. Objects are produced by classes and are the units that act in an application. The definition of a class is made up of attributes and operations. The behavior of an object is described by the possible messages it is able to understand. For each message, the object needs the appropriate operations. Message and operation are often used as though they had an identical meaning, although this is not correct.

Difference message/
operation ⇒ p. 37

As well as attributes and operations, a class also includes the definitions of potential constraints, tagged values, and stereotypes.

Constraints ⇒ p. 206
Tagged values ⇒ p. 211
Stereotypes ⇒ p. 213

Notation

Classes are represented by rectangles which either bear only the name of the class (in bold), or show attributes and operations as well. In the second case, the three rubrics – class name, attributes, operations – are divided from each other by a horizontal line. Class names begin with an upper case letter and are singular nouns (collective classes or similar may be in the plural form, if required).

ATTRIBUTES.   Attributes are at least listed with their name, and may additionally contain specifications of their type (that is, their class), an initial value, and potential tagged values and constraints.

```
          «Stereotype»
          Package::Class
          {PropertyValues}
  attribute:Type=InitialValue {Constraint}
  operation(Parameter) {Constraint}
```

```
  Class
```

Attributes ⇒ p. 195
Operations ⇒ p. 198

OPERATIONS.   Operations are also noted at least with their name, and additionally with their possible parameters, class and initial values of these parameters, and potential tagged values and constraints.

In the top rubric (class name) we find, above the class name and enclosed in guillemots, the class stereotypes (for example *«DomainClass»*), while below the class name and enclosed in braces, we find the tagged values (for example *{abstract}*). The class name can be prefixed with the name of a package, with a double colon separating package and class names.

Abstract classes
⇒ p. 190

Example

A class *Circle* might, for example, include the attributes *radius* and *position* together with the operations *display(), remove(), setPosition(pos),* and *setRadius(newRadius)*. No package name is specified in the illustration, but it might, for example, read *Graphics::Circle*. The constraint *{radius > 0}* requires the value of the attribute *radius* to be always greater than 0. A circle with a negative radius or with a radius equal to 0 is not allowed. The specification of the initial value *(10, 10)* for the attribute *center* means that when an instance is generated, the value of the attribute is preset to this value.

Packages ⇒ p. 217

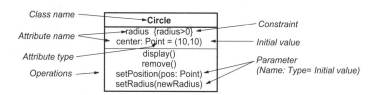

Some programming languages support the classification of attributes and operations in so-called categories; see the example in the section on stereotypes.

Stereotypes ⇒ p. 213

Metaclasses

advanced

In Smalltalk (and also in CLOS), classes too are simply objects, that is, classes can be sent messages, and they can include (class) attributes. In C++, class attributes and operations can be emulated by declaring them as static.

Class operations
see ⇒ p. 199

However, in C++ classes cannot be treated like objects. An example for a class message or a class operation is `new`, which is used to create a new instance of a class. In Smalltalk, for example:

```
newObject:= Class new.
anEmployee:= Employee new.
```

Classes of class objects are called metaclasses and, similarly to a normal class, noted with the stereotype *«metaclass»*.

Stereotypes ⇒ p. 213

```
«metaclass»
CustomerClass
```

In Smalltalk, classes are principally instances of their metaclasses. The metaclasses themselves are instances of the class *MetaClass*, which in turn is an instance of the class *MetaClassClass*. The latter, however, is again an instance of the class *MetaClass*, which brings the cascade to an end. (Summary based on Enfin-Smalltalk, see Wallrabe and Oestereich, 1997.)

Class operations
⇒ p. 199

In UML, class operations need not be noted within the metaclass; they may also be contained in the class itself, where they are underlined in order to distinguish them from normal operations.

Class attributes
⇒ p. 197

The same applies to class attributes.

advanced

Parameterized Classes

Related terms: *generic class, template, bound element*.

Definition

Template

A parameterized class is a template equipped with generic formal parameters, which can be used to generate common (that is, non-parameterized) classes. The generic parameters serve as placeholders for the actual parameters which represent classes or simple data types.

Description

In a parameterized class, no concrete class is defined, but only a template for generation of classes. These templates are usually a type of macro technique which has no special function, apart from text replacement. In statically typed languages, parameterized classes are an important means for writing re-usable code. C++ and Eiffel support parameterized classes.

A class generated with the aid of a parameterized class is called a *bound element*.

Bound element

Example

A typical application are collection classes, that is, classes in which a set of objects can be stored. A possible example is the following waiting queue template (C++):

```
template <class Element>
class WaitingQueue {

  ...

  public:
    void add(<Element>* i);
    void remove(<Element>* i);
    ...

};
```

This waiting queue can be parameterized for different types of elements, for example for patients in a waiting room or cars in a traffic jam:

```
class Patient;
class Car;

...

WaitingQueue<Patient> WaitingRoom;
WaitingQueue<Car> TrafficJam;
```

Notation

In the graphical notation, parameterized classes are represented in the same way as classes, with an additional dashed rectangle in the upper right-hand

Refinement relation
⇒ *p. 248*

corner that shows the parameters. Classes generated with the aid of a parameterized class have a refinement relation with the stereotype «bind» to the parameterized class.

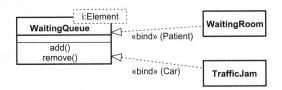

Another notation variation is shown in the next figure, in which the parameterized class is shown without the «bind» relation (also known as *bound element*).

Abstract Classes

Related terms: *virtual class*.

Definition

Classes ⇒ *p. 186*

An abstract class is never used to generate object instances; it is intentionally incomplete and thus forms the basis of further subclasses which can have instances.

Description

Abstract classes often represent a general term, a generic term for a set of concrete terms. Thus, *vehicle* can be an abstract generic term for *bicycle*, *car*, *truck*, *train*, and *airplane*. Real instances exist of the concrete terms *bicycle*, *car*, and so on, but there is no such thing that would be simply a *vehicle*. Vehicle is merely an abstraction, a generalization.

Superclass
Inheritance ⇒ *p. 222*

An abstract class is always a superclass. An abstract class that has no subclasses makes no sense. Either it is superfluous, or it lacks a concrete class as subclass.

Notation

An abstract class is represented in the same way as a normal class, but in addition, the tagged value *abstract* is written below the class name. Alternatively, the class name can also be set in italics. As usual, attributes, operations, constraints, and so on can be part of the class.

Tagged values
⇒ *p. 211*

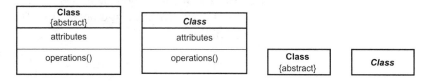

For hand-written presentations, it is somewhat time consuming to mark classes as abstract. On the one hand, it is difficult to produce hand-written italics. On the other hand, you need to know beforehand whether a class is abstract; later marking-up is not possible. In the old Booch notation, you could add an 'A' in a triangle standing on its top, which was easier for hand-written notes because it used up less space. In line with the old Booch notation, I often use the short form *{A}* to mark a class as abstract.

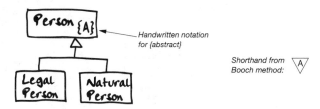

Example

The class hierarchy shown in the figure below represents the abstract super-class *GeomFigure*. In practice, a geometric figure will always be a triangle, a circle, or a rectangle, and this is why these are its concrete subclasses. The discriminator in this context is the figure shape.

Discriminator
⇒ *p. 222*

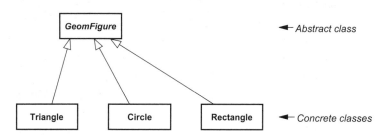

Classes ⇒ p. 186

Utility Classes

Related terms: *function collection*.

Definition

Utility classes are collections of global variables and functions which are combined into a class and defined there as class attributes and operations. The stereotype *«utility»* marks a class as a utility class.

Stereotypes ⇒ p. 213

Description

Utility classes are not true classes, but collections of global variables and functions which are, however, noted in the form of a class.

Notation and Example

Class attribute ⇒ p. 195
Class operation ⇒ p. 198

Utility classes are noted in the same way as normal classes, but have the stereotype *«utility»*. They contain class attributes (global variables) and class operations (global functions/operations).

```
        «utility»
        MathFun

    sin(angle):Real
    cos(angle):Real
    tan(angle):Real
    cot(angle):Real
```

Utility classes allow facts to be expressed in a procedural object-oriented way. They frequently occur in connection with hybrid programming languages such as C++, which also contain procedural modes of expression. In object-orientation, they are usually not needed; thus, the trigonometric functions shown in the example would fit well as common operations into the corresponding numerical classes.

OBJECTS

Related terms: *instance*.

Definition

An object is a unit which actually exists and acts in the current system. Each object is an instance of a class. An object contains information represented by attributes whose structure is defined in the class. An object can receive the messages defined in the class, that is, it has appropriate operations for each message defined. The behavior defined through the messages applies equally to all objects of a class, as well as to the structure of their attributes. The values of the attributes, however, may change individually from object to object.

Classes ⇒ p. 186

Attributes ⇒ p. 195
Operations ⇒ p. 198

Description

An alternative term for *object* is *instance*. A class contains the definition of objects, that is, their abstract description. The behavior of an object is described through the possible messages it can understand. For each message, the object needs appropriate operations. Message and operation are often used synonymously, although this is incorrect.

 In *multiple classification*, an object is simultaneously an instance of more than one class (a fairly theoretical case, not contemplated in C++, Java, and Smalltalk). In Smalltalk, however, you can achieve the same effect via the actor–role design pattern.

 In *dynamic classification*, an object can become consecutively an instance of more than one class (mainly possible in Smalltalk, but again a fairly theoretical case).

Instance

*Difference message/
operation ⇒ p. 37*

*«overlapping», multiple
classification ⇒ p. 224*

*Actor roles
⇒ pp. 175 f.*

*«disjoint» (dynamic
classification)*

Notation

Objects are represented by rectangles which either bear only their own name, or which in addition show the name of their class, or the values of specific or all attributes. If attribute values are indicated, the rectangle is subdivided into two rubrics separated by a horizontal line. To differentiate it from the class

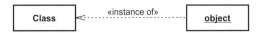

*Collaboration
diagrams* ⇒ *p. 257*
Sequence diagrams
⇒ *p. 262*

notation, the name of the object is underlined; furthermore, the object name usually begins with a lower-case letter.

Attributes are shown with their names and an exemplary value or their current value in the actual context. Operations are not shown because they have no object-individual manifestations and are identical for all objects of a class. In collaboration and sequence diagrams, the concrete message exchange between objects is shown instead.

Dependency relation
⇒ *p. 247*

Instantiation relationships, that is, class–object relationships are represented by a dashed arrow. The object points to its class.

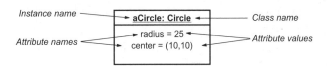

Example

See Class ⇒ *p. 186*

The illustration shows an object of the name *aCircle*, which is an instance of the *Circle* class. It is described by the two attributes *radius* and *center*, with the radius having a value of *25* and the center *(x,y)* a value of *(10,10)*.

Instance name ——→ aCircle: Circle ←—— Class name

radius = 25 ←

Attribute names ——→ center = (10,10) ←—— Attribute values

The following illustration shows a so-called multiobject; it can, for example, be used in collaboration diagrams to indicate that a message is sent simultaneously to a set of objects (of the same class).

ATTRIBUTES

Related terms: *data element, instance variable, variable, member*.

Definition

An attribute is a (data) element which is contained in the same way in each object of a class and is represented by each object with an individual value. In contrast to objects, attributes have no identity of their own outside the object they are a part of. Attributes are completely under the control of the objects of which they are a part.

Classes ⇒ p. 186
Objects ⇒ p. 193

Description

Each attribute is at least described by its name. In addition, a data type or a class, plus an initial value and constraints may be defined. The definition of the attribute type is programming language dependent: in Smalltalk, the value of an attribute is again an object; in C++ it can also be a pointer, or a composite or an elementary data type (for example `integer`). Usually, the type or class of an attribute is indicated.

In languages with dynamic binding (such as Smalltalk), in which attributes (instance variables) are not bound fixed to one type, the class specification describes which class membership may be expected for the attribute, even though the language remains noncommittal.

Instance variable

Constraints can be used in addition to the type specification to further restrict the value range or value set of the attribute, or to make it dependent on other conditions.

Constraints ⇒ p. 206

Tagged values can be used to specify additional special properties. Thus, for example, the tagged value *{readonly}* indicates that an attribute may only be read.

Tagged values ⇒ p. 211
State diagrams ⇒ p. 265

Optional and mandatory attributes can be differentiated by specification of the appropriate multiplicity:

Multiplicity specification

```
optionalAttr[0..1]: Class
mandatoryAttr[1]: Class
```

Optional and mandatory attributes

Multiplicity specification should only be noted when they are not *[1]*, which is the default value, that is, normally all attributes are mandatory. Sets (for example dynamic arrays) can be noted with *[*]*, which means that we are dealing with a composition (that is, the elements of the set have their own identity), which should therefore be used, or in other words, modeled.

Dynamic arrays
Composition

Derived attributes

advanced

DERIVED ATTRIBUTES. A particular variation are the so-called derived attributes. Inside an object, these are not represented physically by a value, but are calculated automatically. The calculation prescription is specified in the form of a constraint. For derived attributes too a type can be indicated. Specification of an initial value does not apply; indication of a tagged value is usually dispensable too.

Derived attributes are principally not directly modifiable. Since attributes should in no case be directly modifiable, derived attributes can also be realized by means of appropriate operations. Derived attributes should only be derived from object-internal elements and do without accessing neighboring objects. Otherwise, it is preferable to define appropriate calculation operations.

Caching

Performance

Definition of derived attributes is useful to indicate that intermediate storage (caching) of values is sensible at that point. Usually, this is done wherever calculations must not be repeated unnecessarily, for performance reasons.

Class attributes

advanced

CLASS ATTRIBUTES (CLASS VARIABLES). These do not belong to an individual object, but are attributes of a class (for example, in Smalltalk). This means that all objects of a class can access such a common class attribute. Class attributes can, for example, be used to count or number the generated objects of a class. With each newly generated object of a class, for example a counter is incremented.

Visibility mark: public, protected, private

advanced

Depending on the programming language, the external visibility of attributes can be restricted. In Smalltalk, this is superfluous, because attributes can only be addressed by the object itself; any external access is only possible via operations. In C++, the access possibilities can be declared as follows:

Access restriction

- `public`: visible and usable for all.
- `protected`: access is allowed to the class itself, its subclasses, and the classes declared as `friend`.
- `private`: only the class itself and the classes declared as `friend` can access private attributes.

`friend` is a mechanism in C++ with which a class can grant access rights to selected other classes.

Attributes should be used only by the class in which they are defined. Other classes (superclasses, subclasses, and associated classes) should always use operations to access them (`private`).

Notation

Attribute names begin with lower-case characters and class names with upper-case ones, while tagged values and constraints are enclosed in braces.

attribute : Package::Class =
   InitialValue {PropertyValue} {Constraint}

Derived attributes are marked by a prefixed slash (/). Class attributes are underlined, and (C++) visibility specifications, such as `public`, `protected`, and `private` are marked with '+', '#' and '−'. Public, protected, and private marks can also be assigned to class attributes.

Class operations
⇒ *p. 199*

/derivedAttribute
classAttribute
+publicAttribute
#protectedAttribute
−privateAttribute

Inside a class, attributes are separated from the class name by a horizontal line and are thus located in the second category within the class rectangle.

Person
name : String = 'Unknown' firstName : String = ' ' birthDate : Date /age {age=today-birthDate}

Examples

name : String = ′Unknown′
invoiceDate : Date = today
birthDate : Date
color : {red, blue, green}
radius : Integer = 25 {readonly} {radius > 0}
/age : Integer {age = today − birthDate}
/numChildren {numChildren = childrenSet count}
age {transient}
defaultName = ′Noname′
-versionNo : Integer
-counter : Integer
time : DateTime::Time
dynamArray[*]
name[1] : String
firstName[0..1] : String
firstNames[1..5] : String

OPERATIONS, METHODS

Related terms: *method, service, procedure, routine, function, message.*

Definitions

Operation

Operations are services which may be required from an object. They are described by their signature (operation name, parameters and, if needed, return type).

Method

A *method* implements an operation; it is a sequence of instructions.

Message

A *message* passes an object the information on the activity it is expected to carry out, thus requesting it to perform an operation.

Differently from these definitions, the terms operation and method are often used synonymously or according to the definition of the programming language used.

Description

A message consists of a selector (a name) and a list of arguments, and is directed to exactly one receiver. The sender of a message is as a rule returned exactly one response object. Inside a class definition, an operation has a unique *signature* composed of the name of the operation, potential parameters (arguments), and a potential return value (function result). The parameters of an operation correspond in their definition to the attributes, that is, they bear a name and, where needed, additional indications of type and default value.

Signature
Parameters
Attributes ⇒ p. 195

Operations may be provided with *constraints* which, for example, describe the conditions to be met at the call or the values the arguments may have.

Constraints ⇒ p. 206

Tagged values can be used to describe additional special features. Tagged values are, for example, *{abstract}* to indicate an abstract operation, or *{obsolete}* to indicate that this operation exists only for compatibility with previous versions and should no longer be used otherwise.

*Tagged values
⇒ p. 211*

Abstract operations

ABSTRACT OPERATIONS. These are operations which are represented only by their signature and whose implementation takes place only in a subclass. In C++, abstract operations are also called purely virtual operations.

*Abstract classes
⇒ p. 190*

Abstract operations can exist only in abstract classes. Abstract operations that are not repeated and implemented in a subclass make no sense, unless it needs to be ensured that an object can understand the corresponding message without requiring any active intervention.

Objects communicate with each other by exchanging messages. Each object understands exactly the messages for which there is a corresponding operation (which is the reason why the terms message and operation are often used synonymously – which is, however, incorrect). However, in classes that define an object, this operation may be defined multiply. Further explanations can be found in the section on polymorphism.

Difference message/ operation ⇒ p. 37

Polymorphism ⇒ p. 40

Notation

The signature of an operation is given as follows:

> name(argument : ArgumentType = DefaultValue, ...):
> ReturnType {PropertyValues} {Constraints}

Example:

> setPosition(x : Integer = 1, y : Integer = 1):
> Boolean {abstract} {(x > 0) and (y > 0)}

The name of the operation begins with a lower-case letter. Arguments have names that begin with a lower-case letter and are described further by specifying a data type or a class, if required. In this case, argument name and type are separated by a colon. Default values may be specified for arguments, although this is only sensible when using programming languages with optional parameter passing. The body of an operation contains the implementation code and is therefore programming language specific.

Tagged values and constraints are enclosed in braces. Abstract operations are either set in italics or assigned the tagged value *{abstract}*:

Abstract operations

> *display()*
> display() {abstract}

CLASS OPERATIONS. Class operations (for example in Smalltalk) are indicated by underlining, while the external visibility of operations is marked by prefixed special characters:

advanced

Visibility mark

> <u>classOperation()</u>
> +publicOperation()
> #protectedOperation()
> –privateOperation()

In C++, public means visible and usable for all, protected allows operations to be accessed by the class itself, its subclasses, and classes declared as friend, while private means that only the class itself and classes declared as friend are allowed access. friend is a mechanism in C++ with which a class can grant access rights to selected other classes. It should be noted that the meaning of these keywords in C++ and Java do not match completely; the best thing to do is use the meaning from the actually employed programming language.

Smalltalk

In programming languages that cannot differentiate operations with regard to their access possibilities, operations are instead given names that begin with *private* (for example *privateShowAt*). This naming convention is mostly sufficient (... and what you really should never use are *veryPrivate* operations ...). In the class model, granting of access rights is uniform and language-independent: access restrictions are noted as tagged values.

Tagged values
⇒ *p. 211*

Examples

See class ⇒ *p. 186*

Within a class, the operations are listed in the lower part of the rectangle, as shown in the following example:

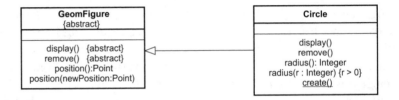

position(x, y)
position(x : Integer, y : Integer)

resize()
resize(byFactor)
resize(): GeomFigure
resize(byFactor : Real): GeomFigure

addPhoneNumber(phoneNumber : String, type : CallType = #Fax)

payIn(amount : Amount):Amount {amount > 0}

release():ContractStatus

Naming Conventions

Be extremely careful with the naming of operations. No tool and no methodology can relieve you from this responsibility. The meaning of names of operations is often underestimated. If necessary, discuss them with your colleagues. You will become more conscious about what the operation is supposed to do and for which outcomes it is responsible.

Always try to use active verbs, be careful with adjectives, and – above all – be precise! For example:

- *dataHasChanged()* returns *true* if the data has changed, whereas *checkDataChange()* or *dataIsOK()* return *true* if the check has been executed successfully, which may also be the case with unchanged data. *dataHasSuccessfullyChanged()* returns *true* if the last data change has been concluded successfully.
- *pageChange(page)* gives unfortunately no precise information as to whether the page is in the process of being changed or whether the page change has already been concluded. Better alternatives might be: *changedTo(page)*, *changingTo(page)*, and *changeTo(page)*.

The difference between the right word and the almost right word is the difference between lightning and the lightning bug.

Mark Twain in a letter dated 10/15/1888

INTERFACES, INTERFACE CLASSES

Definition

Interfaces describe a selected part of the externally visible behavior of model elements (mostly of classes and components).

Interface classes are abstract classes (more precisely, types), which define abstract operations exclusively.

Description

Interface class

Interfaces are specifications of the external behavior of classes (or other elements) and contain a set of signatures for operations that classes (or others) wishing to provide this interface need to implement.

Tagged value
⇒ p. 211

They are marked with the stereotype «*interface*». Their operations need not be explicitly marked as *{abstract}*, because this is mandatory.

Common classes that wish to implement an interface need to provide all the operations defined in the corresponding interface class.

A common class can implement several interfaces and, in addition, contain further properties. In other words: an interface usually describes a subset of the operations of a class. Between implementing class and interface class

Realization ⇒ p. 248

there is a realization relationship.

Extension of interfaces

Interface classes can extend other interfaces, that is, inheritance relationships between interface classes are possible. Care must be taken to ensure that only abstracts are added.

It is illegal to restrict the semantics of the interface superclass. All invariants must be kept. Additional invariants are allowed. It is also possible to specify restrictions for parameters and return types.

Multiple inheritance
⇒ p. 226

An interface class can extend several other interfaces, that is, it can have several superclasses. In contrast to multiple inheritance in common classes, this is unproblematic because only sets of signatures are combined.

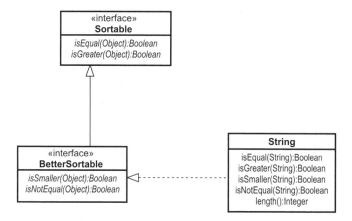

Common classes can implement several interfaces, however, it should be ensured that the different interfaces do not contain homonymous signatures because it would be very risky if their semantics too were defined identically.

In any case, the interfaces to be implemented must be free of contradictions within each other. This can, for example, be achieved by factorizing out common features of the interface classes.

To make the interface concept even more powerful, you can, for example, specify the following additional constraints for each signature defined in an interface:

◆ *Precondition.*   Description of the conditions to be satisfied prior to the call of the operation, which may (tacitly) be assumed by the operation.
◆ *Postcondition.*   Description of the conditions to be satisfied by the operation after having terminated.
◆ *Invariants.*   Description of the conditions which must always be satisfied.
◆ *Exported exceptions.*   List of exceptions that may be triggered by an operation.

Notation

Interface classes are noted in the same way as common classes, except that they bear the stereotype *«interface»*. They do not need a department for attributes, because they contain only operations. Operations in interface classes define only signatures; they are abstract and should therefore be set in italics.

As shown in the illustration on the previous page, interfaces can extend other interfaces; for this purpose, an inheritance relationship is drawn with the arrow pointing towards the interface to be extended.

The fact that a class implements an interface can be represented in two different ways. On the one hand, a realization relationship can be noted, as shown in the upper part of the following illustration. The realization relationship looks like an inheritance relation, however, the line is dashed. If your modeling tool does not support this, just take an inheritance relation and mark it with the stereotype *«implements»*.

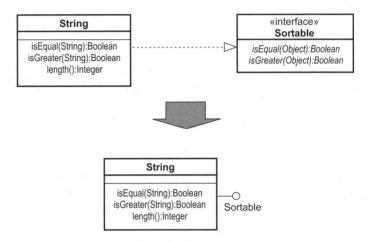

The other possibility of representing the implementation of an interface is the so-called interface 'lollipop.' Interfaces are noted with the lollipop symbol (a small empty circle joined by a line to the class that provides the interface). Next to it, the name of the interface is shown; it corresponds to the name of the corresponding interface class.

Both variations are equivalent. The notation with the realization relationship offers the possibility of reading the operations required by the interface class. The lollipop variation is a short notation; the operations required by the interface are not directly visible, only the name of the interface class is shown. See the illustration shown in the *Example* section.

Dependency relation
⇒ p. 247

Exploitation of an interface by other classes can be noted by means of a dependency relationship (dashed arrow) towards the interface class. Usage of an interface presumes that the user knows the interface provider, that is, usually there is also an association, for which the dependency relationship is not a replacement.

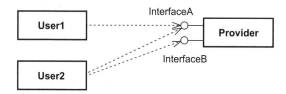

As well as classes, components too can provide interfaces, with the same conventions applying to their notation.

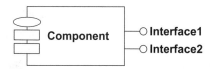

Example

The first illustration of the *Notation* section shows that the class *String* implements the interface *Sortable*. Both notation variations are equivalent.

The *Sortable* interface requires two operations: *isEqual()* and *isGreater()*. Objects which have these two operations can be sorted. The *String* class satisfies the requirements for this interface because it has the two required operations.

Further examples
⇒ *pp. 131, 134, 146, 247*

The following illustration shows the class *String* which provides an interface named *Sortable*. This interface is used by the class *SortedStringList* which is noted by the dashed relationship with the interface symbol. This means that *SortedStringList* uses the properties of *String*, which are defined in the interface class *Sortable*.

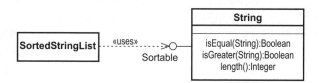

The definition of interfaces is helpful to explicate and reduce coupling between classes. Thus, in the above example, *SortedStringList* as the interface user is only dependent on two operations of the *String* class.

All other operations of the *String* class could be changed without impairing sortability – an information one would only have been obtained with an intensive study of the *SortedStringList* class.

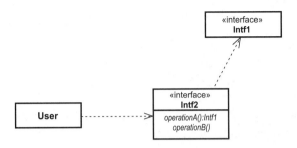

The above illustration shows a dependency relation between two interface classes. The definition of interface *Intf2* contains an operation *operationA()*, which returns an object of type *Intf1* as a result. Via this operation, the user of the interface *Intf2* also becomes a user of the interface *Intf1*, which is represented by the dashed relationship between the two interface classes.

In strongly typed languages such as Java, modeling of such dependencies is usually of no importance because the compiler carries out the necessary type checks. In languages with dynamic typing such as Smalltalk, this may be of interest for a restrictive handling of interface and type export.

CONSTRAINTS

Related terms: *restriction, integrity rule, condition, tagged value, stereotype, note, dependency, invariant, assertion.*

Definition

A constraint is an expression which restricts the possible contents, states, or the semantics of a model element and which must always be satisfied. A constraint may consist of a stereotype or of tagged values, a formal OCL (*Object Constraint Language*) expression, a semi-formal or a free formulation (note), or a dependency relationship. Constraints in the form of pure Boolean expressions are also called *assertions*.

Description

Integrity rule

A constraint describes a condition or integrity rule. It can describe the legal set of values of an attribute, specify pre- or postconditions for messages or operations, request a special context for messages or relationships, define a specific order, put a chronological condition, and the like.

Constraints are formulated freely (as free text or a formula-like/semi-formal description), or they are noted more stringently as tagged value, stereotype, or dependency. Constraints request or prohibit specific properties. Depending on the possibilities of the modeling tool, they can be appended to arbitrary notation elements, amongst others to attributes, operations, classes, and all kinds of class relationships.

Feature ⇒ p. 211
Stereotype ⇒ p. 202
Note ⇒ p. 216
Dependency ⇒ p. 247

Constraints represent additional semantic information on a model element. Freely formulated constraints, however, generally remain uninterpreted, that is, they are used by designers as information storage and bookmarks, but their contents are, for example, not converted automatically into code.

Constraints and tagged values overlap somewhat in their use. Tagged values cannot be formulated freely, but are specific key/value pairs. In contrast to freely formulated constraints, in most cases they directly influence code generation. Thus, if a corresponding tagged value can be defined instead of a constraint, this should be preferred with a view to a more precise meaning and to code generation. This liberty is intentional and allows pragmatic adaptation to the capabilities of the modeling tools.

Notation

Constraints are enclosed in braces:

{ Constraint }

Constraints that define a direct dependency of two elements (mostly association), can be noted by a dashed line between the elements involved. If one element is dependent on the other, instead of the line an arrow is drawn which points towards the independent element.

Constraints can generally also be described within a note from which dashed lines lead to the model elements involved. This form is chosen above all when the constraint concerns several model elements, so that a direct association to an element is neither possible nor sensible, for example in a constraint between three associations.

Examples

DEPENDENCY. The following example, which shows associations between the classes *Project* and *Employee*, asserts that the project leader is recruited from the set of project members. The dashed arrow expresses a dependency, in this case the *{subset}* constraint in the sense of *ProjectLeader* ∈ *ProjectMembers*

Dependency ⇒ p. 247

Subset constraint

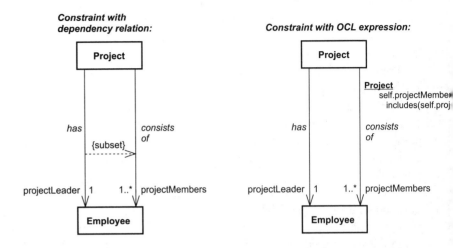

of a project. The dependent association contains only the object relations that are also contained in the association pointed to by the arrow.

The right-hand side shows the alternative with an OCL expression. OCL (*Object Constraint Language*) is a formal language for the description of constraints and navigations (see Chapter 11).

The OCL expression

> Project
> self.projectMembers->includes(self.projectLeader)

means that the set operation *includes()*, applied to the set of project members with the project leader as an argument, must return *true*. *self* as an instance of the class *Project*.

In this example, the variation with the dependency arrow appears to be simpler, and the OCL expression much more expensive. This is only due to the simplicity of the example. In Chapter 11 on OCL, you will find more complex examples.

CONSISTENCY. The following example is similar. Here, it is stated that an invoice belongs to the same customer as the contract on which it is based.

This ensures that the customer receives only invoices for existing contracts. The association between *Invoice* and *Customer* is redundant in this example; therefore, its consistency must be defined by means of a constraint. Usually, one tends to avoid redundant relationships. However, where they are necessary or sensible, problems resulting from the redundancy can be handled with the aid of such consistency constraints.

advanced

OCL ⇒ p. 276

OCL ⇒ p. 276,

further OCL examples
⇒ pp. 141, 154

Consistency constraint

advanced

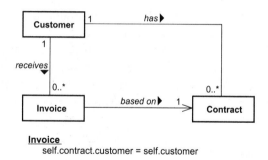

Invoice
self.contract.customer = self.customer

The OCL expression also makes clear who is responsible for consistency, namely the context which initiates the expression and to which *self* refers, in this case the instances of the *Invoice* class.

OR. Another example for constraints between relationships is the following, which asserts that a person has either domestic or foreign country addresses (thus, an exclusive OR, or XOR). Persons having both domestic and foreign country addresses are excluded. This example is admittedly somewhat artificial. OR constraints for associations are not properly regarded as elegant design and should be used sparingly ;-)

OR constraint
See p. 143

advanced

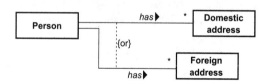

VALUES. In the following illustration, constraints are put on the possible values of the attributes of the *Rectangle* and *Triangle* classes. In the rectangle, all values must be greater than *0*; in the triangle, it is stated that values can only assume constellations that are valid for triangles.

Value constraint

Rectangle
a {a > 0}
b {b > 0}

Triangle
a {c-b < a < b+c}
b {a-c < b < a+c}
c {a-b < c < a+b}

ORDER. In the next example, an order is stated: the list of names is sorted by the last names of the persons.

Order constraint

advanced

Aggregation
⇒ *p. 243*

Formula constraint
~~advanced~~

FORMULAS.   Another example for the use of constraints is the definition of calculation rules for derived attributes. The following illustration shows the class *Person*, in which the age represents an attribute derived from the date of birth and the current date. Derived attributes are marked with a prefixed slash. On the left-hand side, the constraint is written directly after the attribute; on the right-hand side it is put in a note. Both forms of notation are allowed.

Derived attributes
⇒ *pp. 195 f.*

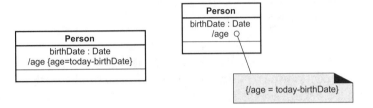

Enumeration
~~advanced~~

ENUMERATIONS.   Enumerations are also enclosed in braces, for example:

> color : {red, blue, green}

However, enumerations can usually be avoided and should be described, instead, by a class (here, the *color* class).

Gerontological constraint

To conclude this section, we introduce another example with a constraint on an aggregation. It shows a collection of people who take part in an off-shore duty-free shopping spree. To ensure that the OAPs remain together, it has been established that participants must be over 65: a duty-free shopping tour is an aggregation of elderly people.

The question arises where and how such constraints, and in particular object-transcendent constraints, should finally be implemented. An important factor is to determine the responsibility for satisfying the constraint, that is, to answer the question as to which class has to bear the responsibility. In the customer/contract/invoice example discussed earlier, the OCL expression tells us that it is the invoice.

In the above example, the responsibility question is also easy to answer. As we can see from the navigation direction, the *ShoppingSpree* class is responsible for the aggregation. Thus, this is where the constraint should be located. The *ShoppingSpree* class will provide an operation for adding further people to the set of participants, for example *addParticipant(participant:Person)*. Within this operation, the age needs to be checked. Here is an outline of the conversion into Java:

```
Class ShoppingSpree {
    private Vector participantSet;

    public void addParticipant(Person : participant) {
        if (participant.age > 65} {
            participantSet.addElement(participant);
        }
        ...
```

Since participants cannot become younger, this form of conversion is alright. It should be noted that in this example the constraint is only checked when adding a new participant, but that the constraint must also be maintained at any later point in time.

TAGGED VALUES

Related terms: *property string, tagged value, feature, characteristic, constraint*.

Definition

Tagged values are user-defined, language and tool specific keyword/value pairs which extend the semantics of individual model elements with specific characteristic properties.

Keyword/value pairs

Description

Tagged values add specific additional properties to existing model elements. In the same way that attributes describe the properties of a class in more detail, tagged values can further specify the properties of an arbitrary model element (for example, of a class or an attribute). They detail the semantics of a model element and, in many cases, influence code generation. Some tagged values have been explicitly designed to control code generation, mostly on the basis of specific design or code patterns.

Although tagged values can be assigned completely arbitrarily, it is, however, sensible, for example in a project or an enterprise, to agree on a limited and well-defined set of tagged values for a tool. In view of the relationship with code generation, this usually happens automatically.

Constraints ⇒ p. 206

Abstract classes
⇒ p. 190
Abstract operations
⇒ p. 198 f.

Probably, the most frequently used tagged value is *abstract* (unless it is not defined as a freely formulated constraint, which would also be possible), which marks abstract classes and abstract operations. For attributes, the property *readonly* may be sensible. In operations and attributes, the keyword *private* can indicate that the element should not be used, while the keyword *obsolete* indicates that the element in question exists for compatibility with older versions only and should no longer be used.

It is also possible to specify information on the author or the version number of a class as a property.

Code generation

In the examples mentioned above, connections to code generation are obvious: usually, abstract classes and operations must also be declared as abstract or virtual in the program code, and the same applies to private operations and attributes. For read-only attributes, at most a read operation is generated, but not an operation for setting the attribute value.

Thus, tagged values are a very powerful and easy-to-handle tool for definition of semantic details and automatic conversion of design patterns.

Stereotypes ⇒ p. 213

The difference with the stereotype consists in the fact that a stereotype extends the metamodel by a new element. Tagged values, instead, allow individual instances of existing model elements (for example, a specific operation) to be extended by specific properties.

Notation

Tagged values consist of a keyword and a value and are enclosed in braces either individually or as an enumeration. They can be attached as a kind of label to all model elements, for example to associations, classes, attributes, and operations.

```
┌─────────────────────────────────┐
│          GeomFigure             │
│      {abstract Version=1.3}     │
├─────────────────────────────────┤
│   visible : Boolean {readonly}  │
├─────────────────────────────────┤
│      display() {abstract}       │
│      remove() {abstract}        │
│      getPosition(): Point       │
│      setPosition(p: Point)      │
│      setPos(x, y) {obsolete}    │
└─────────────────────────────────┘
```

If the value is a Boolean which is *true*, it may be omitted; thus

    {transient=true}

is identical with

    {transient}

Instead of braces, tools may also use other kinds of marking up, such as colored highlights, italic type, and so forth.

Examples

{abstract}
{readOnly}
{private}
{obsolete}
{Version=2.1}
{Author=Tara King}
{transient}
{persistent}

STEREOTYPES

Related terms: *usage context*, *constraint*.

Definition

Stereotypes are project-, enterprise-, or method-specific extensions of pre-existing model elements of the UML metamodel. According to the semantics defined with the extension, the model element to which the stereotype is applied are semantically directly affected.

Metamodel extension

In practice, stereotypes mainly specify possible usage contexts of a class, a relationship, or a package.

See feature ⇒ p. 211
Constraints ⇒ p. 206

Description

Stereotypes classify the possible uses of a model element. This does not mean modeling of metaclasses, but ascribing specific common features to one or more classes. One might object that multiple inheritance serves the purpose; however, stereotypes are once again different because they have no type semantics, they are neither types nor classes. Instead, they allow a mental and sometimes visual differentiation and give hints on ways of use, connections with existing application architectures, development environments, and so on.

A model element can be classified with an arbitrary number of stereotypes. Semantics and visual representation of the element can be influenced by assignment of stereotypes. In practice, this is realized for example by modeling tools which vary their code generation in function of stereotypes.

Code generation

Stereotypes should not be freely and arbitrarily invented and assigned by individual developers, but should be defined in a project-, enterprise-, or tool-related fashion.

Attributes and operations too can be provided with stereotypes. This allows attributes and operations to be subdivided into appropriate groups within the class (see the *Example* section further below).

Relationships may also be classified by means of stereotypes.

Tagged values
⇒ *p. 211*

The difference between stereotypes and tagged values lies in the fact that with a stereotype, the metamodel is extended by a new model element. With tagged values, in contrast, individual instances of existing model elements (for example a specific operation) are extended by specific properties.

With Joos *et al*. (1997), four types of stereotypes can be distinguished:

*Use case diagrams,
actors* ⇒ *p. 180*

◆ *Decorative stereotypes.* These may be used to make tools and diagrams look more colorful and visually appealing, for example actors and the like in use case diagrams.

◆ *Descriptive stereotypes.* These are stereotypes which are mainly used to describe contexts of usage and which represent a kind of standardized comment, for example, to associate classes to specific architecture layers («business class», «process control», and so on). See the illustration further below.

◆ *Restrictive stereotypes.* These stereotypes mean formal restrictions to be applied to existing model elements. They define restrictions on existence or non-existence of specific properties, thus extending the metamodel.

Interface class
⇒ *p. 213*

The most prominent exponent is UML's predefined stereotype «interface», whose restriction consists in the fact that classes marked as such are abstract classes and must only contain abstract operations.

◆ *Redefining stereotypes.* These are metamodel modifications which would allow the fundamental concepts of the original language (UML) to be violated and which should therefore be avoided.

Descriptive and restrictive stereotypes are sensible on the whole; decorative stereotypes make sense as long as they are used in homeopathic doses. New stereotypes should principally be defined, that is, invented only with extreme case and not without need.

Many stereotypes are already predefined in UML. Self-created and tool-specific stereotypes are problematic as they may be used to doublecross the standardization of UML.

Yet another problem may arise with the modification of (the meaning of) stereotypes, because no version concept exists for the resulting stereotypes.

Notation

The stereotype is placed before or above the element name (for example a class name) and enclosed in French quotes or *guillemots* («»).

Alternatively to this purely textual notation, special symbols may be used (decorative stereotypes), as shown below with the stereotypes *«actor»*, *«control»*, *«boundary»*, and *«entity»*.

Furthermore, tools are free to use specific color or other visual highlighting.

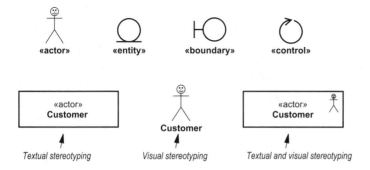

Examples

Stereotypes can, for example, be used to indicate the meaning of a class in the application architecture, such as:

«presentation», «process», «domain class».

Further examples:

«model», «view», «controller», «exception», «primitive», «enumeration», «signal», «complete», «incomplete», «overlapping», «disjoint», «implements», «uses», «extends».

NOTES

Related terms: *annotation, comment.*

Definition

Notes are comments to a diagram or an arbitrary element in a diagram, without any semantic effect.

Description

Notes are annotations to classes, attributes, operations, relationships, and the like. Some analysis and design tools provide the possibility of creating notes with user-defined structures and names.

Thus, it is possible to deposit information on, for example, development state, version of a class, developer responsible for the class or its last modification, and so on. Data concerning project management, such as cost incurred so far and estimated remaining cost can be managed. Some tools also provide evaluation mechanisms for user-defined note structures, which turns notes into a powerful and practical instrument.

Notation and Example

Example
Constraint ⇒ p. 207

Notes are represented by earmarked rectangles containing text. Optionally, a line or a dependency relationship may be drawn from the rectangle to the diagram element to which the note refers, for example to an attribute.

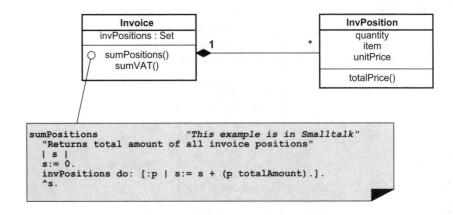

EXPLORATIVE PROTOTYPES

Explorative prototypes are in most cases sequences of dialog designs which illustrate previously elaborated use cases. Dialog designs are executable dialogs in which data can be entered, but which do not include all features of a finished application, such as help functions, error handling, database storage, performance, robustness, an undo functionality, and so on. Use cases describe concrete user actions, including potential exceptions and special cases.

Dialog designs, formula designs

Explorative prototyping is used for analysis. It is a medium for communicating with future users about the planned application system. Frequently, explorative prototypes are dialog designs. They can, however, also be evaluations, printing samples, form designs, simulations, or calculation rules. The latter could be, for example, realized as spread sheets and reviewed together with experts from the application domain.

First, it has to be established which dialogs are needed and on the basis of which use cases they are required. Sometimes, doubts can arise as to whether in a specific situation one or several dialogs are needed, or whether in two different situations the same dialog might be used. In such cases, the requirements must be carefully compared. If in doubt, it might be better to opt for the simpler solution, that is, the one with fewer dialogs. Potentially, this may lead to conflict at a later stage, which suggests a different structure is required. But at least you will know why.

Explorative dialog prototypes show users and specialists actual aspects of the future system. Depending on the users' power of abstraction and imagination and their experience with software systems, you may also get some critical reactions on the dialog designs, such as 'this field needs to be shifted further up, and that one is far too small.' You as a system analyst, however, might be glad to have identified the dialogs at all, and do not really wish to hear these comments at this stage.

In such situations, it may be helpful not to show dialog designs, but to discuss brief textual descriptions which in a few keywords summarize the most important functions of the dialogs.

Customer search

> ‣ *Input of various search terms, such as customer number, name, phone, place*
> ‣ *Start search*
> ‣ *Select customer*
> ‣ *Delete all search terms*

Customer file

> ‣ *Display; processing of customer attributes, if required*
> ‣ *Customer number, name, addresses, phone numbers, and so on*
> ‣ *List of all reservations, contracts, invoices, damages, and so on, with corresponding branching possibilities*
> ‣ *Store modifications*

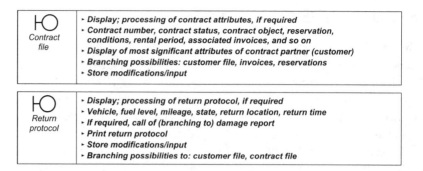

*Dialog specification
⇒ p. 136*

In a similar way, you can also describe existing marginal systems and interfaces. This does not make precise interface specifications superfluous, but for a first sketch of the surroundings of the new application, this form of description can be very useful.

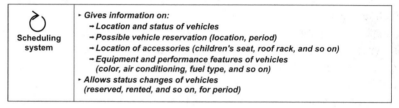

In use case diagrams, the individual use cases can be assigned the dialogs they require. The same process also applies to external systems, as shown in the illustration below.

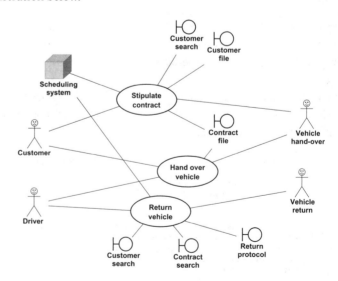

Chapter 8

Class Diagrams (Relational Elements)

This chapter gives a detailed description of the individual elements of the Unified Modeling Language used for representation of static modeling features – each subdivided into definition, description, notation, and examples.

GENERALIZATION, SPECIALIZATION

Related terms: *inheritance, concretization.*

Definition

Mechanism (Inheritance)

Inheritance is a programming language concept, that is, an implementation mechanism for the relationship between superclasses and subclasses by means of which attributes and operations of a superclass also become accessible to its subclasses.

Structuring principle (generalization, specialization)

Generalization and specialization are abstraction principles for hierarchical structuring of the semantics of a model.

Generalization (or specialization) is a taxonomic relationship between a general and a special element (or vice versa), where the special element adds properties to the general one and behaves in a way that is compatible with it.

Description

In generalization or specialization, properties are structured hierarchically, that is, properties of general significance are assigned to more general classes

Superclass

Subclass

(superclasses), and more special properties are assigned to classes that are subordinate to the general ones (subclasses). Thus, the properties of the superclasses are bestowed on the subclasses, that is, subclasses inherit properties from their superclasses. Therefore, a subclass contains both the properties specified in itself and the properties of its superclass(es).

Discriminator

Differentiation into superclasses and subclasses is often performed by means of a distinctive feature (or characteristic) called *discriminator*. The discriminator denotes the aspect relevant for hierarchical structuring of the properties. This is not given *per se*, but the result of a modeling decision. For example, one might categorize vehicles on the basis of how they are powered (combustion engine, electrical, horse power), but also on the basis of the medium of locomotion (air, water, rail, road).

Whether a discriminator is chosen and, if so, which one, depends on the semantic contents of the generalization relation. If the subclasses can be seen as elements of a defined enumeration (air, water, ...), the discriminator usually suggests itself. It is helpful to bring the discriminator explicitly to mind during modeling, and to integrate it into the graphical or textual model description. Thus, the discriminator becomes a documented design decision.

Partition

The entirety of subclasses based on the same discriminator is called a partition.

Within the class hierarchy, the attributes and operations are located in exactly those classes in which they actually represent a property of the class, that is, that the semantics ascribed to them represent an objective property of precisely that class (under consideration of the structuring aspect). This may also be an abstract property.

In other words, an attribute or an operation is not located in a class with the sole purpose of guaranteeing its re-use in derived subclasses – although this is usually the effect of this kind of hierarchical structuring. The same applies to optimization and normalization effects known from data modeling (ERM). The decisive factor is the presupposed semantics.

Delegation ⇒ *p. 145*

Notation

The inheritance relation is represented by means of a large empty arrow pointing from the subclass to the superclass. The arrows may alternatively be drawn directly from the subclasses to the superclass, or combined to a common line. The direct arrows allow for a more flexible layout and can also be easily drawn by hand. The combined arrows emphasize the collectivity of the sub-classes, namely that they are specializations of a superclass on the basis of a discriminator.

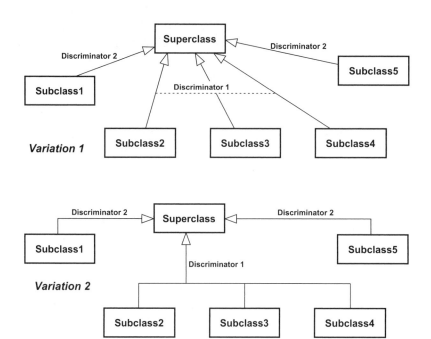

*See multiple
inheritance ⇒ p. 266*

In the direct arrow variation, the inheritance relations to which the discriminator applies are either joined by a dashed line which is then labeled with the name of the discriminator, or each individual inheritance arrow is labeled with the discriminator. If the specification of discriminators is omitted, it is unclear whether the subclasses are independent specializations or the outcome of a common discriminator.

The discriminator is a virtual attribute of possible concrete objects. It does not appear as an attribute in any of the classes, but it is implicitly contained in the relation between superclasses and subclasses: the names of the subclasses created through this discrimination would be the attribute values of the implicit discriminator attribute.

Constraints ⇒ p. 206
advanced
UML

Generalization relations can be provided with the following predefined constraints:

*Multiple inheritance
⇒ p. 225*

Predefined constraints

- ◆ *overlapping*
  This constraint has been specially designed for multiple inheritance to control combination of common properties from separate inheritance paths. For more details, see the section on multiple inheritance below.
- ◆ *disjoint*
  This is the inverse constraint of *overlapping* and the default.
- ◆ *complete*
  All subclasses are specified, further subclasses are not expected. Independently of this, it is not necessary for all subclasses to be present in a diagram.
- ◆ *incomplete*
  Further subclasses are expected, but have not yet been modeled. This must, however, not be confused with the situation where a defined subclass is merely not shown in a diagram. In the following illustration, *{incomplete}* is used to express that an additional subclass is expected, but has not yet been defined.

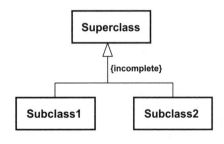

Example

In a screen display window, circles, rectangles, and triangles are supposed to be displayed and moved. The concepts of *circle*, *rectangle*, and *triangle* can be generalized and very generally denoted as *geometric figures*. The classes *Circle*, *Rectangle*, and *Triangle* would therefore be specializations of the common superclass *GeomFigure*; the discriminator would be the figure shape. In the abstract superclass, the operations *display()* and *remove()* are marked as abstract, that is, all geometric figures have these operations, but they are only implemented in the concrete subclasses.

Discriminator: figure shape

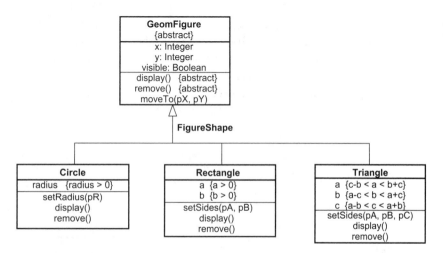

See discussion ⇒ pp. 25 ff.

    The attributes *x*, *y*, and *visible* are part of all geometric figures and are therefore located in the superclass. The *radius* and the sides *a, b,* and *c*, in contrast, are special properties of the concrete geometric figures.

    The concrete attributes are equipped with the necessary constraints for the geometric figure in question. For example, in a circle, the radius must not be equal to or less than zero, and in a triangle, the sum of any two sides must be greater than the remaining third side.

Multiple Inheritance

advanced

The previous section showed simple inheritance with the aid of the geometric object example. Each class has at most one superclass. In multiple inheritance, a class may have more than one superclass. Instead of a class hierarchy, in this case one could speak of a class heterarchy.

Not all programming languages need or support multiple inheritance (Smalltalk and Java, for example, do not). It should also be viewed with a fairly critical eye, as it creates problems. What happens if different superclasses contain homonymous properties (which obviously may behave differently)? Of which superclass will the subclass take the property? This conflict can as a rule only be avoided by addressing the property in a fully qualified way, that is, including the denomination of its superclass.

Conflicts in multiple inheritance

Further conflict situations may be constructed. For example, the two superclasses that possess a common subclass could in their turn be derived from a common superclass, so that a property would be passed on in two directions and then combined again through multiple inheritance. Here too, the property may be overwritten in any intermediate class lying between the two. An alternative to multiple inheritance is delegation.

Delegation ⇒ p. 145

An example for multiple inheritance: a pig is both a mammal and a terrestrial animal. It therefore inherits the properties of the *Mammal* class and the *Terrestrial* class.

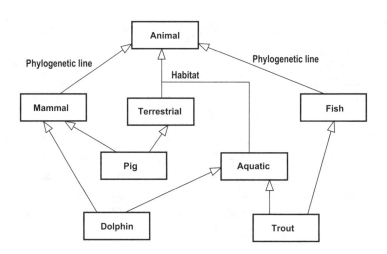

Overlapping Versus *Disjoint*

The two inverse constraints *overlapping* and *disjoint* are relevant in connection with multiple inheritance. The class diagram shown below will help with the explanation. It shows the specialization of vehicles following the two discriminators *LocomotionMedium* and *KindOfPower*. The only concrete class in the example is *SailingBoat*; only instances of this class may be generated.

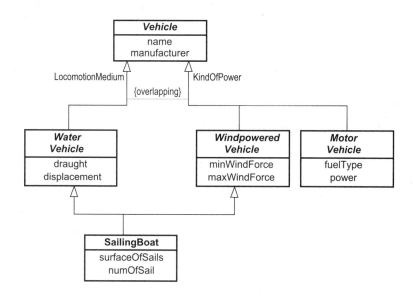

The *SailingBoat* class inherits the properties of its superclasses. The properties of the *Vehicle* class can be inherited in two ways, on the one hand, via *WaterVehicle*; on the other hand via *WindpoweredVehicle*.

By default, inheritance relationships are always *disjoint*. This means that *SailingBoat* would doubly inherit the attributes *name* and *manufacturer* from *Vehicle*, that is, the instances of *SailingBoat* would keep them twice.

The *overlapping* constraint ensures that these attributes are only inherited once. The two objects shown below illustrate the difference between *disjoint* and *overlapping*.

overlappingSailingBoat
name
manufacturer
draught
displacement
surfaceOfSails
numOfSails

disjointSailingBoat
waterVehicle.name
windpoweredVehicle.name
waterVehicle.manufacturer
windpoweredVehicle.manufacturer
draught
displacement
surfaceOfSails
numOfSails

ASSOCIATION

Aggregation ⇒ p. 243
Composition ⇒ p. 245

Related terms: *aggregation, composition, link, object connection, relation.*

Definition

As a relation between classes, an association describes the common semantics and structure of a set of object connections.

Description

Object connections

Associations are needed to enable objects to communicate with each other. An association describes a connection between classes. The concrete relation between two objects of these classes is called *object connection* or *link*. Thus, links are the instances of an association.

Recursive association

Usually, an association is a relation between two different classes. In the main, however, an association may also be of a recursive nature; in this case, the class has a relation with itself, where it is usually assumed that two different objects of that class are linked. However, even three or more different classes can be involved in an association. Special variations of an association are aggregation and composition.

Aggregation ⇒ p. 243
Composition ⇒ p. 245

Temporary links

Usually, an association is valid for the entire life span of the involved objects, or at least for the duration of a business event. However, it is also possible to model associations that are valid only temporarily. For example, because an object is the argument of a message and is only locally known to the receiving object inside the corresponding operation. In this case, the stereotype *«temporary»* should be used.

Visibility specifications
⇒ p. 199

> ◆ **Cardinality**
>   Number of elements
> ◆ **Multiplicity**
>   Range of allowed cardinalities

The multiplicity of an association specifies the number of objects of the opposite class to which an object can be associated. If this number is variable, the range, that is minimum and maximum, is specified. If the minimum is 0, the relation is optional.

Each association can be given a name which should describe the relation in more detail (usually a verb). On each side of the association, role names can be used to indicate which roles the individual objects assume in the relation.

Roles, constraints

Constraints may be used to restrict the relation under specific aspects.

Notation

Relations are represented by a line drawn between the involved classes. At the respective ends, the multiplicity of the relation can be indicated. Each relation should be given a name (set in italics) which describes what this relation consists of or why it exists. To be able to read the class names and the name of the relation in the correct direction, a small solid triangle pointing in the reading direction can be drawn next to the relation name.

Reading direction

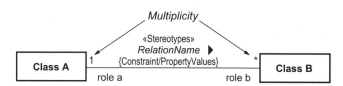

Relation names can be noted for both reading directions. At each end of a relation, additional role names can be specified (naming conventions as with attributes). A role name describes how the object is seen by the opposite object in the association.

Attributes ⇒ p. 195

Furthermore, an association can be described in more detail by means of constraints, tagged values, and stereotypes. Stereotypes are noted before or above the relation name, constraints and tagged values after or below the name.

Constraints ⇒ p. 206
Tagged values
⇒ p. 211
Stereotypes ⇒ p. 213

Classes can be joined by direct lines, that is, the shortest way, or by lines following a rectangular grid. This is a matter of personal taste or the drawing capabilities of the design tool.

On each side of the association, the multiplicity is noted as an individual number or as a value range. Value ranges are noted by specifying the minimum and the maximum value, separated by two dots (for example 1..5). An asterisk * is a wildcard and means 'many.' Different alternatives are listed, separated by a comma.

Multiplicity

One-way associations or directed associations, in which only one side knows the other, but not vice versa, are described in the section on directed associations.

Directed associations
⇒ p. 241

Example

The following illustration shows a relation between a company and its employees. The relation is read as follows: '1 company employs * employees.' The asterisk * stands as a wildcard for an arbitrary number of instances.

While different relation names can be specified per reading direction (thus '* employee works for 1 company' too), the multiplicity applies to the entire association, that is, to both directions. In addition, role names may be appended to the relation, since objects of such classes often interact with each other in specific roles. In this case, the company plays the role of employer, while the employee is the employee [...].

Roles

Further examples of multiplicity specifications:

1	exactly one
0, 1	zero or one
0..4	between zero and four
3, 7	either three or seven
0..*	greater than or equal to zero (default, if the specification is omitted)
*	ditto
1..*	greater than or equal to one
0..3, 7, 9..*	between zero and three, or exactly seven, or greater than or equal to nine

Associations are usually realized by assigning appropriate reference attributes to the classes involved. In the above example, the class *Employee* would receive an attribute *employer* as a reference to an object of the class *Company*, and the class *Company* would get an attribute *employee* with a collection object (or a subclass) for referencing the *Employee* objects. Some modeling tools use the role names of the relation for the corresponding automatically generated attributes. Therefore, role names often correspond to the corresponding attributes.

Recursive Associations

Related terms: *self-related association*.

Definition

Recursive associations are associations in which only one class is involved.

Description

A particular variation of association is the recursive association in which objects of the same class enter a relation with each other. It should be assumed that two different instances of the class are associated with each other, because otherwise no association would need to be formulated.

The example shows employees who can assume the role of *manager* in which they guide a set of office clerks, and who can assume the role of *office clerks* who report to a single manager. In directly recursive associations, either role names or relation names must be specified, because otherwise the relation does not become apparent.

Role names
Relation names

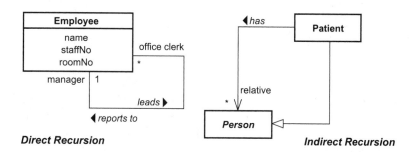

Direct Recursion   **Indirect Recursion**

Besides the directly recursive associations, there are also the indirect ones in which the recursivity is not recognizable at first sight. In the example, *Person* is an abstract class, that is, there can only be instances of *Patient*. *Patient*, however, can associate a set of relatives which in this case must also be patients. Here too, it should be assumed that different instances are associated with each other.

Attributed Association

advanced

Related terms: *association attributes, association class.*

Definition

A model element which has both the properties of a class and an association. It can be viewed as an association with additional class properties (attributed association) or as a class with additional association properties (association class).

Description

Besides the forms of association described until now, there is yet another one in which the relation itself has attributes. An attributed association suggests itself in cases where attributes are found which can be associated neither to one nor to the other class, because they are property of the relation itself.

Association class

The properties of the relation are modeled as a class which is notationally attributed to the association. Semantically, association and association class are identical, that is, the name of the association class corresponds to the name of the association. The instances of the association class are the concrete object relations between the (normal) classes involved in the association.

A peculiarity of attributed associations is that two involved objects may at most have one relation with each other. This will be explained further below with the aid of an example.

Notation

Attributed associations are represented in the same way as normal associations. In addition, via a dashed line that starts from the association line, a further class is assigned, the so-called association class. Otherwise, the association class is noted like a common class.

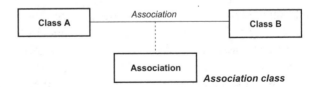

Examples

The association between employee and company of the previous section can, for example, be extended in a way that information on employment periods can be taken into account.

The attributes which describe these periods belong neither to the class *Company* nor to the class *Employee*, but are part of the relation between those two. In the same way, operations could be part of association classes. Since the instances of the association classes are identical to the concrete object relations, they cannot exist on their own, but are dependent on the two actual objects involved.

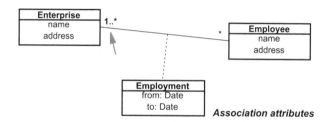

Association attributes

Occasionally, we also speak of implicit association classes; implicit because the class does not describe independent objects and needs not bear a name (associations do not require names). Obviously, in this case it is very sensible to specify a name. The names of the association and the association class are always identical.

Implicit association classes

What makes attributed associations so special is that two involved objects can at most have one relation with each other. The multiplicities specify that a company may have *1..** employees and that an employee must at least be employed by one company.

Special semantics of multiplicity

In real life an employee may have worked several times, in different periods, for a company. In an attributed association like the one shown above, this is not possible! Any two involved objects may only have one relation with each other. Thus, an employee cannot have two relations with the same company. If this is required, an attributed association is not suitable.

The following illustration shows an example in which the special semantics of the attributed association are required. Each employee is assigned specific abilities combined with a degree of competence. Here, an employee can be assigned an ability only once, because the employee cannot have the same ability with different degrees of competence; one would always choose the higher degree (this example is, by the way, taken up again in the section on qualified associations).

In fine-grain design, such relations are usually broken up, and the association class becomes a proper class. It must, however, be ensured that the special semantics of the attributed association are maintained, that is, replaced

Qualified association ⇒ *p. 236*

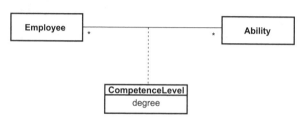

by corresponding constraints. This will indeed be the first example in the following section.

Please also note the transfer of the multiplicities.

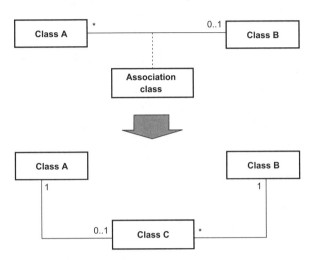

Association Constraints

If it is required that an association satisfies specific conditions, these may be noted, enclosed in braces, as constraints next to the association line. The constraints may have an arbitrary content and may be formulated freely, semi-formally, or formally (as OCL expressions).

OCL ⇒ p. 276

The following example takes up the situation discussed in the previous section. It was required that each employee can be assigned an ability only once (with a corresponding degree of competence). The constraint shown in the illustration below makes use of the fact that in a *Set*, an element may only be contained once (in contrast to the *Bag*). Thus, even if the sets are identical, no ability occurs twice.

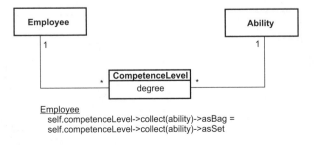

Employee
self.competenceLevel->collect(ability)->asBag =
self.competenceLevel->collect(ability)->asSet

The attributed association '*Enterprise employs employees*' as shown already in the previous section, is shown in the following illustration as a broken-up variation with two common associations. Here, the constraints are to ensure that the employment periods of an employee do not overlap. This has just been freely formulated. The constraint gives no information on how this should be implemented.

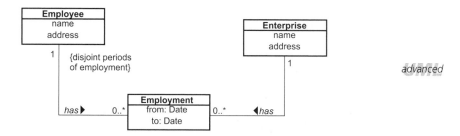

advanced

Here, an OLC expression could be more precise. Why don't you try to formulate it!

See ⇒ pp. 149, 151

Another example is the *{ordered}* constraint which specifies that the objects inside the relation are ordered. The way this order is implemented is usually not mentioned. Another possibility is sorting the objects: *{sorted}*. The constraint may also describe by which attributes the objects are ordered or sorted, for example *{ordered by contract date}*. Complex sorting rules should be noted as separate constraints.

Ordered association

Constraints are usually also needed for the description of referential integrity when deleting objects; here, they specify whether during deletion of an object:

Referential integrity

- ◆ the opposite object is also deleted
  {delete related object},
- ◆ only the relation between the objects is to be deleted
  {delete link},
- ◆ deletion is only allowed if no more relations exist
  {prohibit deletion}.

The section on constraints contains further examples of constraints inside and between associations.

Constraints, further examples ⇒ p. 207

advanced

Qualified Associations

Related terms: *associative array*, *dictionary*, *qualifying association*, *partitioned association*.

Definition

A qualified association is an association in which qualifying attributes are used to subdivide the referenced set of objects into partitions where, viewed from the initial object, each partition may occur only once.

Description

Relations in which an object can associate *many (*)* objects of the opposite side are usually implemented by means of a container object in the initial object. This could, for example, be a dictionary (associative array, look-up table in a database, or the like). In a dictionary, access is carried out by specifying a key. The qualified association is the UML counterpart to the programming construct dictionary. Further explanations are given further below with the aid of an example.

Notation

The qualifying attribute used for the association is noted in a rectangle attached to the side of the class that accesses the target object via this qualifier. Several attributes may be specified in this rectangle. The notation corresponds to that of attributes in classes; however, the specification of default values does not apply in this case.

Example

The illustration shows employment of people in an enterprise. Besides their names, employees also have their initials. From the normal association shown on top, it can be seen that each employee belongs to a single enterprise and that an enterprise has a set of employees.

In the qualified association, the sets of employees are partitioned, that is, divided into subgroups. Partitioning is carried out on the basis of the specified qualifying attribute, in this case, the initials. All employees of an enterprise

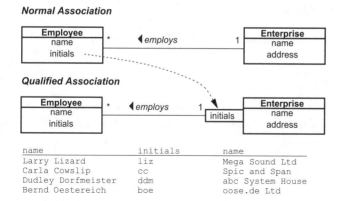

that have the same initials belong to one partition. If all employees of an enterprise have different initials, the number of created partitions will be the same as the number of employees in the enterprise.

Employees of different enterprises may also have identical initials without, however, landing in a partition, because partitioning is enterprise-specific.

If one wanted to ensure that all employees of an enterprise have different initials, it would be sufficient to set the multiplicity on the side of the employee to 1, since this multiplicity specification always refers to a partition and not to the enterprises. Multiplicity always refers to an instance of the qualifier.

The following illustration shows a further variation of an example that has already been discussed in the section on attributed associations. In the example shown below, an employee may have abilities [Oh!] where each ability is assigned exactly one degree of competence. This excludes the possibility of specifying several contradictory degrees of competence for one ability. Furthermore, the association is directed, that is, the competence levels know nothing about the employees' abilities.

Example attributed association ⇒ p. 231

Derived Associations

Related terms: *calculated association, derived element.*

Definition

A derived association is an association whose concrete object relations can be at any time derived (calculated) from the values of other object relations and their objects.

Notation

Derived associations are noted just like common associations, except that their name is prefixed with a slash (/). The derivation rule can be noted as a constraint.

Description and Example

The following illustration shows a derived association, that is, this relation is not stored, but is calculated when required. Thus, through a detour via the *Department*, each *Employee* is assigned one *Enterprise*. The */works for* association marking this fact can therefore be derived, that is, calculated. This situation should not be confused with the *Customer–Invoice–Contract* examples in the section on constraints, where actually existing redundant associations were supposed not to contradict each other.

Constraints, examples
⇒ pp. 207 f.

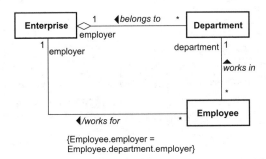

{Employee.employer =
Employee.department.employer}

N-ary Associations

Related terms: *ternary association*.

Definition

An n-ary association is like a common (binary) association, except that more than two association roles are involved in it.

Description

As well as the usual binary relations, and apart from attributed associations, there are also ternary and n-ary associations, that is, associations in which three or more classes (more precisely: association roles) are equally involved. An association role is represented by a class. A class may also be multiply involved in an n-ary association.

Ternary association

The illustration below shows an example of seat reservation on passenger trains. In the simplest case, a reservation consists of a passenger (for whom the seat is reserved), a seat (which is being reserved), and a train (time of reservation). Our example goes a bit further, it also allows group reservations, that is, several (possibly contiguous) seats for several passengers. Since the number of reserved seats should match the number of passengers, an appropriate constraint has been noted. Who will actually sit on which seat is a problem that, in this example, the group must decide internally.

This example can be extended: many passengers travel only for a section of the route whereas, in the above example, seats are reserved for the entire route. In this – now quaternary – association, we can find the new class

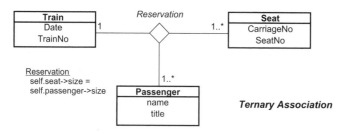

Ternary Association

Date	TrainNo	Name	Title	Carriage	Seat
4.3.97	ICE681	Anne Meadows	Ms	3	26
4.3.97	ICE681	Will A. Worm	Mr	5	10
7.3.97	ICE530	Anne Meadows	Ms	2	13
9.3.97	ICE135	Carl Titmouse	Dr	7	46

Section being involved. This allows seats to be reserved also for sections of the route. To ensure that these sections are disjointed for the reservation of an individual seat, a further constraint needs to be noted, this time in free text.

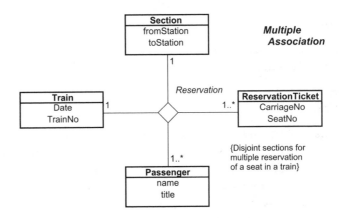

N-ary associations can usually be transformed into normal associations. The following illustration shows the conversion of the ternary association of the previous page.

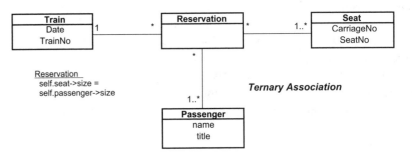

And because there is some space left on the page, here is an example which shows that the number of association roles need not match the number of classes involved.

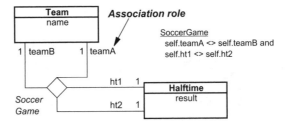

Directed Associations

Related terms: *unidirectional association, navigability*.

Definition

A directed association is an association in which you can directly navigate from one of the involved association roles to the other, but not vice versa.

Notation

A directed association is noted in the same way as a common association, with the exception that on the side of the class towards which navigation is possible, it shows an open arrow head. Multiplicity and role names are only relevant on the side of the association towards which you can navigate.

Description and Example

The following illustration shows an association which can only be navigated in one direction. In this example, the invoice can access the address, but the address does not know with which invoices it is associated.

All associations are unidirectional, that is, are directed associations. Bidirectional associations are actually two inverse associations, as shown in the following illustration.

Unidirectional and bidirectional relations

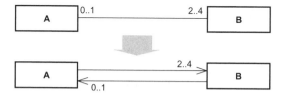

Inverse association

Thus, object-oriented associations have different semantics as compared with relational connections in Entity Relationship Modeling (ERM), where bidirectional relations are assumed. Particularly OO rookies with a 'relational background' often continue to perceive associations with relational semantics.

Confusion with relational connections

Thus, if in object-oriented associations only one association line without navigational direction is drawn (upper relation between *A* and *B* in the previous illustration), this is practically only a simplification and short notation. In reality, we are dealing with two independent relations. For one relation, class *A* bears the responsibility; for the other, class *B*. Different semantics or distribution of responsibilities would both violate the encapsulation principle and reduce possibilities of re-use.

UML currently allows both interpretations:

◆ Associations without navigational specification are bidirectional, that is, they implicitly consist of two inversely directed associations.
◆ Associations without navigational specification are underspecified, that is, their navigability is not known.

Personally, I prefer the second interpretation. Other UML authors, for example Fowler and Scott (1997), also prefer this variation.

Derived association
⇒ *p. 238*

The following example shows the relations between customers, invoices, and contracts. The relation '*invoice for customer*' is a derived association. How it is calculated, that is, how one navigates from the invoice to the customer, is specified by the constraint *{Invoice.Customer = Invoice.Contract.Customer}*. Furthermore, the illustration shows two directed associations. The invoice has relations with the customer (derived) and with the contract (factual) and therefore knows the other two classes. Vice versa, only the contract knows about the *Invoice* class.

{Invoice.Customer = Invoice.Contract.Customer}

AGGREGATION

Related terms: *entirety–part relation, association*.

Definition

An aggregation is an association in which the involved classes represent an *entirety–part hierarchy*.

Association ⇒ p. 228

Description

An aggregation can be understood as the combination of an object out of a set of individual parts, in form of an entirety-part hierarchy.

 A distinctive feature of all aggregations is that the entirety assumes tasks in substitution of its parts. The aggregate class contains operations, for example, which do not cause a change in the aggregate itself, but forward the message to its individual parts. This is known as *propagation of operations*. In contrast to the association, the involved classes do not maintain an equal-right relationship, but one class (the aggregate) assumes a special role for delegation of responsibility and leadership.

 In an aggregation relation between two classes, exactly one end of the relation must be the aggregate, and the other stand for the individual parts. If no aggregate was present on any of the sides, we would have a normal association; if both sides accommodated an aggregate, this would be a contradiction, with the two aggregates contending with each other for the leading role.

 In some cases, aggregations describe relations in which the parts are existence-dependent on the entirety. This means that if the aggregate (the entirety) is deleted, all individual parts are deleted with it. If an individual part is deleted, the aggregate survives. This strict form is called *composition* and will be discussed in the next section.

Entirety–part hierarchy

Composition ⇒ p. 245

Propagation of operations

Delegation ⇒ p. 145

Composition ⇒ p. 245

Notation

In the same way as an association, an aggregation is represented by a line drawn between two classes; in addition, it is marked with a small empty diamond. This diamond is located on the side of the aggregate, that is, the entirety. It almost symbolizes the container object in which the individual parts are collected. Otherwise, all notation conventions of the association apply.

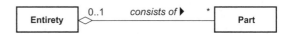

The cardinality specification on the side of the aggregate is usually 1, so an omitted specification can by default be interpreted as 1. A part can belong to several aggregations at the same time.

Similarly to inheritance relations, aggregations too can be represented as tree structures, that is, on the side of the aggregate, the individual lines are combined into a common line with a common diamond.

Examples

The *Enterprise–Department–Employee* example shows that a part (*Department*) can in turn be an aggregate.

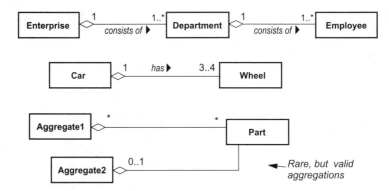

Constraint {ordered}
⇒ *p. 207*

The following illustration shows an aggregation represented in the form of a tree-structure:

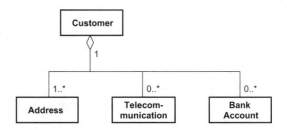

Composition

Related terms: *aggregation, association.*

Definition

A composition is a strict form of aggregation, in which the parts are existence-dependent on the entirety.

Existence-dependent parts

Description

Since a composition is a special variation of the aggregation, most of the assertions applying to the aggregation also apply to the composition. The composition too is a combination of an object out of a set of individual parts. As with the aggregation, in the composition too the entirety assumes tasks in representation of its parts. The following differences should, however, be noted.

The cardinality on the side of the aggregate can only be 1. Each part is only part of exactly one composition object; otherwise the existence-dependency would become contradictory. The life span of the parts is subordinate to that of the entirety, that is, the parts are generated together with the aggregate or subsequently, and they are destroyed before the aggregate is destroyed.

If a variable multiplicity is specified for the parts (for example *1..**), this means that they do not need to be created together with the aggregate, but can also come into being later. However, from the very moment of their creation, they belong to the entirety; they are not allowed an independent existence of their own. In the same way, they can also be destroyed by the aggregate at any time; at the latest, however, together with the aggregate itself.

In C++, the differentiation between aggregation and composition leads to a corresponding implementation (*pointer* or *value*). Smalltalk and Java do not have this differentiation, because there are no such things as pointers or the like; they are principally references (sic!).

Notation

In the same way as the aggregation, the composition is drawn as a line between two classes, equipped with a small diamond on the side of the entirety. In contrast to the aggregation, however, the diamond is not empty, but solid.

See aggregation
⇒ *p. 243*

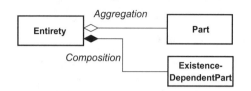

Composition relations can be noted with a multiplicity specification, a relation name (with an optional reading direction arrow), and with role names. Several composition relations with an entirety can be combined into a tree structure. In two further notation variations, the parts are noted inside the class symbol of the entirety, as shown in the following illustration.

Alternative notation

advanced

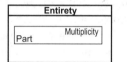 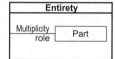

Example

Further examples
⇒ *pp. 143 ff., 154*

A typical example of a composition is the invoice with its invoice positions. The invoice positions are existence-dependent on the invoice. As soon as the invoice is deleted, all invoice positions that it contains would also be deleted. The invoice assumes specific tasks for the entirety; for example, the *Invoice* class supposedly contains operations such as *numberOfPositions()* or *sum()*. The following illustrations show yet another example in different notation variations.

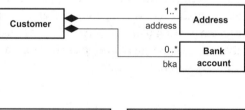

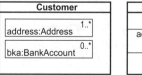 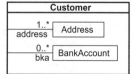

DEPENDENCY RELATIONS

Definition

A dependency is a relation between two model elements which shows that a change in one (the independent) element requires a change in the other (the dependent) element. This dependency refers to the model elements themselves and not to potential instances of these elements.

Description

Dependencies may have various causes. Some examples are:

- A class uses a specific interface of another class. If this interface is changed, that is, if properties are modified in the interface-providing class that are part of the interface, changes become necessary in the interface-using class as well.
- A class is dependent on another class, that is, a change in the independent class necessitates changes in the dependent class.
- An operation is dependent on a class, that is, a change in the class potentially necessitates a change in the operation.
- A package is dependent on another package. The cause may lie in the fact that a class in one of the packages is dependent on a class in the other package.

The dependency refers neither to the objects nor to the moment of program execution, but directly to the model elements. Thus, the dependencies between individual components may determine the order of compilation required. *Component ⇒ p. 245*

Thus, dependency relations are not designed to represent dependencies such as those that are the subject of the design pattern *Observer*, for example. *Design pattern ⇒ p. 44*

Notation

A dependency is represented by a dashed arrow pointing from the dependent element to the independent element.

Example

The illustration shows examples of dependencies between classes and interfaces, between two packages, and between an operation and a class.

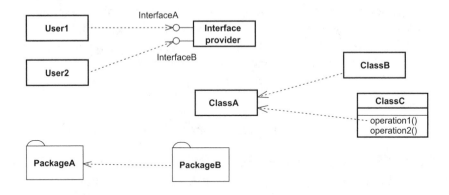

REFINEMENT OR REALIZATION RELATIONS

Definition

Refinement relations are relations between similar elements of different degrees of detail. Realization relations are relations between an interface and its implementation.

Description

Refinement relations can, for example, be used to express the following modeling situations:

Analysis/design
Clean/optimized

◆ A relation between the analysis version and the design version.
◆ A relation between a clean implementation and an optimized, but potentially difficult variation.
◆ A relation between an interface class and a class which implements this interface.
◆ A relation between two differently-grained elements.

Refinement relations allow better documentation of specific design decisions: 'The XY class was neatly designed, but we had to optimize it [...].' The result is usually an improved representation of the modeling history.

Since project budget and duration are usually limited ('They aren't at your place? Contact me! My email address is boe@oose.de.'), one should not document every conceivable refinement of such relations, but only those cases where the knowledge of the refinement or the previous variation appears to be of real significance.

Provided that a principal difference is made between an analysis model and a design model, refinement relations can also document the corresponding dependencies. When design decisions are made that require the analysis model to be updated, the refinement relation points to the analysis element affected.

If no explicit analysis model exists, but only different versions of a continuously evolving comprehensive model, refinement relations between the analysis and design versions of an element are sensible only in exceptional cases. Refinement relations are not designed for version maintenance of model elements.

Notation

The refinement relation is represented as a dashed generalization arrow pointing toward the 'original' variation, that is, toward the coarser or less optimal element.

Generalization
⇒ *p. 222*

Example

The illustration above shows an interface class and its implementation. In many cases, a note with an appropriate text, attached to the refinement relation, is probably of some help. The following illustration shows an optimization refinement.

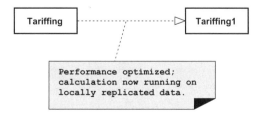

Chapter 9

Behavioral Diagrams

This chapter explains in detail the individual elements of the Unified Modeling Language used for the representation of dynamic model features – each structured into definition, description, notation, and example.

ACTIVITY DIAGRAMS

Related terms: *object state, action state, state diagram*.

Definition

Object-oriented procedure plans

Activity diagrams describe the procedural possibilities of a system with the aid of activities.

An activity diagram is a special form of a state diagram, which mostly or exclusively contains activities.

An activity is a state with an internal action and one (or more) outgoing transition which automatically follows the termination of the internal activity. An activity is a single step in a procedure. An activity can have several outgoing transitions if these can be identified through conditions.

Description

Activity: step in a procedure

An activity is a single step in an processing procedure. It is a state with an internal action and at least one outgoing transition. The outgoing transition implies termination of the internal action. An activity may have several outgoing transitions if these can be identified through conditions.

Activities can be part of state diagrams, but are usually employed in separate activity diagrams. Activity diagrams are similar to procedural flow charts, except that all activities are uniquely associated to objects.

Parallelism

Activity diagrams support the description of parallel activities. For activity paths running in parallel, the order is irrelevant. They can run consecutively, simultaneously, or alternately.

Activities and activity diagrams are associated either to:

- a class,
- an operation, or
- a use case.

They describe the possible internal procedures for these model elements.

Swim lanes

Activity diagrams can be subdivided into responsibility domains, the so-called *swim lanes*, which allow activities to be assigned to other elements or structures. For example, the class or component the activities belong to can be stated. If activity diagrams are employed for analysis and business process modeling, swim lanes can also be used to map organizational structures.

Multiple transitions

Another possibility of representing parallel processes are multiple transitions or triggers. If, for example, all individual positions need to be checked in a part list before the list can be closed, it is possible to model so that the individual positions are checked independently from each other, that is, in arbitrary order and potentially also in parallel.

Activity diagrams are therefore suitable for representing the most disparate types of procedures. In contrast to sequence diagrams, they are able to describe completely the technical connections and dependencies underlying a use case. An activity diagram can even satisfy several use cases or be use-case transcendent. Business rules and decisional logics can also be represented.

Activity diagrams can be used both in a fairly fuzzy and conceptual way and for detailed specifications with a view to implementation.

Notation

An activity is shown as a shape with a straight top and bottom and with convex arcs on the two sides. The activity description, which can be a name, a freely formulated description, a pseudocode or a programming language code, is placed in the symbol.

Incoming transitions trigger an activity. If several incoming transitions exist for an activity, each of these transitions can trigger the activity independently from the others.

Outgoing transitions are drawn in the same way as event arrows, but without an explicit event description. Transitions are triggered implicitly by the termination of the activity.

Outgoing transitions can be provided with conditions enclosed in square brackets. Such conditions should be Boolean expressions; alternatively, branching points may be used. Instead of binding the conditions directly to the transitions leaving the activity, an empty diamond is drawn from which the different conditions leave together with their conditions. This diamond too represents a (decisional) activity.   *Conditions*

Decision

*Synchronization
Splitting*

Moreover, transitions may be synchronized and split. These situations are represented by short thick lines into which transitions bump or from which they leave.

Synchronization   Splitting

Activity diagrams have only recently found their way into UML. Maybe this is the reason why some important and desirable constructs are still missing. Synchronization, for example, is defined in such a way that all incoming transitions must be present before the leaving transition fires (AND synchronization). There is no possibility of describing the fact that one incoming transition is sufficient for firing (OR synchronization). Or that two out of four transitions are needed, and so on.

OR or AND?

I remedy this by writing appropriate constraints next to the synchronization, as shown in the following illustration.

See ⇒ p. 60

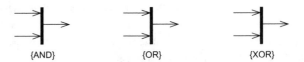

{AND}   {OR}   {XOR}

In the following illustration, the notation of multiple transitions is shown. The asterisk * stands for 'many transitions,' which means that the subsequently mentioned activity is carried out several times. Furthermore, how the multiplicity comes about is also noted. The example shown is taken from the context of an insurance contract. A premium adjustment is to be made for the individual positions of the insurance. Thus, the *Premium adjustment* activity is started once for each existing individual position. Whether these activities are performed sequentially or in parallel is not specified. In any case, the different, potentially parallel activities need to be synchronized again. Thus, a synchronization bar is drawn and a synchronization condition specified.

For splitting, I always write 'for each …' and for subsequent synchronization, 'all …' (or '$\sum$ …'). This is my personal convention; UML does not deal with these situations in great detail.

Object State

Often, activities cause changes in object states. Object states are represented as rectangles that contain the name of the object and, enclosed in square brackets, the object state.

Activities and object states are joined by dashed transition lines. If the line leads from an object state to an activity, this means that the activity presumes or requires an initial state. If the line leads from an activity to an object state, this shows the state resulting from the activity.

State changes of objects need not be modeled; notation of object states is merely a way of emphasizing them when this is of particular significance.

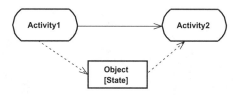

Example

The following illustration shows a business process *first application for an insurance*. The activity diagram is subdivided into three vertical swim lanes which indicate the responsibilities for the activities in question.

Further examples
⇒ *pp. 129, 131, 137*

Application processing, for example, is responsible for acquisition of the insurance data (start of contract, policy holder, and so on). Responsibility for contracts with a premium greater than 500 and for contracts drawn as samples lies with another unit. The activities of the center lane are performed mechanically, that is, without responsibility of a specific user.

The upper left-hand part shows that the clerk first needs to specify the contract start date, because in the following procedure, only those insurance products (for example contents) can be assigned that are valid for that point in time. Subsequently, the decision is left to the clerk whether to assign the policy holder first, or to select the product and create the cover. This is an example for representation of a business rule.

Below the activity *define contract start date*, we will find a splitting bar which splits the activity flow. Below the activities *create cover* and *assign policy holder*, we will find the synchronization bar. Only after all incoming transitions are present, the next action is triggered.

Below the *create cover* activity, the constraint *[cover complete]* is added, which means that this condition must be satisfied when leaving the activity.

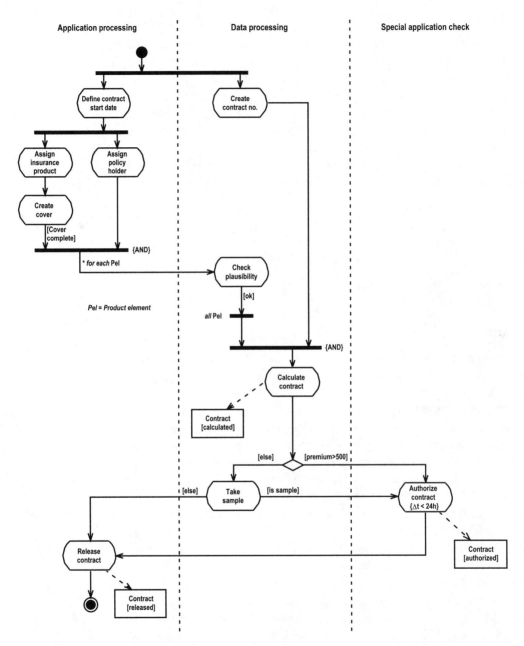

An activity can have several outgoing transitions with different conditions. If none of the conditions can be met, nothing more will happen, that is, subsequent activities and final states can no longer be reached.

After complete cover has been created and the policy holder assigned, each product element is checked for plausibility. The notation * *for each Pbs* indicates that the individual product elements may be checked in any order or in parallel. Thus, for each product element, a thread might be started. After all threads have been terminated with positive outcome (*[ok], all Pbs*) and the contract number has been generated, the contract is calculated.

If the calculation of the contract yields an insurance premium > 500, the contract must undergo a special application check by another instance, for example the group manager. The same applies if the contract was drawn as a sample.

Finally, the contract is released by the office clerk.

Activity diagrams need not necessarily be structured so that the activities are ordered chronologically from top to bottom (similar to sequence diagrams). But it seems quite sensible to do so.

COLLABORATION DIAGRAMS

Related terms: *cooperation diagram, interaction diagram, object diagram.*

Definition

A collaboration diagram shows a set of interactions between selected objects in a specific, limited situation (context), focusing on the relations between the objects and their topography.

Objects ⇒ p. 193

Description

Basically, a collaboration diagram shows the same facts as a sequence diagram, but from another perspective. The collaboration diagram emphasizes the objects and their cooperation with each other; between them, selected messages are shown. The chronological course of communication between the objects, focused upon in the sequence diagram, is marked in the collaboration diagram by numbering the messages. For two objects to communicate with each other, the sender of the message must have a reference, that is, an association, to the receiver object.

Sequence diagram ⇒ p. 262

Object relation, association ⇒ p. 228

The object relation may either exist permanently, or only temporarily or locally (for example as argument of a message). Without an association having to be present, the object can always send messages to itself.

Association ⇒ p. 228
Aggregation ⇒ p. 243

Collaboration diagrams show the chronological sequence of the messages, their names and responses, and their possible arguments. They can equally be used to represent iterations and message loops. Furthermore, they can be employed for the representation of design issues and, in a slightly more detailed form, of implementation issues.

Collaborations are always projections of the underlying complete model and are consistent with it.

Like sequence diagrams, collaboration diagrams too are suited for describing individual procedural variations. They are, however, not suitable for a precise or complete definition of behavior. For this purpose, activity and state diagrams are the better choice.

Collaboration diagrams are a very good tool for explaining or documenting a specific procedural situation. They can be quickly sketched and discussed on a flip chart or a whiteboard. Employment of a CASE tool for creation of a collaboration diagram is sensible if one wishes to incorporate the diagram into the documentation for a particular description of an issue.

Notation

Notation, objects
⇒ *p. 193*

Between the objects, association lines are drawn on which the messages are noted. A small arrow indicates the direction of the message from sender to receiver. If arguments are passed together with the message, they are listed too. Possible responses can be shown as well; they are put in front of the actual message in the form *response:= message()*.

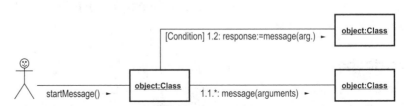

The chronological sequence of the messages is indicated by sequence numbers. The first message begins with number 1. The starting message, that is, the external message that triggered the interaction is shown without a number. This message may also start from an actor symbol.

Message descriptions are based on the following syntax:

```
PredecessorCondition SequenceExpression ReturnValue :=
                 MessageName (ArgumentList)
```

The individual elements have the following meaning:

◆ *Predecessor condition.*   This is an enumeration of the sequence numbers of other messages that need to have been sent before this message may be sent. This allows synchronization to be achieved. The sequence numbers are listed separated by commas and terminated with a slash /. The predecessor condition is optional. Example:

```
1.1, 2.3/
```

◆ *Sequence expression.*   To show the sequence of messages, they are numbered in ascending order. If new messages are sent within an operation which interprets a received message, they are given a new subsequence number separated by a dot. Thus, messages show their depth of nesting inside other messages. Example: message 2.1.3 follows message 2.1.2. Both were sent during interpretation of message 2.1.

Instead of numbers, strings of characters can be used. The sequence expression, if specified, is terminated with a colon.

Iterations, that is, repeated sending of a message, are marked with an asterisk *. To describe the iteration in more detail, for example, to specify the number of iterations, an appropriate indication in pseudocode or the programming language used can be added in square brackets. Example:

```
1.2.*[i := 1..n]:
```

In the iteration, it is assumed that all messages are sent sequentially. If a parallel execution is to be indicated, the asterisk is followed by two vertical lines:

```
1.2.*||[i := 1..n]:
```

In the same way, a condition noted in pseudocode or in the actual programming language can be added, which needs to be satisfied for the message to be sent. This not only allows individual scenarios to be represented, but also more general interaction structures. Example:

```
1.2.*[x > 5]:
```

◆ *Response.*   The response supplied by a message can be given a name. This name can then be used as an argument in other messages. Its scope is the same as that of local variables inside the message to be sent and may indeed be such a variable. It may also be the name of an object attribute.

◆ *Message name (parameter list).*   Name of the message, usually homonymous with a corresponding operation that interprets the message. The signature of the operation is specified.

Predecessor

Sequences

Iterations

Response

Signature, operation
⇒ *p. 199*

Objects that are generated within the described scenario are marked as *«new»*, objects that are destroyed are marked as *«destroyed»*, and objects that are generated and destroyed in the scenario are marked as *«transient»*.

The relation between two objects, which forms the basis for the message exchange, may have various causes which can be marked in the diagram. Where the connecting line meets the message-receiving object and the role name (attribute name) is noted, one of the following stereotypes can be indicated:

Stereotypes ⇒ p. 213

♦ *«association»*
   The object relation is based on an association, aggregation, or composition. This is the default; the specification can therefore be omitted.

Visibility specifications

♦ *«global»*
   The receiving object is global.
♦ *«local»*
   The receiving object is local in the sending operation (and thus *«new»* or *«transient»*).
♦ *«parameter»*
   The receiving object is a parameter in the sending operation.
♦ *«self»*
   The receiving object is the sending object.

Synchronization features

Various arrow shapes have been defined for specifying particular synchronization conditions. They have the following meaning:

⟶	simple, sequential
⟶×⟶	synchronous
⟵	restricted
⟶	time-dependent
⟶	asynchronous

♦ The sequential message is accepted by the receiver and processed completely. Only then can the sender continue.
♦ With a synchronous message, the sender waits until the receiver has accepted the message.
♦ With a restricted message, the exchange is aborted if the receiver does not immediately accept the message.
♦ With a time-dependent message, the exchange is aborted if the receiver does not accept the message within a specific delay.

♦ Asynchronous messages end up in the waiting queue of the receiver. The sender is not interested in when the receiver accepts the message.

Example

The following example shows the message exchange between four different objects during reservation of a mail order article. The first *reserve(o)* message contains the object *o* (the *order*) as an argument, therefore the relation with the *order* object bears the stereotype *«parameter»*.

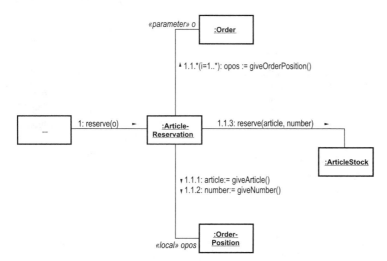

Message *1.1* to the order object is repeated in a loop *[i=1..*]*; as a response, an order position *opos* is returned each time. This is sent the messages *1.1.1* and *1.1.2* whose responses (*article, number*) are used as parameters in the subsequent message *1.1.3* to the *ArticleStock*.

Further examples of messages:

♦ *Simple message*
    2: display(x, y)
♦ *Nested message with response*
    2.3.4: i := count(block)
♦ *Conditional message*
    [x > 7] 1: check()
♦ *Synchronized and iterative message*
    2, 4.2, 4.3/ 5.1.*: notify(x)

SEQUENCE DIAGRAMS

Related terms: *interaction diagram, event trace diagram, scenario, message diagram.*

Definition

A sequence shows a series of messages exchanged by a selected set of objects in a temporally limited situation, with an emphasis on the chronological course of events.

Description

Collaboration diagram
⇒ p. 257

The sequence diagram basically shows the same facts as a collaboration diagram, but from another perspective. In the collaboration diagram, the emphasis lies on the cooperation between objects. The chronological course of communication between objects is indicated by the numbering of messages.

Lifelines

In the sequence diagram, the emphasis is on the chronological course of messages. Objects are merely shown by vertical lifelines. This highlights the chronological sequence of the messages. Time runs from top to bottom.

Notation

Objects are represented by dashed vertical lines. On top of the line, we find the name or the object symbol. Messages are drawn as horizontal arrows between the object lines, on which the message itself is noted in the form *message(arguments)*. Similarly to the collaboration diagram, the response is shown in textual form (*response:= message()*) or as a separate, but dashed arrow with an open head.

Overlapping of the dashed lifelines with broad, empty (or gray) bars symbolizes the control focus. The control focus specifies which object currently holds program control, that is, which object is currently active. The left- or right-hand borders can be used to note freely formulated explanations, time requirements, and the like.

Creation and removal of objects can also be represented in sequence diagrams. The construction of a new object is indicated by a message that meets an object symbol; the destruction of an object by a cross at the end of the control focus.

Condition

As in state and collaboration diagrams, messages can be additionally provided with conditions in the notation *[Condition] message()*. This notation

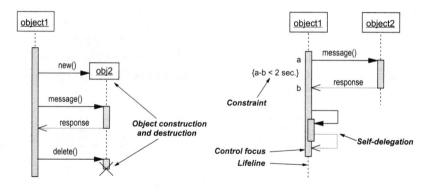

originates from Buschmann *et al.* (1996). Since, in the meantime, UML has introduced activity diagrams which are much better suited for expressing a multitude of different procedural alternatives, the use of conditions in sequence diagrams is no longer recommended.

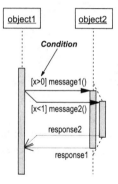

To indicate iterations, that is, multiple sending of a message, an asterisk *   *Iteration* is placed in front of the message (iteration mark).

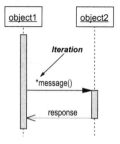

Example

Collaboration diagram
Example ⇒ p. 261

Further examples
⇒ p. 160

The following example shows the same situation as the example in the section on collaboration diagrams, where you will find further explanations about this example. The sequence diagram with control focus shows clearly which objects are active and when.

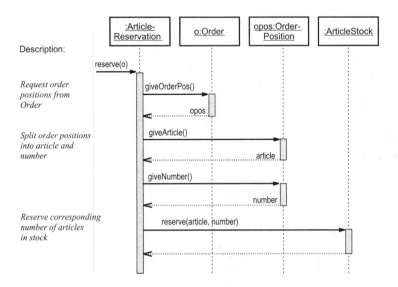

The next illustration shows a section containing indirectly recursive messages. Here, the existing message focus is overlaid with an additional one (shown slightly shifted to the right).

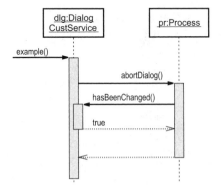

The corresponding program instructions would look like this:

```
class DialogCustService {
  Process pr;
  boolean changed;

  public void example() {
    ...
    if (pr.abortDialog(self)) {
      ...
    }
  }
  public boolean hasBeenChanged() {
    // returns true, if data has been changed
    return(changed);
  }
}
class Process {
  void abortDialog(DialogCustService dlg) {
    if (dlg.hasBeenChanged()) {
      ... // abort dialog
    }
  }
}
```

STATE DIAGRAMS

Related terms: *state machine, state transition diagram, finite automaton.*

Definition and Description

A state diagram shows a sequence of states an object can assume during its lifetime, together with the stimuli that cause changes of state.

A state diagram describes a hypothetical machine (finite automaton) which at any given time is found in a set of finite states. It consists of:

- a finite, non-empty set of states;
- a finite, non-empty set of events;
- functions which describe the transition from one state to the next;
- an initial state;
- a set of final states.

The individual elements are explained in more detail in the following sections.

Example

Further example
⇒ *p. 161*

The following example shows the state transitions for a flight reservation. Where the event names correspond to the action operations, only the operation is shown. On opening the flight, the initial state leads to the *NoReservation* state. When this state is entered, the *Reset* operation is executed. If a reservation is made for this flight, the object changes to the state *PartiallyReserved*. The *Reserve* event is associated to the homonymous *Reserve* action (implemented as an operation). In this operation, the actual reservation takes place, and the internal reservation counter is updated. After termination of this action, we will find the object in the *PartiallyReserved* state.

Each additional reservation leads to the same action. As long as free seats are available, the object remains in the *PartiallyReserved* state. If only one seat is left, it changes into the *FullyBooked* state. Cancellation of reserved seats is carried out in a similar way. Thus, the state diagram describes which actions are triggered by which events and under which conditions these (and together with the call of the corresponding operations) are permitted.

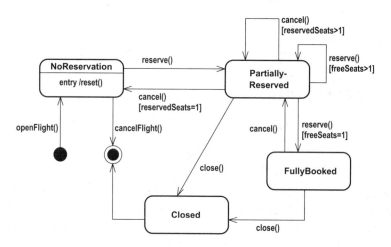

States

Related terms: *initial state, final state.*

Definition

A state belongs to a single class and represents an abstraction or a combination of a set of possible attribute values that the objects of this class may assume. State diagrams describe the internal state model of an object.

Description

Not every change of an attribute value is perceived as a change of state. The abstraction consists of considering only those events that significantly affect the behavior of the object. A state can therefore also be seen as a time span between two events.

Two particular types of state are the initial and final states. No transition may lead to an initial state, and no event allows leaving the final state.

Initial state and final state

States have either unique names or they are anonymous states. Anonymous states are different from each other, that is, two unnamed states in a diagram are two different states. In all other cases, states bearing the same name are actually the same state.

Anonymous states

Each state may contain a set of state variables. State variables are attributes of the class to which the state belongs. The set of state variables is therefore a subset of the class attributes. In a state, only those attributes are listed as state variables that are essential for the description or identification of the state.

State variables
Attributes ⇒ p. 195

Not every class needs to have states; it needs to show a significant behavior. If all operations of an object can be called in an arbitrary order independent of its internal state, state modeling is not required.

Transitions from one state to the next are triggered by events. An event consists of a name and a list of possible arguments. A state can attach conditions to an event which must be satisfied before the event can cause the transition into this state. Conditions may be formulated independently of a specific event. Events can trigger actions inside the state that are realized through appropriate operations. Three special triggers are predefined:

Events, conditions, operations

- ◆ *entry* fires automatically when entering a state,
- ◆ *exit* fires automatically when leaving a state,
- ◆ *do* fires repeatedly as long as the state is active, that is, not left.

Notation

States are represented by rounded rectangles. They may contain a name and be optionally subdivided by horizontal lines into up to three rubrics.

State
stateVariables
event / ActionDescription

State
event / ActionDescription

State

State
stateVariables

The top rubric contains the name of the state. It may be omitted; in that case, the state is an anonymous state. For clearer visual structuring of diagram layouts, states may occur more than once in the same diagram.

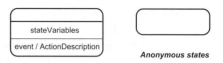

Anonymous states

Attribute ⇒ p. 195

In a second rubric, existing state variables may be listed. Since state variables are attributes of the class, they are noted in exactly the same way:

variable : Class = InitialValue {Feature} {Constraint}

The third available rubric of the state symbol contains a list of possible internal events, conditions, and operations resulting from them. They are noted in the following format:

event / ActionDescription

The action description can be the name of an operation, or it can be formulated freely. It may contain state variables, attributes of the class, or parameters of the incoming transitions.

Initial states are drawn as small solid circles, final states as empty circles surrounding smaller solid circles.

● *Initial state*   ◉ *Final state*

Example

The illustration shows a state of the class *Contract*. Once a customer has been assigned and the state left, selected customer data are to be automatically inserted into the contract form.

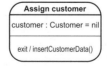

Substates

States can be nested into further, either sequential or parallel substates. In simultaneous, concurrent substates, the state symbol is subdivided into additional rubrics with the aid of dashed lines.

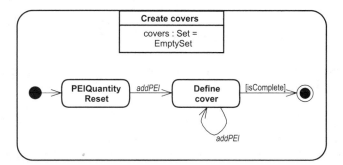

The above example shows a sequential nesting. When an insurance contract is stipulated, a product is selected (for example, contents), which consists of several product elements (PEl), such as furniture, glass, and so on. For each product element, a cover must be created. The illustration shows the *Create covers* state of this context.

The following illustration shows the notation of parallel substates.

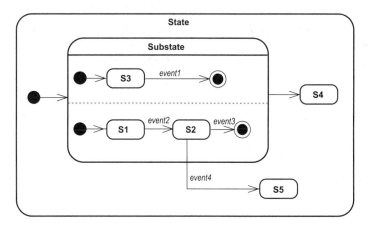

Events and Transitions

Related terms: *state transition*.

Definition

An event is an occurrence which has a particular significance in a given context, can be localized in space and time, and needs to be taken into account because it triggers a state transition.

Event

Transition

Description

An event may have the following causes:

- A condition (defined for a transition) is satisfied.
- The object receives a message.

In contrast to states, events do not belong to a specific class.

States and events can be used to draw up state diagrams which describe when an object is allowed to receive specific events, and which consequences this has for the status of the object. Specific events can only be processed sensibly if the object is in a suitable state for doing so. It may also be stated that an event may lead to different actions, depending on the state the object is in, and on the conditions attached to the event.

ε transition

State transitions are usually triggered by events which are noted on the arrows that connect the states. Transitions without event specifications are triggered automatically as soon as the actions belonging to a state are terminated.

Conditions

Events may be provided with conditions. The conditions attached to an event must be satisfied for the state transition to occur. Conditions may be formulated independently from the events. Moreover, an event may in turn trigger events in other objects.

Notation

Event and action

Events are represented by arrows leading from one state to the next. An arrow may also point back to the state it started from.

On the arrows, the transition descriptions are noted in the following form:

```
event(arguments)
[condition]
/operation(arguments)
^targetObjects.sentEvent(arguments)
```

Chapter 10

Implementation Diagrams

This chapter describes in detail the elements of the Unified Modeling Language used for the representation of implementation issues.

COMPONENT DIAGRAMS

Related terms: *component, subsystem, module, package.*

Definition

A component represents a physical piece of program code, either as source code, binary code, DLL, or executable program.

Component diagrams show the interrelations between components.

Description

Interfaces ⇒ p. 202

In practice, components are very similar to packages: they define boundaries, and group and structure a set of individual elements. Components may have interfaces.

Dependencies ⇒ p. 247

Components or component diagrams may under certain conditions also be needed to protocol compiler and runtime dependencies.

The files that are to contain the program code for the individual classes must be defined at the latest at implementation start – depending on the programming language used. In Smalltalk, where no module concept is needed, this problem is different from C++, where the appropriate *.cpp and *.h files need to be created.

I generally use components for description of larger sets of technically related classes, such as, all classes that have to do with partner management. The Partner component could, for example, contain the classes *Person, LegalEntity, NaturalPerson, PartnerRole, PremiumPayer, PolicyHolder, MailRecipient, Mediator, InsuredParty, Address, BankAccount, PhoneNumber,* and so on – just anything that technically has to do with Partner and has no better place to go.

Interfaces

However, the combination of a set of elements to a bigger unit is only one aspect. Another one is providing one or more common interfaces. Thus, while all elements contained in a component know each other well, that is, practically completely, only a section is made externally available. The properties a component exports are defined by its explicit interfaces.

Packages versus components

Packages and components can be used for very similar purposes. While packages represent a more logical view, components emphasize the physical perspective.

Notation and Example

A component is represented as a rectangle that has two small rectangles on its left-hand side. The name of the component and, where required, its type are written inside the component. Furthermore, the component may in turn contain other elements (objects, components, nodes).

Physical architecture

Dependencies between individual modules are represented by means of the corresponding dependency relations (dashed arrows).

Further examples ⇒ pp. 131, 134

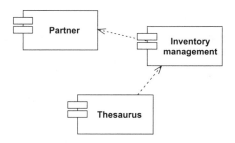

DEPLOYMENT DIAGRAMS

Related terms: *node, configuration diagram*.

Description

A node is an object which is physically present at runtime and has computing power or memory, such as computers (processors), devices, and the like.

Deployment diagrams show which components and objects run on which node (processes, computers), that is, how they are configured and which communication relations exist between them.

Notation and Example

Components ⇒ p. 272
Components are represented by bricks. Nodes that communicate with each other, that is, have the appropriate relations, are connected with one another by association lines. Optionally, components or runtime objects (processes) *Interfaces ⇒ p. 202* may be placed inside the bricks. Interfaces and dependency relations between *Dependency ⇒ p. 247* these elements are also allowed.

Nodes are identified either by their sole name or by a name followed by a specification of the node type:

> Name
> Name:NodeType

This kind of diagram is often created with the aid of conventional drawing programs. Instead of ordinary bricks, more colorful clip-art is used (pictures of printers, computers, and the like).

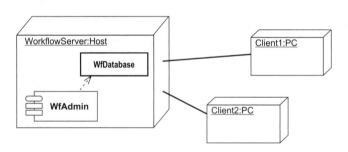

Chapter 11

Object Constraint Language

This chapter explains the most important elements of the Object Constraint Language.

OBJECT CONSTRAINT LANGUAGE (OCL)

The Object Constraint Language (OCL) is a simple formal language which allows additional semantics to be added to UML models which, with the remaining UML elements, can be either not expressed at all or only insufficiently.

The OCL has emerged from the IBEL (Integrated Business Engineering Language), an IBM development. The OCL formalism is based on set theory and is very similar to the Smalltalk language.

With the OCL, it is possible to:

♦ specify constraints of a model;
♦ indicate invariants, preconditions, and postconditions of operations and similar;
♦ describe navigation paths of an object network.

This chapter does not provide a complete OCL reference, but only explains the most important elements.

Simple Examples

Attribute access

The first two examples define constraints on the values of attributes (*employee*, *boss*, and *person* are classes, *salary* and *age* are attributes):

```
employee.salary < boss.salary
person.age > 18
```

Set access

The following expressions represent set operations. Set operations begin with an arrow '->':

```
person.addresses->isEmpty
person.addresses->size
employee->select(age > 30)
```

When navigating along associations, the role name of the opposite class is used for accessing the opposite association side. If no role name is present, the class name may be used.

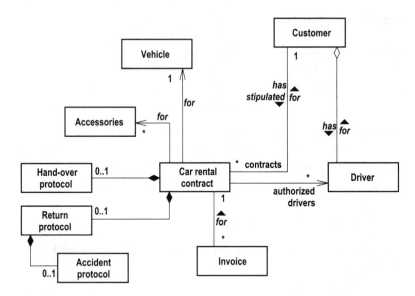

Considering the class model shown above, the following expressions would be equivalent:

CarRentalContract
    self.authorizedDrivers

CarRentalContract
    self.driver

Self

OCL expressions are usually initiated by a context for a specific instance in the form:

Context
    self.property

where *self* is a specific instance of context. Examples:

Person
    self.age

Enterprise
    self.employee->size

Enterprise : e
    e.employee->size

Complex Examples

The following example contains the constraint that all drivers included in the rental contract of a rented car must be at least 18 years old:

CarRentalContract
self.driver->forAll(d | d.age >= 18)

In the expression contained in *forAll*, the variable *d* is substituted in turn with all the elements of the *driver* set. For each *d*, the expression in *forAll* is evaluated. *forAll* returns *true* if the logical expression contained in it is true for all elements. The following formulation is an equivalent short notation:

CarRentalContract
self.driver->forAll(age >= 18)

The following formulation returns the set of all drivers aged over 70:

CarRentalContract
self.driver->select(age > 70)

The following expression returns the set of all male drivers younger than 25 (assuming that the *isMale* operation is defined in the Driver class):

CarRentalContract
self.driver->select(d | d.age < 25 and
    d.isMale)

The next two examples each return a bag of the first names of all drivers whose birthday is today:

CarRentalContract
self.driver->select(d | d.birthDate =
    today).firstName

CarRentalContract
self.driver->select(d | d.birthDate = today)
    ->collect(firstName)

The next expression ensures that all drivers specified in the rental contract belong to the same customer:

CarRentalContract
self.driver->forAll(d1, d2 | p1 <> p2 implies
    p1.customer = p2.customer)

The existence of a hand-over protocol presumes the existence of at least one driver:

CarRentalContract
self.handoverProtocol->notEmpty implies
self.driver->size > 0

The next example yields the set of all drivers of the customer of the present rental contract:

CarRentalContract
self.customer.driver

The number of contracts of a customer stipulated after 1/1/1997 can be determined by means of the following formulation:

Customer
self.contracts->
select(c | c.stipulationDate > '1/1/1997' asDate)

Predefined Basic Types and Operations

The following basic types are predefined in the OCL:

Type	Example
Boolean	true, false
Integer	1, 2, 23, 12045
Real	3.14, 0.266
String	'Starship'
Set	{55, 23, 47}, {'red', 'blue', 'yellow'}
Bag	{55, 23, 47, 5}, {12, 8, 8}
Sequence	{1..10}, {8, 17, 25, 26}

Set, *Bag*, and *Sequence* are subclasses of *Collection*. *Set* is a set in which no element occurs more than once, while in a *Bag* elements may occur any number of times. *Sequence* is a *Bag*, except that the elements are ordered.
The following evaluation order applies:

1. Dot operations ('.') have the highest precedence.
2. Unary operators ('not').

3. Binary operators ('+', 'and').
4. Among binary operators, the usual order applies: dot before plus and minus, from left to right, and so on.
5. Bracketing '(' and ')' forces a different order.

The following operations are predefined for the basic types.

Integer, Real

Expression	Type of Result	Description
i1 = i2	Boolean	Yields true if i1 and i2 are equal
i1 + i2 : Integer	Integer	
i1 + i2 : Real	Real	
r1 + i1	Real	
r1 round	Integer	

Boolean

implies

Expression	Type of Result	Description
a and b	Boolean	Yields true, if a and b are true
a or b	Boolean	Yields true, if at least one of the two values a and b is true
a xor b	Boolean	Yields true, if exactly one of the two values a and b is true
not a	Boolean	Yields the negation of a
a implies b	Boolean	(not a) or (a and b), that is, if a is true, b shall also be true
if a then a1: OclExpr else a2:OclExpr	a1.type	If a is true, expression a1 is evaluated otherwise a2
a = b	Boolean	Yields true, if a and b are equal

Collection

Expression	Type of Result	Description
s1 = s2	Boolean	Do s1 and s2 contain the same elements?
s.size	Integer	Number of elements of s
s.sum	Integer or Real	Sum of all elements of s, provided they are numerical
s.includes(e)	Boolean	Is e an element of the set s?
s.isEmpty	Boolean	Is the set empty (size=0)?
s.exists(Expr)	Boolean	Does the set s contain an element for which the expression yields true?
s.forAll(Expr)	Boolean	Does the expression yield true for all elements of the set?

Set

Expression	Type of Result	Description
s1.union(s2)	Set	Union of s1 and s2
s1.intersection (s2)	Set	Intersection of s1 and s2
s1 – s2	Set	All elements of s1 not contained in s2
s.include(e)	Set	All elements of s plus the element e
s.exclude(e)	Set	All elements of s without the element e
s1.symmetric Difference(s2)	Set	All elements of s1 and s2 that do not occur simultaneously in s1 and s2
s.select(Expr)	Set	Subset of s composed of the elements for which the expression yields true
s.reject(Exprr)	Set	Subset of s composed of the elements for which the expression yields false
s.collect(Expr)	Bag	Bag of the results of the expression applied to all elements of s

Set *(continued)*

Expression	Type of Result	Description
s.asSequence	Sequence	Returns s as a sequence
s.asBag	Bag	Returns s as a bag

Bag

Expression	Type of Result	Description
b1.union(b2)	Bag	Union of b1 and b2
b1.intersection (b2)	Bag	Intersection of b1 and b2
b.include(e)	Bag	All elements of b plus the element e
b.exclude(e)	Bag	All elements of b without the element e
b.select(Expr)	Bag	Subbag of b composed of the elements for which the expression yields true
b.reject(Expr)	Bag	Subbag of b composed of the elements for which the expression yields false
b.collect(Expr)	Bag	Bag of the results of the expression applied to all elements of b
b.asSequence	Sequence	Returns b as a Sequence
b.asSet	Set	Returns b as a Set

Sequence

Expression	Type of Result	Description
s1.append(s2)	Sequence	Sequence s1, followed by the elements of s2
s1.prepend(s2)	Sequence	Intsersection of s1 and s2
s.first	Element.Type	First element of s

Sequence *(continued)*

Expression	Type of Result	Description
s.last	Element.Type	Last element of s
s.at(i)	Element.Type	i-th element of s
s.include(e)	Sequence	All elements of b plus the element e inserted at the end
s.exclude(e)	Sequence	All elements of b without the first occurrence of the element e
s.select(Expr)	Sequence	Subsequence of b composed of the elements for which the expression yields true
s.reject(Expr)	Sequence	Subsequence of b composed of the elements for which the expression yields false
s.collect(Ausdr)	Sequence	Sequence of the results of the expression applied to all elements of s
s.asBag	Bag	Returns s as a Bag
s.asSet	Set	Returns s as a Set

Part IV

Appendices

Appendix A

Glossary

This glossary defines the most important terms of object-orientation and UML.

Abstract class

No object instances of an abstract class are ever generated; it is intentionally incomplete, thus forming a basis for further subclasses that can have instances. C++: virtual class.

Abstract data type (ADT)

The concept of abstract data type is similar to that of class. An abstract data type is the combination of data and operations that can be performed with this data.

Abstract operation ⇒operation

An operation for which only a ⇒signature is defined, but no sequence of instructions; that is, the operation is defined, but not yet implemented. It is implemented in a derived class. C++: virtual operation.

Abstraction

Abstraction is a method in which the essential features of an object or a concept are singled out under a specific point of view.

Action state (activity)

A state with an internal action and one or more outgoing transitions which automatically follow termination of the internal action. An activity is a single step in a process. It may have several outgoing transitions provided that these can be distinguished through conditions.

Active class ⇒active object

A class whose instances are executed in parallel and have their own thread.

Active object ⇒active class

Instance of an active class.

Activity diagram

An activity diagram is a special form of state diagram which pre-eminently or exclusively contains ⇒action states (activities).

Actor

An actor is a ⇒class lying outside the system which is involved in an interaction with the system described in a ⇒use case. Actors usually assume a well-defined role in the interaction. An actor is a ⇒stereotyped class.

Aggregation ⇒association, ⇒composition

An aggregation is a special form of association in which the involved classes do not have an equivalent relation with each other, but represent an entirety–part hierarchy. An aggregation describes how an entirety is composed of its parts.

Analysis

(Object-oriented) analysis is the name for all activities in the framework of a software development process that serve determination, clarification, and description of the requirements towards the system (that is, clarification of what the system is supposed to perform).

Application component ⇒component

Application components are technical ⇒subsystems.

Architecture

Specification of the fundamental structure of a system.

Argument

Concrete value of a ⇒parameter.

Assertion ⇒constraints

Assertions are Boolean expressions that should never become untrue and, if they do, indicate errors. Typically, assertions are only activated during the development phase.

Association ⇒directed association, ⇒bidirectional association

An association describes a relation between classes, that is, the common semantics and structure of a set of ⇒object relations. We differentiate between ⇒directed associations (directly navigable only in one way) and ⇒bidirectional associations (directly navigable in both directions). The two ends of an association are ⇒association roles.

Association class ⇒attributed association, ⇒resolved association, ⇒implicit association class

A model element that disposes of the properties of both a class and an association. It may be seen as an association with additional class properties (attributed association) or as a class with additional association properties (association class).

Association role

> The role a type or a class plays in an ⇒association. This means that a role represents a class in an association. The distinction is important because a class may also have an association relation with itself and in this case, the two association ends can only be distinguished by means of their role specifications.

Attribute

> A named property of a type. An attribute is a data element equally contained in each object of a class and represented by each object with an individual value. In contrast to objects, attributes have no own identity outside the object of which they are a part. Attributes are completely under the control of the objects of which they are parts.

Attributed association ⇒association, ⇒association class

> An association that has its own attributes.

Base class ⇒superclass

Bidirectional association ⇒association

> A bidirectional association is an association directly navigable both ways, that is, an association in which it is possible to navigate directly from each of the involved ⇒association roles to the opposite one.

Binding ⇒dynamic binding

bound element ⇒parameterized class

Business class ⇒class

> ⇒instantiation ⇒business objects.

Business event (process)

> A (business) object (for example a concrete contract), triggered by an event (for example receipt of application form), which is processed by means of the activities described in a business process.

Business model (business class model)⇒domain class model

> Class model which pre-eminently or exclusively contains ⇒business classes (domain-specific elementary terms in form of classes).

Business object ⇒object

> A business object represents an object, a concept, a place, or a person out of real business life in a technically rough degree of detail, that is, in an

elementary concept or term (contract, invoice, and so on). For practical realization, business objects are aggregations of fundamental domain objects (⇒domain classes: invoice positions, address, and so on) reduced to technically motivated properties, to which everything else is delegated. Typically, they define interfaces and are a kind of façade.

Business process ⇒workflow

A combination of organizationally potentially distributed, but technically related activities needed to process a business event (for example a concrete application form) in a result-oriented fashion. The activities of a business process are usually chronologically and logically related to each other. A business event is usually triggered by an event (for example receipt of an application form).

Cardinality ⇒multiplicity

Number of elements.

Class

A class is the definition of attributes, operations, and semantics of a set of objects. All objects of a class correspond to that definition.

Class attribute, class variable ⇒attribute

Class attributes do not belong to an individual object, but are attributes of a class (for example in Smalltalk).

Class diagram

A class diagram shows a set of static model elements, in particular classes, and their relations.

Class library

A class library is a collection of classes.

Class operation, class method ⇒operation

Class operations are operations which do not operate on an object, but on a class (for example in Smalltalk).

Class template ⇒parameterized class

Collaboration ⇒collaboration diagram

A collaboration is the context of a set of interactions.

Collaboration diagram

A collaboration diagram shows a set of interactions between a set of selected objects in a specific limited situation (context) with an emphasis on the relations between the objects and their topography. Similar to the ⇒sequence diagram.

Collection

Collections are objects that reference a set of other objects and provide the operations needed to access those objects.

Component

A component is an executable software module with its own identity and well-defined interfaces (source code, binary code, DLL, or executable program). Outside UML, components are often defined differently, more in the sense of a ⇒package. See ⇒application component.

Component diagram

A component diagram shows organization and dependencies of ⇒components.

Composite ⇒Aggregation

A composite is a strict form of aggregation in which the parts are existence-dependent on the entirety.

Concrete class

A ⇒class that can instantiate ⇒objects. See ⇒abstract class.

Concretization ⇒specialization.

Concurrency

Two or more activities are performed simultaneously (in parallel).

Configuration diagram ⇒deployment diagram.

Consistency constraint ⇒constraint

A constraint between several associations which represent partly redundant facts. The constraint specifies the consistency condition.

Constraint

A constraint is an expression which restricts possible contents or states, or the semantics of a model element and which must always be satisfied. The expression may be a ⇒stereotype or ⇒property values, a free formulation (⇒note), or a ⇒dependency relation. Constraints in the form of pure Boolean expressions are also called ⇒assertions.

Container class ⇒collection

CRC card

Filing cards on which the name of the class, its responsibilities, and its collaborations are described.

Data abstraction

The principle of making only the operations applicable to an object externally visible. The actual internal realization of the operations and the internal structure of the object are hidden. This means an abstract view of the semantics without considering the actual implementation.

Default implementation

Concrete implementation of an actual abstract operation for providing subclasses with a default behavior.

Delegation

A mechanism by which an object does not (completely) interpret a message itself, but forwards it to another object.

Dependency

A relation between two model elements which shows that a change in one (the independent) element requires a change in the other (the dependent) element.

Deployment diagram

A diagram which shows the configuration of the ⇒nodes and their ⇒components, processes, and objects present (employed) at runtime.

Derived association ⇒association, ⇒derived element

A derived association is an association whose concrete object relations can at any time be derived (calculated) from the values of other object relations and objects.

Derived attribute ⇒attribute, ⇒derived element

A derived attribute is calculated from the values of other attributes. Derived attributes cannot be modified directly and are implemented or set by means of a calculation operation.

Derived element

A model element which can at any time be calculated from another element and is shown only for clarity, or added for design purposes, without, however, adding any semantic information.

Design

(Object-oriented) design is the name for all activities in the framework of the software development process in which a model is logically and physically structured, and which serve to describe how the system fulfills the requirements described in the ⇒analysis.

Design pattern

Generalized solution ideas for repeatedly occurring design problems. They are not ready-coded solutions, but merely describe the solution approach.

Directed association ⇒association, ⇒navigation

An association in which it is possible to navigate directly from one of the involved ⇒association roles to the other, but not vice versa.

Discriminator

Differentiation feature for structuring of the model semantics into ⇒generalization or specialization relations.

Domain

Application or problem area inside which the technical modeling takes place. Usually, the part of the entire model is viewed as an application area model (domain model) that relates to the actual subject-specific problems. Implementational, cross-sectional and other aspects are not part of it. In the context of application architecture, it usually refers to the domain class model (that is, without framework, GUI, controller, and other classes).

Domain class ⇒class

Usually technically motivated class that represents a concept of the problem domain. Used in contrast to ⇒business classes.

Domain model

A class model pre-eminently or exclusively containing domain classes.

Dynamic binding, late binding

> This term denotes that a ⇒message is assigned only at runtime to a concrete ⇒operation which then interprets it.

Dynamic classification

> An object is consecutively an instance of different classes of a subtype structure, that is, it can change its class membership during the course of its lifetime.

Event

> An occurrence which, in a given context, has a meaning and which can be localized in space and time.

Framework

> Set of cooperating classes which under specification of a process ('Don't call the framework, the framework calls you') provides a generic solution for a number of similar problems or tasks.

Fundamental class ⇒domain class

Generalization ⇒specialization/concretization

Generic class ⇒parameterized class

Generic design

> Use of templates and macros for design (in CASE tools).

Generic programming

> Use of templates, ⇒parameterized classes, and the like in programming.

GUI

> Graphical User Interface.

Information hiding

> Deliberate hiding of implementation details. Externally, an interface is provided, but the internals (for example of a class) are not visible. Thus, the way in which the interface is served remains invisible.

Identity ⇒object identity

Implicit association class

> The (nameless) ⇒association class of an ⇒attributed association.

Inheritance ⇒simple inheritance, ⇒multiple inheritance, ⇒multiple classification, ⇒dynamic classification

Inheritance is a programming language concept for the implementation of a relation between a superclass and a subclass in which subclasses can share properties of their superclasses. Inheritance usually implements ⇒generalization and specialization relations. Alternatives: ⇒delegation, ⇒aggregation, ⇒generic programming, ⇒generic design.

Instance ⇒object

For domestic use, instance and object can be regarded as synonyms.

Instantiation

Creation of an object of a class.

Interaction diagram

Collective term for ⇒sequence diagram, ⇒collaboration diagram, ⇒activity diagram.

Interface ⇒interface classes

Interfaces describe a selected part of the externally visible behavior of model elements (mainly of classes and components), that is, a set of signatures.

Interface classes

Interface classes are ⇒abstract classes (more precisely: types) which exclusively define ⇒abstract operations. Interface classes are classes marked with the ⇒stereotype «interface». They are specifications of the externally visible behavior of classes and contain a set of ⇒signatures for operations which classes desiring to implement this interface must provide.

Interface inheritance

Inside a ⇒specialization relation, only an ⇒interface is inherited.

Invariant

A property or an expression which needs to be satisfied across the entire lifetime of an element, for example an object.

Link

> A concrete relation between two objects, that is, the instance of an ⇒association. An object has a link to another object when it has a reference to it. Such references are usually implemented as ⇒attributes, which, however, does not matter to the modeling.

Message ⇒operation, ⇒method

> Mechanism by means of which objects can communicate with each other. A message conveys object information on the activity the object is expected to carry out, that is, a message prompts an object for execution of an operation. A message consists of a selector (a name) and a list of arguments, and is addressed to exactly one receiver. The sender of the message can have a response object returned. Through ⇒polymorphism, a message can lead to the call of several homonymous ⇒operations.

Metaclass

> A class whose instances are in turn classes. This concept exists only in some object-oriented languages (for example in Smalltalk).

Metamodel

> A model which defines a language that can be used to define a model.

Metatype ⇒powertype

Method ⇒operation

> In Smalltalk, operations are called methods. In UML, a method is defined as the implementation of an operation. In practice, the use of method and operation as synonyms is not critical.

Multiple classification

> An object is an instance of several classes at the same time (not possible in C++, Java, and Smalltalk).

Multiple inheritance

> A class has several direct superclasses (not possible in Java and Smalltalk).

Multiplicity

> Range of allowed ⇒cardinalities.

N-ary association

> An ⇒association in which more than two ⇒association roles are involved.

Navigation, navigability ⇒navigation specifications

> Navigation refers to the possible ways of accessing objects (and their attributes and operations) in a network of objects. Access routes consisting of a single relationship are called directly navigable.

Navigation specifications

> Description of access paths and access restrictions and their results (for example, by means of ⇒OCL).

Node

> A physical runtime object that uses a computer resource. Runtime objects and components can reside on nodes.

Notes

> Comments or annotations to a diagram or one or more arbitrary model element/s without semantic effect.

Object

> An actual existing and acting unit with its own identity and defined boundaries which encapsulates state and behavior. The state is represented by ⇒attributes and ⇒relations, the behavior by ⇒operations or ⇒methods. Each object is an instance of a class. The defined behavior equally applies to all objects of a class, as does the structure of their attributes. The values of the attributes, however, are individual for each object. Each object has its own identity, unchangeable and independent from its attributes and the like.

Object-based

> A programming language or a database is called object-based if it supports the concept of data abstraction, but partly or entirely lacks more advanced concepts such as class, inheritance, polymorphism, and so on.

Object diagram

> A diagram that shows objects and their relations at a given point in time. Usually a ⇒collaboration diagram or a special variation of the ⇒class diagram.

Object identity

Property which distinguishes an object from any other object, although it can have the same attribute values.

Object-oriented programming language

Object-oriented programming languages satisfy the following basic concepts:
- objects are abstract units,
- objects are instances of a class, that is, they are derived from a class,
- classes inherit properties, thus forming an inheritance hierarchy,
- objects are referenced dynamically, that is, binding is dynamic, thus allowing polymorphism.

OCL, Object Constraint Language

OCL defines a language for description of ⇒constraints, ⇒invariants, ⇒pre- and postconditions, and ⇒navigation inside UML models.

OO

Abbreviation for object-orientation.

Operation ⇒method, ⇒message

Operations are services, which may be requested of an object by means of a ⇒message, intended to cause a specific behavior. They are implemented by means of ⇒methods. In practice, operation and message are often used as synonyms.

OR constraint ⇒constraint

A constraint between associations which all lead from a common class to other different classes. This constraint specifies that the objects of the common class support ⇒object relations (or, more precisely, ⇒association roles) with only one of the other classes (exclusive OR).

Ordered association ⇒association

Association in which the object relations are ordered in some specific manner.

Ordering constraint ⇒constraint

A constraint of an association which specifies that its elements (⇒object relations) are ordered in some specific manner.

Package

Packages are collections of arbitrary model elements used to structure the entire model into smaller, clearly visible units. A package defines a namespace, that is, inside a package the names of the elements contained must be unique. Each model element can be referenced in other packages, but belongs to exactly one (home) package. Packages may in turn contain packages. The topmost package contains the entire system.

Parameter

Parameters are specifications of variables which pass operations, messages, or events, and are modified or returned by them. A parameter may consist of a name, a type (class), and a passing direction (in, out, inout).

Parameter list

Enumeration of the names of arguments and, where needed, their types, initial values, and the like.

Parameterized class

Template equipped with generic formal parameters used for generation of normal (non-generic) classes. The generic parameters serve as placeholders for the actual parameters which represent classes or simple data types.

Partition ⇒discriminator

Entirety of subclasses based on the same discriminator.

Pattern ⇒design pattern

Persistent object

Objects whose lifespan exceeds the running time of a program session. For this purpose, such objects are stored on non-volatile media (for example in databases).

Polymorphism

Polymorphism means that homonymous messages to compatible objects of different classes may trigger a different behavior. In dynamic polymorphism, a message is assigned to a concrete operation not at compile time, but at reception during program runtime. The precondition for this is ⇒dynamic binding.

Postcondition

A condition which describes a state that must be given after termination of an operation or the like.

Powertype

Type (class) whose instances are subtypes (subclasses) of another type (class).

Precondition

A condition which describes a state that must be given before the start of an operation or the like.

Propagation ⇒delegation

Extension of the properties of a class through use of operations of other classes.

Property, tagged value

Properties are user-defined, language- and tool-specific keyword/value pairs (tagged values) which extend the semantics of individual model elements with special characteristic features. The difference to the ⇒stereotype is that a stereotype extends the metamodel with a new element. Property values, in contrast, allow individual instances of existing model elements (for example, a specific operation) to be extended with specific features.

Protocol

A set of signatures.

Qualified association ⇒association, ⇒qualifier

Association in which the referenced set of objects is subdivided into partitions with the aid of qualifying attributes, and where, viewed from the initial object, each partition may only occur once.

Qualifier ⇒qualified association

The attribute via which, in an association, the opposite side is accessed. The qualifier is defined as a part of the association, however, this attribute must be defined in the class it is used to access.

Referential integrity

Rule which describes the integrity of object relations, in particular if one of the objects involved or the object relation itself is to be deleted.

Refinement

Relation between similar elements of different degree of detail or specification. Refinement relations are stereotypes of ⇒dependency relations.

Relationship

Connection between model elements with semantic contents. Generic term for ⇒association, ⇒aggregation, ⇒composition, ⇒generalization, and ⇒specialization.

Resolved association ⇒association, ⇒association class

An ⇒attributed association in which the attributes have been converted into a common class, and the attributed association has been transformed into two common associations including the newly created class.

Responsibility

Includes the attributes and the interpretable messages of an object.

Role ⇒association role

Scenario

A specific sequence of actions. For example, a concrete process path in a use case (so-to-say, an instance of the use case) (⇒sequence diagram).

Self

self (Smalltalk) and this (Java, C++) are predefined programming language keywords. With this or self, an object can send a message to itself, that is, it calls another of its own methods. Messages that an object sends to itself with this or self are treated in exactly the same way as external messages.

Self-delegation

For the execution of an operation, a partial task is delegated to another operation of the same class (that is, an object sends a message to itself).

Sequence diagram

A sequence diagram shows a set of interactions between a set of selected objects in a specific limited situation (context) with the emphasis on chronological sequence. Similar to the ⇒collaboration diagram. Sequence diagrams may exist in generic form (description of all possible scenarios), or in instance form (description of exactly one specific ⇒scenario).

Signature

The signature of an operation is composed of the name of the operation, its parameter list, and the specification of a potential return type.

Simple inheritance ⇒inheritance

In simple inheritance, a subclass inherits only from a direct superclass.

Specialization, generalization ⇒inheritance

Generalization (or specialization) are taxonomic relations between a general and a special element (or vice versa), where the more special element adds further properties, extends the semantics, and behaves in a compatible way with the general element. Generalization and specialization are abstraction principles for hierarchic structuring of the model semantics under a discriminating aspect (⇒discriminator).

State

Abstraction of the possible attribute values of an object. A state belongs to exactly one class and represents an abstraction or combination of a set of possible attribute values that the objects of this class may assume. In UML, a state is a condition or situation in the life of an object during which a specific condition is satisfied, activities are carried out, or an event is expected.

State diagram, state machine

A state diagram shows a sequence of states an object can assume during its lifetime, and the stimuli that make state changes happen. A state diagram describes a hypothetical machine (finite automaton) which at any point of time is found in a set of finite states. It consists of:

◆ a finite, non-empty set of states;
◆ a finite, non-empty set of input symbols (events);
◆ functions which describe the transition from one state to the next;
◆ an initial state;
◆ a set of final states.

Static classification

An object is and remains an instance of exactly one class, that is, it cannot change class membership during its lifetime. See ⇒dynamic classification.

Stereotype

Stereotypes are project-, enterprise-, or method-specific extensions of existing model elements of the UML metamodel. According to the semantics defined with the extension, the modeling element to which a stereotype is applied is semantically directly affected. In practice, stereotypes indicate in particular the possible usage conditions of a class, a relation, or a package. Other extension mechanisms in UML are ⇒properties and ⇒constraints.

Subclass

A subclass is a specialization of a superclass and inherits all properties of the superclass.

Subset constraint ⇒constraint

A constraint/dependency between two associations. The elements (⇒object relations) of one association must be part of the elements of the other association.

Subsystem ⇒component

A subsystem is a very large component or a component composed of a large quantity of individual components. Helpful for structuring of very large systems.

Super

super (Smalltalk, Java) is a programming language keyword. It ensures that the message always goes to the next higher class that disposes of the specified operation.

Superclass ⇒generalization

A superclass is a generalization of selected properties of its ⇒subclass(es).

Superstate ⇒state

A superstate contains other states or substates.

Swimlane

Areas separated by lines in ⇒activity diagrams, which describe the responsibilities of the elements contained in the diagram.

Tagged value ⇒property

Template ⇒parameterized class

Ternary association ⇒n-ary association

An association in which three association roles are involved.

This ⇒self

Type

Definition of a set of operations and attributes. Other elements are type-conformant if they dispose of the properties defined by the type. In practice, often used as an equivalent to description of ⇒interfaces.

Transition

Passage from one ⇒state to another, often triggered by an ⇒event.

Use case

A use case describes a set of activities of a system that leads to a tangible result for the actors from the point of view of these actors. A use case is always initiated by an actor. Otherwise, a use case is a complete, indivisible description.

Use case diagram

A diagram which shows the relations between ⇒actors and ⇒use cases.

Use case model

A model which describes the functional requirements to a system in the form of use cases.

Utility

Utility classes are collections of global variables and functions which are combined into a class and defined there as class attributes and operations. Thus, utility classes are not proper classes. A class is marked as a utility by means of the ⇒stereotype «utility».

Virtual class ⇒abstract class

Virtual operation ⇒abstract operation

Visibility marks

Restrict accessibility of attributes and operations (private, protected, public, and so on).

Workflow ⇒business process

Computer-aided automation and support of a business process or a part of it.

Workflow engine

Software which controls workflows. Creates, activates, suspends, and terminates workflow instances (that is, computer-aided manifestations of a business event).

Workflow instance

Computer-aided manifestations of a business event; controlled by a workflow engine.

Appendix B

References

Albrecht, A. J. (1979). Measuring Application Development Productivity, Proc. Joint SHARE/GUIDE/IBM Application Development Symposium. Reprinted in: T. Capers Jones, T. (1986). *Programming Productivity – Issues for the Eighties*. IEEE Press, (ISO/IEC DIS 14143).

Alexander, C. (1977). *A Pattern Language*. Oxford University Press, New York.

Alexander, C. (1979). *The Timeless Way of Building*. Oxford University Press, New York.

Beck, K. (1997). *Smalltalk best practice patterns*. Prentice Hall, Upper Saddle River.

Beck, K., Cunningham, H. (1989). A laboratory for teaching object-oriented thinking. *Proceedings of OOPSLA '89, SIGPLAN notices (ACM)* vol. 24, New Orleans, 10/1989.

Beyer, M. (1993). *BrainLand: Mind Mapping in Aktion*. Junfermannsche Verlagsbuchhandlung, Paderborn.

Bittner, U., Hesse, W., Schnath, J. (1995). *Praxis der Software-Entwicklung, Methoden, Werkzeuge, Projektmanagement – eine Bestandsaufnahme*. Oldenbourg, München.

Boehm, B. W. (1981). *Software Engineering Economics*. Prentice Hall, Englewood Cliffs.

Boehm, B. W. (1986). A spiral model of software development and enhancement, *Software Engineering Notes* 11(4).

Booch, G. (1986). *Software Engineering with Ada*. Benjamin/Cummings, Redwood City.

Booch, G. (1991). *Object-oriented design with applications*. Benjamin/Cummings, Redwood City.

Booch, G. (1994). *Object-oriented analysis and design with applications*. 2nd ed., Benjamin/Cummings, Redwood City.

Booch, G. (1996). Properties and Stereotypes, *ROAD*, Feb. 1996, pp. 2 ff.

Booch, G., Rumbaugh, J., Jacobson, I. (1998). *Unified Modeling Language User Guide*. Addison Wesley Longman.

Brooks, F. P. (1975). *The Mythical Man-Month*, Addison-Wesley, Reading, Massachusetts.

Buschmann, F., Meunier, R., Rohnert, H., Sommerlad, P., Stal, M. (1996). *Pattern-Oriented Software Architecture: A System of Patterns*. Wiley, New York.

Chen, P. (1976). The Entity-Relationship Model, Toward a Unified View of Data, *ACM Transactions on Database Systems*, Vol. 1, 1976.

Coad, P., Yourdon, E. (1991a). *Object-Oriented Analysis*. (2nd edn.), Prentice Hall, Englewood Cliffs.

Coad, P., Yourdon, E. (1991b). *Object-Oriented Design*. Prentice Hall, Englewood Cliffs.

Coleman, D., Arnold, P., Bodorff, S., Dollin, C., Gilchrist, H. (1993). *Object-Oriented Development: The Fusion Method*, Prentice Hall, Englewood Cliffs.

Dahl, O.-J., Nygaard, K. (1996). Simula, an Algol-based simulation language, *Communications of the ACM*, 9(9).

Dörner, D. (1989). *Die Logik des Mißlingens. Strategisches Denken in komplexen Situationen*. Rowohlt Verlag, Reinbek.

Fowler, M., Scott, K. (1997). *UML Distilled, Applying the Standard Object Modeling Language*. Addison-Wesley.

Gamma, E., Helm, R., Johnson, R., Vlissides, J. (1995). *Design Patterns: Elements of Reusable Object-Oriented Software*. Addison-Wesley, Reading, Massachusetts.

Goldberg, A. (1982). *The Smalltalk-80 System Release Process*. Xerox.

Goldberg, A., Robson, D. (1993). *Smalltalk-80 The Language and its Implementation*. Addison-Wesley, Reading, Massachusetts.

Goldberg, A., Rubin, K. S., (1995). *Succeeding with Objects, Design Frameworks for Project Management*. Addison-Wesley, Reading, Massachusetts.

Graham, I., Bischof, J., Henderson-Sellers, B. (1997). Associations considered a bad thing. In: *JOOP 2/1997*, pp. 41 ff.

Graham, I., Henderson-Sellers, B., Younessi, H. (1997). *The OPEN Process Specification*. Addison-Wesley (ACM Press), Harlow.

GUI-Guide. Microsoft: *The GUI-Guide*.

Habermas, J. (1987). *Theorie des kommunikativen Handelns*. 2 vol., 4th edn, Suhrkamp, Frankfurt.

Harel, D. (1987). Statecharts: A Visual Formalism for Complex Systems. In: *Science of Computer Programming* 8, pp. 231 ff.

Heisenberg, W. (1942). *Ordnung der Wirklichkeit*. Piper, 1989.

Henderson-Sellers, B., Graham, I. G., Firesmith, D. G. (1997). Methods unification: The OPEN methodology. *JOOP*, May 1997, pp. 41 ff.

Jacobson, I., Christerson, M., Jonsson, P., Övergaard, G. (1992). *Object-Oriented Software Engineering, A Use Case Driven Approach*. Addison-Wesley, Wokingham.

Jacobson, I., Booch, G., Rumbaugh, J. (1997). *The Objectory Software Development Process*. Addison Wesley Longman.

Kilberth, K., Gryczan, G., Züllighoven, H. (1993). *Objektorientierte Anwendungsentwicklung*. Vieweg, Braunschweig/Wiesbaden.

Martin, J., Odell, J. (1992). *Object-Oriented Analysis and Design*, Prentice Hall, Englewood Cliffs.

McMenamin, S. M., Palmer, J. F. (1984). *Essential System Analysis*. Prentice Hall, Englewood Cliffs.

Meyer, B. (1988). *Object-Oriented Software Construction*. Prentice Hall, Englewood Cliffs.

Middendorf, S., Singer, R., Strobel, S. (1996). *Java: Programmierhandbuch und Referenz*. d-punkt-Verlag, Heidelberg.

Miller, G. The Magical Number Seven, Plus Minus Two: Some Limits on Our Capacity for Processing Information. *The Psychological Review*, vol. 63.

Miller, G. (1975). *The Magical Number Seven after Fifteen Years*. Wiley, New York.

Molzberger, P. (1984). *Transcending the Basic Paradigm of Software Engineering*. Hochschule der Bundeswehr München, Bericht Nr. 8405.

Oestereich, B. (1998). Objektorientierte Geschäftsprozeßmodellierung mit der UML. In: *Objekt-Spektrum*, 2/1998, p. 48.

Pasch, J. (1989). Mehr Selbstorganisation in Softwareentwicklungsprojekten. In: *Softwaretechnik-Trends* 2/1989, pp. 42 ff.

Quibeldey-Cirkel, K. (1994). *Paradigmenwechsel im Software-Engineering: Auf dem Weg zu objektorientierten Weltmodellen.* In: *Softwaretechnik-Trends* 2/1994, pp. 47 ff.

Raasch, J. (1993). *Systementwicklung mit Strukturierten Methoden*, 3rd ed., Hanser, München.

Railton, A. *Der Käfer – Der ungewöhnliche Weg eines ungewöhnlichen Automobils. eurotax.*

Rumbaugh, J. (1996a). A state of mind: Modeling behavior. In: *JOOP,* July 1996, pp. 6 ff.

Rumbaugh, J. (1996b). A search for values: Attributes and associations. In: *JOOP*, June 1996, pp. 6 ff.

Rumbaugh, J. (1996c). A matter of intent: How to define subclasses. In: *JOOP,* Sept. 1996, pp. 5 ff.

Rumbaugh, J. (1996d). Packaging a system: Showing architectural dependencies. In: *JOOP*, Nov. 1996, pp. 11 ff.

Rumbaugh, J. (1997b). OO Myths: Assumptions from a language view. In: *JOOP*, Febr. 1997, pp. 5 ff.

Rumbaugh, J. (1997c). Modeling through the development process, in: *JOOP*, May 1997, pp. 5 ff.

Rumbaugh, J., Blaha, M., Premerlani, W., Eddy, F., Lorenson, W. (1991). *Object-Oriented Modelling and Design.* Prentice Hall, Englewood Cliffs.

Rumbaugh, J., Jacobson, I., Booch, G. (1997a). *Unified Modeling Language Reference Manual.* Addison Wesley Longman.

Scharf, T. (1995). Architekturen und Technologien verteilter Objektsysteme. In: *HMD* 186, 1995, pp. 10 ff.

Scheer, A.-W. (1994). *Business Process Engineering – Reference Models for Industrial Enterprise Modeling.* Springer, Berlin.

Scheer, A.-W., Nüttgens, M., Zimmermann, V. (1997). Objektorientierte Ereignisgesteuerte Prozeßkette (oEPK) – Methode und Anwendung. *Veröffentlichungen des Instituts für Wirtschaftsinformatik*, Heft 141, Saarbrücken 1997, URL: www.iwi.uni-sb.de/public/iwi-hefte.

Shlaer, S., Mellor, S. J. (1991). *Object Lifecycles – Modelling the World in States*. Prentice Hall, Englewood Cliffs.

Sims, O. (1994). *Business Objects: Delivering Cooperative Objects for Client-Server*. McGraw-Hill, New York.

Skubliks, S., Klimas, E., Thomas, D. (1996). *Smalltalk with style*. Prentice Hall, Upper Saddle River.

Stein, W. (1993). Objektorientierte Analysemethoden – ein Vergleich In: *Informatik Spektrum*, Vol. 16, pp. 317 ff.

Szyperski, C. (1997). *Component Software, Beyond Object-Oriented Programming*. Addison-Wesley (ACM Press), Harlow.

UML 0.8. Rumbaugh, J., Booch, G. (1995). *Unified Method for Object-Oriented Development, Documentation Set 0.8*. Rational Software Corporation, Santa Clara.

UML 0.9. Rumbaugh, J., Jacobson, I., Booch, G. (1996). *The Unified Modeling Language for Object-Oriented Development, Documentation Set 0.9 Addendum*. Rational Software Corporation, Santa Clara.

UML 1.0. Rumbaugh, J., Jacobson, I., Booch, G. (1997). *The Unified Modeling Language, Documentation Set 1.0*. Rational Software Corporation, Santa Clara.

UML 1.1. Rumbaugh, J., Jacobson, I., Booch, G. (1997). *The Unified Modeling Language, Documentation Set 1.1a6*. Rational Software Corporation, Santa Clara.

UML1.2. OMG UML Revision Task Force (1998). *OMG UML 1.2*.

Valk, R. (1987). Der Computer als Herausforderung an die menschliche Rationalität. In: *Informatik Spektrum*, Vol 10/1987, pp. 57 ff.

Waldén, K., Nerson, J.-M. (1995). *Seamless Object-Oriented Software Architecture, Analysis and Design of Reliable Systems*. Prentice Hall, London.

Wallrabe, A., Oestereich, B. (1997). *Smalltalk für Ein- und Umsteiger*. Oldenbourg, München.

Wirfs-Brock, R., Johnson, R. E. (1990). Surveying current research in Object-Oriented Design. In: *Commun. ACM* 33, No. 9.

Wirfs-Brock, R., Wilkerson, B., Wiener, L. (1990). *Designing Object-Oriented Software*. Prentice Hall, Englewood Cliffs.

Yourdon, E. (1989). *Structured Walkthroughs*. Prentice Hall, Englewood Cliffs.

Index

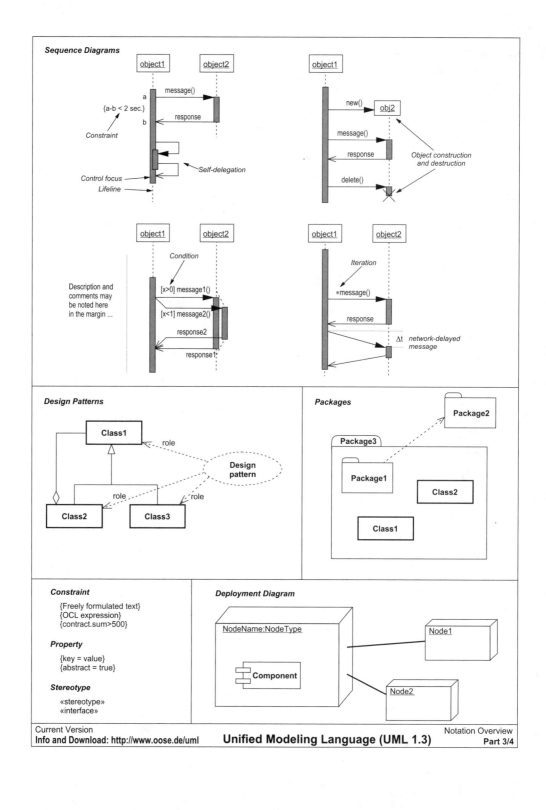

Sequence Diagrams

object1   object2

{a-b < 2 sec.}
Constraint

message()
a
response
b

Self-delegation
Control focus
Lifeline

object1

new()   obj2
message()
response
delete()

Object construction and destruction

object1   object2

Description and comments may be noted here in the margin ...

Condition
[x>0] message1()
[x<1] message2()
response2
response1

object1   object2

Iteration
∗message()
response

Δt *network-delayed message*

Design Patterns

Class1
role
role   role
Class2   Class3

Design pattern

Packages

Package2
Package3
Package1
Class2
Class1

Constraint

{Freely formulated text}
{OCL expression}
{contract.sum>500}

Property

{key = value}
{abstract = true}

Stereotype

«stereotype»
«interface»

Deployment Diagram

NodeName:NodeType
Component
Node1
Node2